GIVE ME EIGHTY MEN

Women in the West

SERIES EDITORS

Sarah J. Deutsch | *Duke University*

Margaret D. Jacobs | *New Mexico State University*

Charlene L. Porsild | *University of New Mexico*

Vicki L. Ruiz | *University of California, Irvine*

Elliott West | *University of Arkansas*

GIVE ME

EIGHTY MEN

WOMEN AND THE
MYTH OF THE
FETTERMAN FIGHT

SHANNON D. SMITH

University of Nebraska Press | *Lincoln & London*

Parts of this book previously
appeared in *Montana, The Magazine
of Western History* (2004).

Library of Congress Cataloging-
in-Publication Data

Smith, Shannon D., 1958–
Give me eighty men: women and the myth
of the Fetterman Fight / Shannon D. Smith.
p. cm. — (Women in the West)
Includes bibliographical references and index.
ISBN-13: 978-0-8032-1541-2 (cloth: alk. paper)
1. Fetterman Fight, Wyo., 1866.
2. Carrington, Frances C. (Frances Courtney),
1845–1911. 3. Army spouses—Wyoming—
Correspondence. 4. United States. Army.
Infantry Regiment, 18th. 5. Fort Phil Kearny
(Wyo.)—History, Military. 6. Fort Phil
Kearny (Wyo.)—History—Sources. I. Title.
E83.866.S65 2008
973.8'1—dc22
2007041261

Set in Swift EF.

⇝ CONTENTS ⇜

ILLUSTRATIONS

⊱ PREFACE ⊰

"With eighty men I could ride through the entire Sioux nation." The story of the Fetterman Fight on December 21, 1866, near Fort Phil Kearny on the Bozeman Trail, is built almost entirely on this infamous declaration attributed to Capt. William J. Fetterman. Accounts of the incident point to this statement to support the premise that Fetterman's arrogance blinded him to the danger of Indian warfare. Historians claim that bravado, vainglory, and contempt for the fort's commander, Col. Henry B. Carrington, compelled Fetterman to disobey Carrington's orders "not to cross Lodge Trail Ridge," thus leading his men directly into a well-planned Indian ambush.

The near universal acceptance of this thesis, presented in scores of books and articles in the more than 140 years since the battle—including most of the classics of Indian Wars history—is striking. Dee Brown's *The Fetterman Massacre,* originally published as *Fort Phil Kearny: An American Saga* in 1962, is widely regarded as the authoritative study of the event. Citing the doomed officer's "reckless boasts" and "cocksureness," Brown portrays Fetterman as so contemptuous of the Plains Indians' military skills that he was oblivious to the overwhelming evidence of their superiority during his short-lived frontier service.

Most historians point to Fetterman's arrogance and the strained relationships between Colonel Carrington and his officers to explain Fetterman's fatal decision to lead his men into ambush. Fetterman is positioned as a catalyst that ignited a long-smoldering resentment held by the fort's officers, all battle-hardened Civil War veterans, toward Carrington, a book-learned militarist who had never seen combat. The subsequent inference is that Carrington had so little military control at the fort that Fetterman felt free to disobey orders out of scorn for his commander. All of these conclusions are drawn from the assumption that Fetterman was driven by a one-dimensional obsession: his belief that a small detachment of white soldiers could easily handle any number of Indian warriors. In seeking to explain the events leading up to the catastrophe, all answers become corollaries to this presumption of Fetterman's undaunted arrogance—completely obscuring any other potential interpretation. These analyses overlook the underlying political, social, and cultural influences that played a critical role in the story. Described by historian Robert Utley as "the opening of the final act of the frontier drama," this incident reflects the complex inter- and intracultural dynamics of the United States and the Plains Indians at a pivotal point in history.[1] Taking these factors into account offers a credible alternative to the traditional story's dénouement that caricatures Fetterman's arrogance and begs the question of how his reputation was so permanently marred.

My quest to answer that question was launched in a documentary editing course in graduate school at the University of Nebraska–Lincoln when I stumbled across a letter in the Eli Ricker Collection in the archives at the Nebraska State Historical Society. In this letter, Frances Ten Eyck, daughter of Tenodor Ten Eyck, an officer who served under Carrington at Fort Phil Kearny, pleaded with Ricker and Carrington to help clear her father's name after he had been portrayed as a coward in a recently published Wyoming history volume. Little did I know that this one letter would lead to a five-year obsession with the Fetterman story.

The professor of the documentary editing course was Dr. Gary Moulton, acclaimed editor of the Lewis and Clark Journals and internationally recognized guru of historical editing. He was also the chair of my master's degree committee. Moulton admonished us to "be as curious as possible" and to annotate to a nearly ridiculous level in order to learn how to make the hard decisions of what to cut, for editing is the disciplined "study of scarcity." Moulton's rules were uncompromising. We were required to look at all aspects of a document and approach each with skepticism. And so it was that I dug so far into the Ten Eyck story that I came out on the other side! My editing project grew from the one letter to seventeen found in three different archives, and by the end of the semester I had read dozens of Fetterman books and articles including the Carringtons' books and Brown's excellent version. I think Moulton gave me an A for effort and sheer volume, as the eighty-one-page document I handed in is a real groaner. My twenty pages of notes were mostly taken from secondary sources and, like everyone else, I believed at that time that Fetterman was an arrogant jerk. But my journey to the Bozeman Trail had just begun because I couldn't leave the story alone.

During the next semester I approached the evidence from two new angles under the direction of two professors who have had a profound impact on my career and life. Dr. Susan Miller, in a challenging seminar titled "Indigenous Perspectives on American History," helped me flesh out the story by exploring it from a Native American perspective. Many years later, I know I have barely scratched the surface of the Indian side of this story—and I have much yet to learn about applying indigenous frameworks in my scholarship—but I hope that some of Dr. Miller's rigorous training comes through and I don't embarrass her too much. The real "aha" in this story came in a Women in the West course with Dr. Charlene Porsild. I knew there was something hiding in the volumes of primary material I had collected and was sure I could make a thesis out of this jumble. My working thesis was that Frances Ten Eyck's letter-writing campaign to Carrington and Ricker had successfully changed the story of the event. Dr. Porsild asked, "How was a Victorian woman able to change the history of a military event?" Her typically astute line of questioning led me to study how women influenced this story—and opened a great big can of worms.

To determine if and how women manipulated the historical

record of this incident, I had to study all of the primary material available and try to build a chronological historiography of the event. Shortly after I began this adventure, I stumbled onto a brief statement by a private who had served under Fetterman in the Civil War and at Fort Phil Kearny. Private F. M. Fessenden, who was a member of Carrington's regimental band, described Fetterman as a warm and friendly man who played with Fessenden's infant daughter.[2] I couldn't shake that image from my head. Fessenden's description of a genial, affable officer controverted the commonly accepted account of a patently arrogant and violent egomaniac. Could this be the same man known for fits of rage and cursing and who had supposedly allowed sergeants to beat privates under his command? A month later I had combed every primary source I could find that described Fetterman. Other than Carrington's reports months after Fetterman's death, every record or description of the man was positive. As I dug deeper and deeper into the records to try to find out when Fetterman's reputation took such a sharp turn, it became clear that women did indeed shape the story we know today.

What has emerged is an alternative explanation to the prevailing version that has clearly evolved from women's work. By combining new research and interpretations with up-to-date scholarship, this book builds on the work of those experts who have come before and revises the familiar story by presenting it from a different perspective—one that eliminates the bias of the women's accounts. In this book, the story is presented chronologically, integrating military, political, social, and cultural influences into the narrative. This places the characters' actions in context and alters the currently accepted rendition of the event. As my exposure to the craft of historical analysis grew, so did my understanding of the significance of this story. I am particularly indebted to the scholarship of Shirley A. Leckie in *Elizabeth Bacon Custer and the Making of a Myth* and Brian W. Dippie in *Custer's Last Stand: The Anatomy of an American Myth*. Their eloquent analyses of the evolution of the Custer myth were invaluable as I struggled to articulate the shaping of the Fetterman myth.[3]

The story concludes with an analysis of the historiography of the incident. Comparing primary and secondary documents illustrates specific examples of the impact women had on the evolution of the historical narrative. By placing a well-documented, plausible version of this dramatic event alongside a historiographical analysis, I seek to show that the story that has been popularized was derived from a history shaped by gender roles. It is a history that I believe was revised and controlled through the efforts of women defending their men with the might of their pen.

I am indebted to the Department of History at the University of Nebraska–Lincoln for taking a gamble on this former software salesperson who wanted to become a historian. The timing of my graduate program was nothing short of perfect, for I was blessed with a series of classes that, in retrospect, seem to have been custom built just for me. Professors John Wunder, Gary Moulton, Charlene Porsild, Ken Winkle, Susan Miller, Emily Greenwald, Gustavo Paz, Alan Steinweis, and Andre Gunder Frank have all left their marks on my training—and my life—and are collectively responsible for anything that resembles historical talent in my work. Gary Moulton supervised my thesis, and I am proud to be one of his last graduate students. Bringing my drafts to his office and picking up his edited chapters was a delight, even though they were dripping with red ink.

I am most grateful to Dr. John Wunder for his patient guidance and enduring support of my career despite the many detours I have taken. He is more than my doctoral committee chair, he is my idol. His intellectual inspiration and gently delivered directives have steered many grad students in the right direction; he is responsible for the successful careers of countless scholars of western and American Indian history. John's lectures are more entertaining than going to a movie, his exams keep students up all night, all while he continues to be a prodigious author and scholar. Above all, John is a genuinely caring mentor and dear friend. In short, he is just the kind of professor I aspire to be.

My family and friends met my apparent midlife crisis with love and support—albeit many thought I was nuts for abandoning a twenty-year career to be a poor grad student. Becky and Kirk Kilpatrick and Michele Haws made it very difficult to leave Denver, but their emotional (and other) support got me through the first years of school. I am sure I would never have survived Lincoln without my sister, Kylie Smith, and her many friends who have since become my dear friends. Once they got over the shock of my career change, my parents and extended family became my greatest champions. Thanks, Dad and Sherry, for your love and encouragement. This book would not exist if my aunt and uncle, Lois and Larry Schaffer, had not read my master's thesis and encouraged me to try to get it published. They passed it around to every western history buff they knew and sent me their feedback. It was a positive note they forwarded from Paul Hedron of the National Park Service that encouraged me to seek publication. At the same time, my sister, Kirsten Vick, took my manuscript home to Chicago and, after reading it, passed it on to her well-read father-in-law, Mike Vick. Their combined enthusiasm and positive comments boosted my confidence enormously. My uncle, Saylor Smith, the real writer in our family, sent his copy back with so many very necessary edits I was floored they had gotten by all the previous readers.

By the time I handed the manuscript to Elizabeth Demers at the University of Nebraska Press, it had been read by dozens of people and no one seemed to hate it. Elizabeth liked the story, too, and I ended up working with a truly great press and truly great people like Heather Lundine and Gary Dunham. I have been blessed with the professional and personal support of some awesome scholars who have become dear friends, including my department chair at Oglala Lakota College, Dr. Holly R. Boomer; Clark Whitehorn, past editor of *Montana the Magazine of Western History;* and the inimitable Patricia Y. Stallard of *Glittering Misery* fame. Indeed, I have had the good fortune to have met many "movers and shakers" in my new avocation of western history and they have been some of the nicest, funniest, and most genuinely helpful people I have ever come across.

Last, but not least, I want to thank my daughter, Katie Calitri, for growing up fast when I needed her to and being a big support to her mother. She has uprooted her life and made personal sacrifices so I could follow my dreams. Now I get to watch her pursue her own and I can't wait.

Any strokes of brilliance in the following pages can be attributed to one or more of the above mentioned people. The mistakes are those of this green historian.

In 1866, near an isolated U.S. Army post in the foothills of the Bighorn Mountains, a well-organized coalition of Plains Indians executed an ambush that killed Capt. William J. Fetterman and his entire detachment of eighty men. The spectacular victory for the Lakota Sioux and their allies would have gone down in history as the greatest defeat ever handed to the frontier army if George Armstrong Custer and his Seventh Cavalry had not ridden into immortality at Little Bighorn ten years later. Like "Custer's Last Stand," the so-called Fetterman Massacre has been mythologized in popular culture and has become one of the most famous events in the history and lore of the American West.

Comparing Custer's and Fetterman's histories is unavoidable because of the proximity in time and location as well as the similarity in outcome. However, many presumed similarities are inaccuracies that have taken on a life of their own, despite the efforts of recent revisions. In spite of the incredible number of studies of the two events, historians have overlooked possibly the most significant correlation between them. Women played an active part in creating the historical record. They did so in order to present their male family members in a favorable light, and their versions of history continue to dominate popular and scholarly accounts.

The Fetterman and Custer stories evolved in the same manner, gradually developing into tales of mythic proportions. Both episodes were initially portrayed as brutal massacres and Fetterman and Custer were immediately cast as fallen heroes. For the next generation, women substantially controlled the reputations of these "heroes" through effective public relations campaigns. Posterity eventually revised both men's reputations, as they are now characterized as overconfident egomaniacs responsible for their own—and their men's—demise. In Custer's case, a woman protected his reputation from scrutiny for half a century. On the other hand, for fifty years women deliberately cast Fetterman as the boastful and disobedient character he remains today.

Custer's widow, Elizabeth Bacon Custer, ensured her husband was revered for decades. Living fifty-seven years after her husband's death, Elizabeth Custer published three books and lectured extensively to defend and embellish his reputation and promulgate an idealized and romanticized home life with her hero. "Her reputation as a 'model wife' and shining example of American womanhood, along with the deference accorded female moral influence, made her, during her lifetime at least, an unassailable character witness," wrote historian Shirley A. Leckie.[1] Her husband's critics were kept at bay for half a century out of respect for the widow's devotion. Historians did not undertake a thorough reassessment of George Armstrong Custer until after her death in 1933. When they did, the historical record changed. Today his name is synonymous with unflattering terms such as "arrogant," "impetuous," and "military blunder."

Women controlled and manipulated the history of the Fetterman fight using the same tactics as Elizabeth Custer—except that instead of shielding Fetterman's reputation, they used him as a scapegoat. Unfortunately, Fetterman had no devoted woman to protect his honor; the bachelor officer was orphaned as a young child and had no siblings. In the aftermath of the Fort Phil Kearny catastrophe, as sensational news reports incited the American public to cry out for someone to blame, Fetterman's commanding officer, Col. Henry B. Carrington, became the fall guy. To protect their beloved and beleaguered colonel, Carrington's first and second wives published books that successfully shifted blame from their husband to the dead captain. That blame has stuck. Today, the well-worn story of the ambush is built almost entirely on the infamous declaration attributed to Fetterman: "With eighty men I could ride through the entire Sioux nation." Citing Fetterman's boast over and over, historians and authors have created an enduring image of an arrogant, contemptuous, self-important buffoon who was disdainful of the Plains Indians' military skills to the point that he abandoned his own military acumen—and common sense—and was easily tricked into disobeying his commander's orders and leading his men to their deaths. History continues to portray Fetterman's arrogance as the primary cause of the massacre of his troops, and his name is as infamous as "Custer."

This characterization of Fetterman was derived from a flawed history and eventually matured into a legend that does not reflect reality. The story we know today was shaped by Victorian-era gender roles and was distorted by subsequent historians and authors as they embroidered it into a national myth. This book reveals the ways women carefully manipulated the public perception of this event and left a permanent and inaccurate imprint on the historical record. Ultimately, it proves that Fetterman does not deserve his infamous reputation as an overconfident fool whose disregard for orders led to the death of his entire command.

These contemporary women were able to control the narrative because they themselves were part of frontier army history. Many of the original writers cited in the creation of our familiar Plains Indian Wars' narrative were women participants in frontier army life, particularly officers' wives. Until recently few knew the role women played in this story. A historian once suggested that "the women of the frontier army suggest an ethereal 'lost battalion.'"[2] Women's historians have begun to rectify this perception by placing women's involvement in the events of this era into the historical narrative. We now know that officers' wives were not the only women present at the frontier forts. Laundresses, servants, enlisted men's wives, and civilian workers' wives and families formed a community in and around the military outpost. Together, this group was referred to by the army as "camp followers." Yet they were highly valued by enlisted men and officers alike.[3]

Officers' wives and female "camp followers" have been a part of American armies from the start. During the American Revolution military historian Edward Coffman reports that women "received authorized rations in Washington's army, and some even fought in battle."[4] Between the years 1815 and 1860, women accompanied their army men to the farthest reaches of the frontier. "Benny Havens," a popular drinking song from the mid-1800s, recognizes these women: "To the ladies of the army, our cups shall ever flow, Companions of our exile, and our shields 'gainst every woe."[5] During the Civil War, wives, laundresses, and other women continued to follow and support the armies on both sides. Some openly served as vivandières, women who marched alongside the men, often going into battle with them to provide medical assistance, to carry water and ammunition, and to relay messages between troops and their commanders. The idea of using vivandières, who were often the only females seen for weeks on end, was adopted from the army of Imperial France, which was, at that time, considered to be the finest in the world.[6] When the war ended, as the army moved to the western frontier, these female "companions of our exile" came along.

At the close of the Civil War, officers who desired to continue their military careers were forced to lobby and jockey for the few available commissions in the postwar army. Most accepted brevet commissions, with a higher nominal rank than that for which they were paid, anticipating future promotions after distinguishing themselves. The romantic image of frontier service convinced many that it held the greatest opportunity for advancement. The men who successfully procured commissions in the post–Civil War frontier army were initially encouraged to bring their wives and families with them. In the spring of 1866, Gen. William T. Sherman urged officers' wives to accompany their husbands and "take with them all needed comforts for a pleasant garrison life in the newly opened country, where all would be healthful, with pleasant service and absolute peace." Having perhaps a sense of the importance of history, the general also fortuitously advised these army wives to keep a record of the history they would be making, for posterity.[7]

Eventually, many women diarists of the frontier army became published authors. According to Coffman, "Even before the frontier disappeared in the nineties, their experiences traveling and living in the West were primitive enough to be exotic, and the Indians, frontiersmen, and soldiers of that day had become curiosities."[8] Although women did not usually write in great detail about the act of battle, their presentation of the story to an interested readership in the East gave them an unprecedented opportunity to control public perception of their men's performance as soldiers. In essence, women were able to "correct" or enhance their men's reputations. Men have dominated historical writing about the Plains Indian Wars of the nineteenth century; however, because many of the primary sources they used are the published and unpublished journals of officers' wives, women have significantly influenced the dramatic and heroic narrative of this era, some of America's best-known history. Women's accounts from this era were unquestioningly embedded in our historical knowledge because Victorian sensibilities, particularly male chivalry, prevented men from challenging a lady's story.

During the Civil War era, the set of ideas known as the "cult of true womanhood" defined a proper woman's role in society. In the early 1800s, as men began to work outside of the home, society considered them engaged in the corrupting influence of commercialism, and the idea that women—who stayed at home and avoided this corruption—were purer than and morally superior to men took hold. The "private sphere" of domesticity was the realm of women, who never entered the "public sphere" of men. Middle-and upper-class women of good character demonstrated piety, submissiveness, purity, and domesticity.[9] Men of good character were chivalrous and respectful to women of their class. In fact, historian John Fraser describes the history of nineteenth-century America as "a progressive overlaying of Enlightenment common sense by chivalric romanticism."[10] Children were taught that "all days may be chivalric, however barren they may seem of opportunity for heroic action. . . . [T]ruth and honor, courtesy and gentleness, purity and faith can never grow old. . . . [V]alor and courage, kindliness of heart and knightliness of soul, are ever the highest orders of nobility."[11] Male chivalry toward women, an extension of men's acknowledgment of the importance of women's virtue, was a defining characteristic of middle-class gender relations throughout the late nineteenth and early twentieth centuries.

Women could, and did, cultivate and leverage this noble, gentlemanly respect. In fact, some women adeptly maneuvered between the public and private spheres by taking advantage of society's respect for their moral authority. Social historians Steven Mintz and Susan Kellog point out that "middle-class women achieved a public voice in such reform movements as temperance and antislavery and succeeded in communicating with a wider public as journalists and authors."[12] Army officers' wives of the late nineteenth century who published laudatory accounts of their husbands' adventures were taking advantage of their position as proper ladies. The mores of the time asserted that well-bred ladies were unquestionably honest, and proper gentlemen would never publicly dispute a woman's story. As we will see, the dramatic history of the Fetterman incident right after the close of the Civil War is a case in point.

GIVE ME EIGHTY MEN

Prelude to Disaster

A t the most fundamental level, the Fetterman battle is the story of a fight over land. Fort Phil Kearny is located in the heart of a land that was known by non-Indians as Absaroka when Fetterman met his fate. Covering more than one hundred thousand square miles in present-day Wyoming, Montana, and South Dakota, it is a majestic country of mountains, valleys, and rolling hills fed by hundreds of rivers and streams. Named for the Crow Indians, the indigenous people at the time European explorers entered this region, Absaroka comes from the name given them by their sister tribe, the Hidatsas. Early French explorers translated the Hidatsa word *Absaroka* into "children of the large beaked bird," which eventually became simply "Crow."[1] The first Euro-American cartographic definition of Absaroka came with the Fort Laramie Treaty of 1851. It was delineated as an "area bounded on the east by the Powder River, on the west by the headwaters of the Yellowstone River, on the north by the Missouri and Musselshell River, and on the south by the Wind River Mountains."[2] Although the Crows' realm was far greater than the forty million acres designated as their land in this treaty, this became the land known as "Absaroka, home of the Crows."[3]

Absaroka was a land of conflict for many years before Euro-

Americans arrived. When Fort Phil Kearny was founded in 1866, the Crow nation had been almost completely removed from Absaroka by an alliance of Plains Indians led by bands of the Teton Lakota Sioux. According to Richard White, historians have been guilty of "viewing intertribal history as essentially ahistoric and static, refusing to examine critically the conditions that prompted Indian actions."[4] This is the case when writers frequently explain the events surrounding the Fetterman battle in terms of the Lakota's fight for their *ancient* homeland. In reality, when the U.S. Army entered Absaroka in the mid-1860s, the Lakota were at their peak of military and political power and had only recently ascended to dominance after fifty years of conflict with the Crows and other tribes of the region. The army then became one of many combatants in a preexisting war zone and permanently altered the dynamics of a decades-long intertribal struggle for the land.

The Crows adopted Absaroka as their homeland at the end of the seventeenth century after an epic migration from present-day Wisconsin that began in the early 1500s. French fur traders spent a year with the Crows in 1742, but for the next fifty years the only exposure the Crows had to whites was disease transmitted through trade with other Indian nations who brought goods, and microbes, from their own trade with Euro-Americans. By the end of the century, smallpox reduced their nation from two thousand to three hundred lodges and forced the Crows to separate into smaller bands. The early 1800s found the Crows reunited and trading with various British and American companies. But they were also fighting to protect Absaroka from the encroachment of other Indian nations who were being pushed out of their own lands by the westward expansion of Euro-American settlers. In 1825, in an effort to prevent Indian trade with the British, the United States sent envoys to negotiate treaties of "friendship" with various tribes, including the Crow nation. The Crows signed the Treaty of Friendship of 1825 hoping the Americans would ally with them in their fight against other tribes for control of Absaroka. Support from their

Prelude to Disaster

new white allies never materialized and for the next twenty-five years the wars escalated between the Crows and a loose coalition of Lakotas, Cheyennes, and Arapahos.

The Plains Sioux consisted of seven divisions joined in a confederation called the Oceti Sakowin, or Seven Council Fires. The Seven Council Fires included the Tetonwan, known as the Teton *Lakota*; the Ihanktonwan and Ihanktonna, known as the Yankton *Nakota*; and Mdewankanton, Wahpeton, Sisseton, and Wapekute, known as the Santee *Dakota*. The Lakota further subdivided into their own Oceti Sakowin consisting of the Oglala, Brulé, Hunkpapa, Miniconjou, Sans Arc, Two Kettles, and Sihaspas. Each of the council fires, or bands, operated independently of the larger nation, and each was generally under the authority of a number of leaders, known as Shirt Wearers. The primary allies in the fifty-year fight with the Crows over Absaroka were the Oglala and Minneconjou Lakota bands along with groups from the Northern Cheyenne and Northern Arapaho nations. Although the Seven Council Fires of the Lakota had never united against an enemy, alliances of several bands against a common foe were not unusual. Over time, representatives from other Lakota council fires such as the Brulés, Sans Arcs, and Hunkpapas joined the alliance in Absaroka, especially when the enemy became the United States.[5]

After gold was discovered in California in 1849, the U.S. government met with the warring Indian nations to negotiate safe passage for the rush of miners and emigrants crossing Indian lands. Anticipating another opportunity to ally with the Americans and diplomatically resolve their conflict with the Lakota, the Crows attended the meeting.[6] In the summer of 1851, more than ten thousand representatives of the Crows, Lakota–Nakota–Dakota Sioux, Cheyennes, Arapahos, Shoshones, Arikaras, and Assiniboines gathered on the banks of the North Platte River in a valley near Fort Laramie. From July to September, tribal delegations converged on the region, and soon a vast city of tepees had developed in the meadows surrounding the fort, with the combined horse herds grazing down the grass for thousands of acres. The spectacle of the largest gathering of Indians in the history of the plains, and probably the nation, had to be amazing—and intimidating—to the few hundred soldiers stationed at the post. Indeed, managing the logistics of the huge gathering soon overwhelmed the officers of the small fort and they ordered the bulk of the encampment to relocate to Horse Creek, about forty miles to the east, as they waited for the gifts to arrive so the negotiations could begin.[7]

The Fort Laramie Treaty of 1851 established the first boundaries ever imposed on the Indian nations of the Northern Plains. The Crow negotiators agreed to relinquish all of their territory east of the Powder River, including the Black Hills, because the Lakota already dominated that area. In return, the Crows asked for enforcement provisions—for the Americans to help protect their claim to the rest of Absaroka—but the American negotiators did not include this stipulation. For accepting the terms and boundaries of the treaty, the Crows were promised fifty thousand dollars in supplies, including weapons for defending their land. But when they returned to Absaroka, the Lakota and their allies continued to raid and hunt in their territory. The Crows were never able to collect the promised annuities because Lakota dominance around the periphery of Absaroka prevented them from getting to the designated forts to claim their goods. On the other hand, the Sioux bands, including the Lakota, had easy access to their promised supplies and constant contact with traders to acquire guns and ammunition. Soon, the Crows were forced to withdraw farther west and north, giving up the heart of their homeland—the Powder River Basin.[8]

In 1862, as the Crows and Lakota continued to clash in Absaroka, gold was discovered just to the north in Idaho Territory. The rush of miners and emigrants from the overcrowded and depleted fields of California and Colorado swelled the area's Euro-American population to twenty thousand by the time Congress created Montana Territory from Idaho Territory in 1864. Routes to the Montana goldfields from the east were costly, circuitous, and time consuming. Steamboats slowly

Prelude to Disaster

made their way up the Missouri River to Fort Benton, Montana, delivering emigrants to stagecoaches and wagon trains for a two-hundred-mile journey across three mountain ranges. An alternate land-based route was no less arduous: taking wagons east on the Platte River road, emigrants traversed the Rocky Mountains and turned north around Salt Lake City. Then they would follow the western slope through Utah and Idaho and recross the mountain range eastward into Montana. In 1863 John Bozeman discovered a more direct overland route, staking a trail from the Platte River road along the eastern slope of the Rocky Mountains directly to the goldfields. Cutting through Powder River country—the heart of Absaroka—the trail took the miners through a war zone where the Lakota and their allies had just wrested control from the Crows. The powerful, dominating Lakota were not inclined to allow Euro-American trespassers on a trail through the last, best hunting grounds of the Northern Plains that they now claimed as their own.[9]

The original political structure of the Sioux nations did not embrace the use of an individual leader, but after years of diplomatic relations with Europeans and Americans, the concept of a single "chief" speaking for all of his people at treaty-making meetings eventually developed. Both Indians and Euro-Americans acknowledged the growing reputation of Red Cloud, an Oglala Lakota, as a leader of the factions with a "stiffening attitude against the whites." Red Cloud was not a formally recognized Lakota leader; he had been passed over as a Shirt Wearer, but at over forty years old, his reputation as a great warrior and leader in battle was renowned among the Lakota and carried enough weight to position him in an undeniable seat of power.[10] Other Lakota leaders, Spotted Tail and Man Afraid of His Horses, to name a few, were more inclined to negotiate with the Americans, and before long Red Cloud was recognized as the primary chief of the so-called hostile bands of Plains Indians.

Conflicts between Indians and Americans added to the incendiary atmosphere on the High Plains. The Sioux Uprising in Minnesota in 1862, the Sand Creek Massacre of Cheyennes in

1864, and Gen. Patrick E. Connor's attack on a peaceful Arapaho camp in 1865 contributed to Red Cloud and his followers' understandable sense of distrust and hostility toward the army and white encroachment. This acrimony, combined with the desire to protect their way of life, drove Red Cloud's Lakota alliance to step up attacks on whites who dared to pass through their hard-won land in Absaroka.[11] Despite the risks, intrepid emigrants and miners flocking to Montana's goldfields continued to use Bozeman's faster, more direct route. Shortly after the close of the Civil War, as the floodgates of western expansion opened, the mass of citizens desiring safe passage to their hoped-for riches in Montana called on their government for protection on the Bozeman Trail.

This public clamor, coupled with the post–Civil War need to replenish the treasury with gold from the Montana fields, compelled the U.S. government to resolve the conflict in Absaroka. However, the newly reunited nation had its own internal strife to contend with before it could effectively turn its attention to the problems in the West. The demands of managing and integrating the South into the Union while controlling and supporting an exploding population in the West nearly overwhelmed the government—especially the military—at this time. Lingering political tensions after four years of war created an atmosphere of distrust and discord at the highest levels of government while barely surmountable bureaucratic problems brought much of its operations to a near halt. This postwar government ineffectualness set the stage for the Fetterman incident.

The reason that nearly every rendition of this story is more myth than reality can be clearly linked to the highly charged post–Civil War political landscape. The vitriolic debate regarding the scope, mission, and size of the peacetime military went on for months and ultimately led to the impeachment of Pres. Andrew Johnson. Although the four-year ordeal of the Civil War was over, scars and animosity ran deep throughout the North and the South. New political forces intending to shape the future of the reunited country were coming to power and

Prelude to Disaster

they had many pressing issues with which to contend. Millions of freed slaves required protection and guidance to enter society, the South had to be supervised while being brought back into the fold of the Union, and the settlement of the remaining western frontier needed support. These problems required the military, but politics and massive war debt stood in the way. So, while the politicians fought, the all-but-abandoned army became bogged down in bureaucracy.

A military historian once labeled this the beginning of "the army's dark ages," during which the disparaged military struggled "almost helplessly against problems that multiplied with each passing day."[12] Congress spent much of the first year after the Civil War locked in debate about the scope, funding, and mission of the peacetime army. Radical Republicans wanted a large army to enforce their vision of a punitive Reconstruction on the conquered South. At the same time, western representatives lobbied for a strong army to protect emigrants and settlers on the frontier. On the other side of the debate, congressmen bent on making their reputations by saving taxpayers money set their sights on shrinking the army even smaller than its prewar force. Minimizing the problems of both the South and the West, President Johnson and his fiscally conservative followers worked to prevent the army from retaining its wartime power and prominence. While simultaneously trying to cut back the military, politicians and their constituents made huge demands on the army. "Whereas the prewar Army of the 1850's was essentially a frontier Army, the postwar Army became something more," writes army historian Maurice Matloff. "To defense of the frontier were added military occupation of the southern states, neutralization of the Mexican border during Napoleon's colonial enterprise under Maximilian, elimination of a Fenian (Irish Brotherhood) threat to Canada in the Northeast, and dispersion of white marauders in the border states."[13] As Carrington and Fetterman's Eighteenth Infantry Regiment began its mission to the frontier, politicians were still grappling with how to address these needs while transforming the army from a war machine of volunteers to a professional branch of the government.

Military and political leaders also struggled with the development of an agreeable Indian policy. The Union army had perfected the Napoleonic "strategy of annihilation" during the Civil War and the army that professional soldiers aspired to was a battle-driven military fraternity, not a national police force. Army officers who set policy and strategy based it on their own ideals and Civil War experiences rather than the reality of the current situation. This left the army without a common recognizable mission. In situations calling for occupation and policing, the army could only respond with blunt force because it was meant to be an offensive instrument. By way of comparison, Canada's Mounted Police had greater success in peacefully controlling the relationships between Indians and settlers because, as historian Joseph Manzione points out, it was "a genuine police force, not an occupational army acting as a national posse." Manzione described Canada's frontier military as a "trained, highly visible, paramilitary police force that used relatively nonviolent tactics of civil regulation and crisis deterrence." On the other hand, the United States' Indian policy utilized a "highly visible, poorly trained army, [and a] crazy-quilt system of local justice and overlapping political venue."[14]

The divided authority of the Department of War and the Department of the Interior over Indian policy was a constant source of conflict for officers in the field as well as those attempting to set policy. The two departments and their employees were locked in a never-ending jurisdictional battle over whether to address Indian problems with force or with patient negotiating. The result of this confusion and fractious infighting was an ambiguous mission and a record of failures including Fetterman's annihilation. The military was in legislative and doctrinal limbo for more than eighteen months after the Civil War, and the Fetterman disaster was a manifestation of the chaos ensuing from the army's massive restructuring without formal approval or direction.

After the Confederate surrender in April 1865, the army began the demobilization process. Nearly one million volunteers were mustered out of service during the next twelve months. Although the regular army had retained its separate identity throughout the Civil War, it had shrunk to a fraction of its prewar enlistment due to the superior benefits and attractions of the volunteer regiments. The first step in regarrisoning the regular army was to rebuild the officer corps. A frenzy of veteran regular army and volunteer army officers vied for commissions. Regular officers who had held high rank in the volunteers reverted to their regular grades, while volunteers who aspired to a regular army career applied for the percent of vacancies apportioned to them. All contended for brevet grades in recognition of wartime services; these were not empty honors, as an officer could be assigned to commands based on brevet rank. Officers who were generals only a few months earlier found themselves as colonels, majors, and sometimes even captains, while colonels and majors found themselves lieutenants. Most officers' initial postwar assignment was recruitment duty, and by mid-1866 the army was re-recruited to more than thirty thousand men, a number hardly sufficient to meet the demands pouring in from the South and the West.[15]

Adding to the postwar chaos of the officer corps's realignment and massive demobilization and recruitment efforts was a complicated reorganization of the army's geographical commands. When examining the accountability and responsibility for the incident at Fort Phil Kearny, historians seldom look higher than Carrington or lower than Fetterman in the military chain of command. Yet, it is the turmoil, disorder, and political gyrations at the top of the military organization—including Pres. Andrew Johnson, Secretary of War Edwin Stanton, General of the Army Ulysses S. Grant, and division commander Gen. William Tecumseh Sherman—that put Fetterman in his precarious position.

A few weeks after the close of the Civil War, Grant appointed Sherman to command the Military Division of the Missouri, basically the territory between the Mississippi River and the Rocky Mountains north of Texas. Sherman, a westerner at heart who lived in California, Kansas, and Missouri in the years before the war, had already moved his family from Ohio to St. Louis in anticipation of this frontier assignment. He knew that cities, roads, and railroads were soon to be built to support the thousands of emigrants seeking their fortunes in the West. According to Sherman's biographer, Robert Athearn, Sherman felt there was only one place for a soldier to be of value: "On the compass of destiny, the magnetic pull came from the West."[16] He quickly established his division headquarters in St. Louis and set to figure out his mission.

It did not take long to determine that the division's main problem was the conflict with hostile Indians who had been surrounded and squeezed by white expansion and were going to fight for every inch of land they had left. However, before Sherman could address "the Indian problem," he had to fight the political machine in Washington for resources and authority. For the next several years, Sherman was battered between his western constituents clamoring for protection and a recalcitrant Congress of eastern city-dwellers who believed Indians should be handled by treaty. Sherman's initial strategies reflected these political problems. He sought to establish policies and procedures that would stretch his meager force as far as possible. He envisioned small army posts supporting cavalry expeditions used to protect emigrants that were to follow regular roads in an orderly fashion. Sherman knew that the intercontinental railroad would be completed in about a year, speeding up the settlement of the West, improving military efficiency, and ultimately sealing the fate of the nomadic Plains Indians. Thus, Sherman's first stance on the Plains was one of defense. He needed a year to eighteen months of peace until the railroad was complete and Congress allocated him adequate resources so he could enlist, equip, train, and mount his new cavalry.

Unfortunately, Sherman was not given a grace period to recruit and train a new frontier army. He had to make many decisions on the fly as situations arose within his territory, and frequently Grant or the War Department made decisions for

🖹 1. Gen. Philip St. George Cooke, ca. 1860. Cooke, known as the "father of the U.S. Cavalry," never recovered from the damage to his reputation after his son-in-law and protégé, the flamboyant J. E. B. Stuart, joined the Confederacy. He learned of his postwar assignment as commander of the newly formed Department of the Platte in an article in his morning newspaper in New York City. National Archives photo no. NWDNS-111-B-2763, Record Group 111: Records of the Office of the Chief Signal Officer, 1860–1982, Series: Mathew Brady Photographs of Civil War–Era Personalities and Scenes, 1921–1940 (Brady Collection).

him. "We cannot afford perfect protection," Sherman admitted; the best he could hope to do was create a "thin blue line" of army posts along the emigrant trails.[17] Sherman was forced to juggle the political and economic demands of his superiors, the cries for support from his constituents, and the appeals for resources from his officers while waiting for Congress to officially define his mission, authority, and budget.

Sherman's first action was to tour his command in the summer of 1865. He determined that his division was too large to effectively control and sought approval to reorganize it into smaller departments. One of the decisions made without Sherman's approval was Grant's appointment of Gen. Philip St. George Cooke to be head of Sherman's newly formed Department of the Platte. By virtue of his rank and years of service in the regular army, Cooke was assigned the command. Sherman complained to Grant that Cooke was too old and that the problems of his favorite frontier department required a younger, more "resolute" commander—he wanted Gen. Winfield Scott Hancock. Grant's hands were tied, though, because Cooke was one of the few brigadier generals of the regular army, a requirement for the command of a department. Hancock, for his part, was a brigadier general in the volunteer army but had not yet been mustered out of the volunteers and commissioned into the regulars.[18] Grant was also concerned that volunteer officers in Indian country might introduce hostilities in order to keep themselves in service with the army. Grant consoled Sherman by telling him Cooke "had experience on the plains however and may do well."[19] Sherman accepted this decision with no further comment and granted Cooke free reign to manage his command as he saw fit. Cooke quickly found out that he had assumed a major portion of Sherman's burden.

Cooke's military career began forty-three years earlier, in 1823, when he entered the United States Military Academy. After Cooke's father died, his family's fellow Virginia gentry rallied to gain Cooke's admission into West Point, "where a young gentleman could obtain his education at the expense of the national government." According to his biographer, Otis E. Young, Cooke never forgot this debt to his country and served "a span of unbroken military duty which even today remains something of a record, and which was to affect the destinies of entire nations."[20] Before the Civil War, Cooke had participated in the foundation of the U.S. cavalry, witnessed the fall of Santa Fe in the Mexican War, played a major role in pacifying the Mormons, and policed the citizens of "Bleeding Kansas." He also spent more than a decade fighting Indians and perfecting cavalry tactics, eventually writing the seminal text on the subject.

Unfortunately, Cooke's many years of military experience did not prepare him for the personal and professional tragedy he endured during the Civil War. Cooke, a Virginian whose parents had owned slaves, remained loyal to the nation that had trained and employed him for nearly forty years. Much to his dismay, his son and two sons-in-law left the army to join the Confederacy and quickly rose to the top ranks, raising questions about Cooke's own loyalty to the Union and exacerbating his understandable heartache over the family's "disunion." In June 1862 Cooke's son-in-law and protégé, J. E. B. Stuart, led twelve hundred troopers of the Confederate cavalry in a daring and highly publicized circuit around McClellan's Army of the Potomac—including Cooke's own command. Stuart delighted in Cooke's humiliation, saying of his father-in-law's allegiance to the Union: "He will regret it but once, and that will be continuously."[21] Cooke spent the rest of the war in inconsequential administrative positions and never fully recovered from the damage to his reputation, his family, and his spirit—by the close of the Civil War he was an embittered man.

The Department of the Platte comprised parts of Nebraska, Colorado, Utah, Dakota, and Montana territories and was defended by a line of eleven posts. When Cooke officially opened his office in Omaha on May 2, 1866, he found that his predecessor had assigned Col. Henry B. Carrington to command an expedition to establish three forts on the Bozeman Trail. In the bureaucratic and politicized postwar officer corps shuffle,

2. Gen. Henry B. Carrington, early in his Civil War Career, ca. 1860. Library of Congress Prints and Photographs Division, Civil War glass negative collection no. LC-DIG-CWPB-06858.

Henry Beebee Carrington came out a winner. About twenty-five hundred men ended up with commissions, and almost all had recent experience commanding soldiers in the heat of battle and the hardships of the field. But not Carrington. In fact, it is difficult to imagine a less qualified senior officer existed in the whole corps for the highly visible frontier mission to which Carrington was appointed.

Carrington was born in Connecticut in 1824 and was raised by his mother and grandmother who indoctrinated him with their own evangelical and antislavery beliefs. While at school in Torringford, Carrington attended a speech by John Brown and later, at a school in Farmington—a small town that was a center of antislavery activity—he witnessed riots, vigilantism, and violence against his fellow abolitionists. These experiences steeled his resolve to become active in antislavery politics. Carrington was attracted to the military life as a boy and wanted to attend the U.S. Military Academy; however, he could not pass West Point's physical fitness requirements because of recurring lung problems (apparently he was a tuberculosis carrier his entire adult life—both of his wives and most of his children died of the disease).[22] Consequently, in 1841, Carrington abandoned his military aspirations and entered Yale, his father's and grandfather's alma mater. He thrived in the academic environment and eventually settled on the study of law. Like many nineteenth-century New Englanders, Carrington moved west to Ohio in 1848. He joined his cousin's law practice in Columbus and established himself as a diligent, dependable worker and church-going Christian. Three years later, he married Margaret Sullivant, who came from a prominent Columbus family.[23]

In 1854 Carrington befriended Ohio senator Salmon Chase at a "fusion" convention of antislavery men. The next year, Chase was elected governor of Ohio as a fusion candidate and two years later was reelected as a Republican. During this time, Carrington occasionally helped Chase in business and financial matters and became increasingly active in the fledgling Ohio Republican Party. Throughout his career Chase used his political power to secure government positions for his abolitionist friends, and Carrington reaped the benefits of this patronage on several occasions. During his second term as governor, Chase appointed Carrington adjutant general of Ohio and called for an overhaul of the citizen militia to make it more organized, disciplined, and reliable. This was a job that fit Carrington's military ambitions and for which his administrative, educational, and oratory skills were perfectly suited. In 1859 Chase returned to the U.S. Senate and his fellow Republican, William Dennison, Carrington's law partner, became governor. Dennison retained Carrington as state adjutant general, a position whose importance increased dramatically at the start of the Civil War.[24]

On April 15, 1861, three days after Confederates fired on Fort Sumter, President Lincoln issued the call for seventy-five thousand state militiamen for three months' duty. Military organizers in both the North and the South were immediately swamped by the buildup of an army that exceeded the capacity of the bureaucracy to equip it.[25] The ensuing month was nothing short of chaos as Carrington's office was overwhelmed with volunteers descending on Columbus. Mustering, feeding, clothing, and transporting thousands of troops in a matter of days was a monumental challenge, even for someone of Carrington's administrative prowess. Newspapers published numerous injurious articles about Carrington's performance, claiming he was excitable and disorganized, but after three weeks he filled Ohio's quota of ten thousand men and had an additional six to eight regiments to offer the War Department. Carrington is credited with devising a plan to use his extra regiments to establish Ohio's defense line beyond the Ohio River border in the mountains of western Virginia to defend railroad terminals on both sides of the river and to protect union loyalists in the area.[26] Dennison's major general of Ohio volunteers, Gen. George McClellan, was subsequently able to use Carrington's quickly assembled regiments to enter and take control of western Virginia.[27] This victory paved the way for West Virginia to become a free state and launched McClellan's meteoric rise to the top of the Union army. It also gave Carrington ammunition to lobby Salmon Chase for a better appointment.

Chase, now Lincoln's secretary of the treasury, found the opportunity to appease Carrington in May 1861 when Lincoln issued a proclamation to add ten new regiments to the regular army. The law required half of the officers of these new two-thousand-man regiments to be appointed from civilian life because more than three hundred commissioned officers had resigned to join the Confederacy and the army was desperately short of officers. Yet many civilians remained reluctant to accept regular commissions because of the superior benefits in the volunteer army. Volunteers received lucrative bounties and pensions for their families, discipline in volunteer units was more informal, and volunteers' commissions expired at the end of the war. By year-end only four thousand men had joined the regular army, and its primary role throughout the war was to serve as an officer pool for the volunteers.[28] Clearly, men who joined the regulars during the Civil War viewed their enlistment as a career decision rather than a temporary service to their nation. Because of the desperate shortage of men and the political nature of the civilians appointed, high-ranking commissions were handed out to men with little or no military experience. Such was the case when Chase secured Carrington a position as colonel of the newly commissioned Eighteenth Infantry Regiment in June 1861.

Although Carrington must have been thrilled to realize his ambition of a military career, he expressed concern to Chase that more experienced officers might resent his rank. Chase assured him that no one who served under him would find any cause to complain and also told Carrington that he would be assigned to positions and climates that "would most certainly preserve you in sound condition." Chase obviously anticipated that Carrington would not be sent to battle. His expectations proved accurate: Carrington spent the remainder of the war in Ohio and Indiana recruiting, processing, and training the soldiers who ultimately earned his regiment's hard-fighting reputation.[29]

3. Capt. William Judd Fetterman. A banker from Delaware at the start of the Civil War, Fetterman was able to realize his true ambition of becoming an officer in the army. Both Carrington women wrote of his gallantry and chivalry. Wyoming State Archives, Department of State Parks and Cultural Resources.

On June 24, 1861, Carrington established regimental head-quarters in Columbus where citizens presented him with a gift of a house in appreciation for his past services. He began recruiting on July 1, and five weeks later established Camp Thomas about four miles north of Columbus. Most of the new officers at Camp Thomas at the outset of the war came from civilian life.[30] Such a man was 1st Lt. William Judd Fetterman, an assistant bank teller who was one of the first men to report for duty in Columbus, arriving just five days after Carrington began organizing the regiment.[31]

Like Carrington, Fetterman had an unfulfilled desire for a military career. His father, who died when Fetterman was nine years old, was a graduate of West Point. The uncle who subsequently raised him was also a West Point graduate and served with distinction during the Mexican War. In 1853 eighteen-year-old William Fetterman applied to the Military Academy but was not successful in securing an appointment. He reluctantly turned to a career in business until the expansion of the regular army at the outbreak of the Civil War gave him a second chance at a life in the military.[32] Historians have overlooked the similarity in Fetterman's and Carrington's careers. Both men were educated civilians with military aspirations who took advantage of the Civil War to gain commissions in the regular army, and they were both recognized as exceptional recruiters.

For nearly five months, Carrington, Fetterman, and the other officers of the Eighteenth recruited, organized, and trained companies of fresh enlistees at Camp Thomas. Fetterman impressed his colonel as being ambitious and proficient. Margaret Carrington observed that Fetterman realized substantial success as a recruiter while "commanding esteem by his refinement, gentlemanly manners, and adaptation to social life."[33] There is no record of Fetterman's opinion of Carrington during this time—he was probably excited and enthusiastic about his new duties as he recruited his company up to quota.

In November 1861 Fetterman, now a captain, took charge of one hundred men in Company A of the Eighteenth Regiment's

Second Battalion and left Camp Thomas for the front. Six months later, in April and May, Fetterman participated in the siege of Corinth, Mississippi. On December 31, 1862, Fetterman led his company into battle at Stones River, Tennessee, where the Eighteenth Regiment lost nearly half its men in an hour of fighting. This launched the reputation of the Eighteenth as a tenacious, hard-fighting unit, and Fetterman received a brevet of major for "great gallantry and good conduct" for his performance in this engagement.[34] Fetterman's superiors recognized his leadership and administrative skills and assigned him to recruiting duty in Pittsburgh in April 1863. With Confederates marching into Pennsylvania and causing a panic throughout the state, the morale of the North was at an all-time low and the army was desperately short of men. Fetterman's assignment at this time was an important duty as the success of recruiting officers was vital to the Union effort.

Fetterman resumed command of his company one year later at his own request. His performance in engagements in Georgia in May 1864 earned him the command of the Eighteenth Regiment's entire Second Battalion—eight companies of about one hundred men each. He held this position during the first months of Sherman's march on Atlanta, Georgia. Again, Fetterman's military skills were recognized as he was appointed acting assistant adjutant general of the nine regiments, or more than ten thousand men, of the Fourteenth Corps to which the Eighteenth Regiment belonged. According to a Union army scholar, the assistant adjutant general of every army corps was, "by the very nature of his office, chief of the staff on which he serves. Under the commanding officer, he directs the service of all other departments of the staff, and of the whole command."[35] As part of the adjutant general staff, Fetterman prepared, classified, received, and transmitted all the reports and records of his command back to the Adjutant General's Department in the War Department. He was involved with and privy to the highest level of tactical and administrative decisions and worked closely with dozens of high-ranking officers. In this capacity he was thoroughly instilled with military procedure and protocol and exposed to every type of commander.

In addition, Fetterman remained in charge of the eight hundred men of the Second Battalion and personally led them in several major skirmishes, including the battle of Jonesboro that precipitated the fall of Atlanta. Fetterman received another brevet, of lieutenant colonel, for his contributions to the Atlanta campaign and continued as acting assistant adjutant general of the Fourteenth Corps until the end of the war. Fetterman's four years of increasing responsibility and experience in both staff and line duties, including leading men in battle and performing administrative duties in a military bureaucracy, ultimately shaped him into the quintessential military officer. Having distinguished himself both in the field and behind a desk as an administrator and recruiter, Fetterman was in an excellent position to rise to the top of the officer corps. Recognizing this potential, Fetterman chose to continue his military career after the war. Not surprisingly, his first commander had made the same decision.

In June 1865 Carrington was already in Columbus when Fetterman found himself joining Carrington back at Camp Thomas where they were assigned to regimental recruiting duty during the postwar rebuilding of the regular army. Carrington had been commissioned brigadier general of volunteers during the war overseeing essential recruitment and policing duties on the home front in Ohio and Indiana. He was kept from battle at the request of Oliver Morton, his friend and Indiana's governor. When the war drew to a close, Carrington's services were no longer required in Indiana, so in April 1865 he took a five-month disability leave and returned to Columbus with Margaret. They took the time to settle in and recover from the death of their infant son, Morton, the fourth of their six children to die before the age of three.[36]

Carrington's contacts and lobbying during this time helped secure his choice assignment to the western frontier. However, he was never able to obtain one of the many brevets being doled out to regular officers, a slight he carried with him for the rest of his life. So, in August Carrington was mustered out as a brigadier general of volunteers and rejoined the regular army at his original rank of colonel of the Eighteenth Infantry Regiment. Although there is no evidence that Carrington and Fetterman met during this summer postwar hiatus in Columbus, as part of a rather small group of officers in the same small city waiting and lobbying for commissions and assignments, it is very likely their paths crossed in social or professional gatherings.

In the fall of 1865 their careers diverged again. Fetterman was assigned recruiting duty in Cleveland, and Carrington was ordered to join his Eighteenth Infantry Regiment in Louisville, Kentucky; the Eighteenth was bound for frontier service in the West. Before Carrington's regiment's ranks could be recruited to full strength, the Department of War ordered the Eighteenth's three battalions to depart Kentucky for Fort Kearney, Nebraska Territory. On November 3, 1865, Carrington and his family accompanied the troops via trains and Missouri River steamships to Fort Leavenworth, Kansas. On November 26 the regiment embarked from Fort Leavenworth on a sixteen-day overland march to Fort Kearney. The Carrington family had never camped or spent a night away from the security and comforts of a city until this brutal early winter march. Margaret Carrington wrote of the miserable journey, "the mercury was twelve degrees below zero and two feet of snow was first to be shoveled aside before a tent could be pitched."[37] After two weeks of grueling bitter-cold days on the march, the Eighteenth arrived at Fort Kearney, Nebraska, on December 11, 1865, where they waited for recruits and orders.

On March 10, 1866, Gen. John Pope issued General Order No. 33, forming the Mountain District to protect the Bozeman Trail, frequently called the Montana Road. The order also assigned "the colonel of the Eighteenth U. S. Infantry" to command this new district.[38] Pope commanded the Division of the Missouri during the last years of the Civil War, but when Grant became general of the army after the war, he gave this command to Sherman and reduced Pope's authority to one of the departments of his old division. The circumstances surrounding General Order No. 33 reflect the confusion and instability of the army command during this postwar era of rebuilding. As Pope issued this order, he knew Sherman and Grant were planning to cut back his territorial command. Between March 3 and March 10—the very day of this order—Sherman and Grant were debating the appointment of Philip St. George Cooke to command a new department to be carved out of Pope's former territory. Sherman implored Grant to reconsider Cooke's appointment. Enclosing a report describing the tensions and potential for conflict throughout the area, Sherman said, "We need a young General, who can travel and see with his own eyes and if need be command both whites and Indians to keep the Peace."[39] Sherman did not prevail in his desire to place his personal choice, General Hancock, in the position, and a few days later Cooke opened his morning newspaper in New York City and was surprised to read he had been assigned to command the Department of the Platte—including the just-formed Mountain District.[40]

Just as Cooke's appointment was the result of his rank and tenure within the regular army at the time, Carrington—a complete unknown to Grant, Sherman, Pope, and Cooke—was appointed commander of the Mountain District in General Order No. 33 by virtue of his original political appointment to the position of "colonel of the Eighteenth U. S. Infantry" at the start of the Civil War. Sherman later told a fellow officer he "had no choice" in the assignment.[41] For his part, Cooke did not know of Carrington's appointment until he reported to Sherman in St. Louis five weeks later, and by that point Carrington had already been notified of his duty and was nearly ready to commence his expedition.

In the nine months that Carrington reported to Cooke, the two never met. Their communications were limited to telegraphs and mail routes that spanned the more than seven hundred miles between Fort Phil Kearny and Omaha. All dispatches from Fort Phil Kearny were passed through Fort Laramie—236 mountainous miles south—and took anywhere from seven days for brief telegrams to six weeks for mail delivery to reach Omaha.

In less than six months Carrington and Fetterman would be reunited for a third time. Fetterman spent the last seven weeks of his life reporting directly to Carrington at Fort Phil Kearny. Few accounts of the "Fetterman Fight" acknowledge the consequential factors that set the stage for the army's failure on the Bozeman Trail. The Department of War was nearly incapacitated by postwar politics and bureaucracy and the army was driven by a naïve, overly optimistic Indian policy. The links in the chain of command from Carrington up to Grant were volatile, untried, and extremely tenuous. Officers were haphazardly assigned to duties in a politically driven, trial-and-error style of decision making, and officers came to their frontier assignments with unrealistic expectations and values shaped by their personal experiences during the Civil War. This explosive combination of factors converged to place Carrington and Fetterman in the situation that resulted in the second most disastrous Indian mission in U.S. history.

☞ CHAPTER ☜

To the Frontier

On May 11, 1866, General Sherman arrived at Fort Kearney as part of a tour of his command. By all accounts he was uncharacteristically relaxed and enjoyed several days of hunting, photographic sessions, military ceremonies, and socializing with the officers and their families. During the previous two months, Carrington had approached his assignment with characteristic efficiency and earnestness. He pored over maps and read everything he could about the West while requisitioning men, equipment, and supplies. According to Margaret Carrington, Sherman reviewed the expedition's progress while "entering into the spirit and plans of the expedition with his usual energy and skill."[1] Paradoxically, just two months earlier Sherman had insisted the Department of the Platte, and especially the Mountain District, was fraught with the dangers and intricacies of Indian relations and required a young, assertive general. Sherman had apparently changed his mind, for now he was reviewing plans for a vital mission into the most contentious territory in his command with an officer who had never seen battle while being entertained by the wives and children who would be accompanying the expedition.

Sherman even encouraged officers' wives to keep journals to record their adventures. If he anticipated any trouble in the

Mountain Division, it is doubtful he would authorize, let alone encourage, these families to go. His change of opinion likely reflects positive reports from Fort Laramie regarding an upcoming conference with Red Cloud and the so-called hostile tribes of the Powder River country.

Most high-ranking officers in the army disdained the treaty-making policy of the Office of Indian Affairs and believed the Plains Indians would be rendered compliant only when they were made to understand the force and determination of the United States. However, in the months after the Civil War the army did not have the manpower or resources to accomplish this task. That is why, in January 1866, the army—not the Office of Indian Affairs—initiated discussions with Red Cloud to meet at Fort Laramie to negotiate terms for a peaceful coexistence in the Powder River country, including rights for white settlers and the army to use the Bozeman Trail. Col. Henry E. Maynadier, commander of Fort Laramie, was ecstatic when the messengers he sent returned from the many different tribes, including Red Cloud's Oglala band, with word that all had agreed to come. E. B. Taylor, from the Office of Indian Affairs, told Maynadier to schedule the conference for early June. Throughout the spring of 1866, news was increasingly positive as Red Cloud and other leaders regularly confirmed that they were ready to discuss peace. Maynadier reported that the Indians were starving, destitute, and willing to agree to anything to avoid another winter as had just passed.[2] As Sherman met with the Carringtons and the other families just prior to leaving Fort Kearney for the Mountain District, he must have been convinced by his own men's reports — corroborated by Indian Affairs — that "a lasting peace" would soon be effected. Margaret Carrington wrote that the prospect of the "long-heralded Laramie council . . . where a solemn peace was to be established and ratified" assured the women. She also commented that the brutal winter march she and the other ladies of the regiment had endured on the way to Fort Kearney the previous November convinced the women they had sufficient experience to undertake the journey and "risk the issues of a Rocky Mountain winter."[3]

On May 19, 1866, a bright and sunny spring day, the Carrington expedition set out for the Bozeman Trail. General Sherman, apparently satisfied with Colonel Carrington's planning and preparations, had returned to his headquarters in St. Louis six days earlier. With more than 1,000 men — 700 soldiers and 300 civilian workers — and 226 mule-drawn wagons filled with the supplies needed to build and garrison three new forts, the procession stretched for several miles. The freight included two sawmills, windows, shingle-making and mowing equipment, and the musical instruments of the thirty-piece regimental band. The household goods of the officers and their families — chickens, turkeys, pigs, rocking chairs, churns, and washing machines — were loaded alongside the soldiers' weapons and ammunition. Several hundred horses and a huge herd of cattle, oxen, and mules brought up the rear of the train. The menagerie traveled less than twenty miles a day and before long someone had dubbed it "Carrington's Overland Circus."[4]

As the huge column snaked its way west along the Platte River they moved farther into Indian country and Carrington's scouts, including the legendary Jim Bridger, became more wary. On Bridger's suggestion, Carrington tightened security and made every effort to "keep clear of Indians along the trail."[5] After eleven days the First Battalion—a little under half of Carrington's soldiers—left the main column for their assigned duty at posts in Kansas, Colorado, and Utah. On June 13 Carrington and the Second Battalion set up camp just outside Fort Laramie. Carrington had hoped to get to the fort while the treaty negotiations with Red Cloud were under way so he could meet the Indians and "form acquaintance of many with whom I will have subsequent relations."[6] The peace council had just reconvened after a weeklong adjournment and Carrington and his circus's arrival clearly set the tone for his "subsequent relations" with Red Cloud. The leader and his fellow Indian negotiators immediately realized that the United States was going to establish a military presence in their territory, and use the Bozeman Trail, with or without a treaty. Red Cloud protested

4. Jim Bridger. Bridger was a famous mountain man, trapper, guide, and scout who was in his sixties when he served as Carrington's trusted scout and advisor. Bridger's storytelling was renowned; both Carrington women wrote of his yarn-spinning and antics and the comfort they took in his presence at the fort. Wyoming State Archives, Department of State Parks and Cultural Resources.

that the Americans intended to steal the road before the Indians said yes or no, and he stormed out of the treaty negotiations.[7] The next morning, Red Cloud and his followers were gone, having dismantled their camp during the night and returned to their hunting grounds on the Powder River in the heart of Absaroka.

The treaty commission obtained signatures from the remaining peaceful Indian leaders, a group who had no interest in Absaroka or the Bozeman Trail and no authority over Red Cloud and his followers. The Office of Indian Affairs negotiators publicly proclaimed the treaty a success, but Carrington and the army officers involved with the peace treaty knew otherwise. On June 16 Carrington sent a message from Fort Laramie to department headquarters in Omaha stating, "All the commissioners agree that I go to occupy a region which the Indians will only surrender for a great equivalent." This was the first of many mixed-message communications Carrington sent to General Cooke. Carrington always balanced his reports of danger—used to justify his urgent requests for ammunition and men—with a statement of confidence in his own ability to prevail. In this message Carrington, who found none of his promised ammunition, horses, or supplies at Fort Laramie, concluded, "I apprehend no serious difficulty. Patience, forbearance, and common sense in dealing with the Sioux and Cheyennes will do much with all who really desire peace, but it is indispensable that ample supplies of ammunition come promptly."[8]

Since he left Fort Kearney, Carrington had become more aware every day of the potential for conflict with the Indians. Barely a month ago Sherman had assured him that this would be a safe assignment and encouraged the officers to take their wives and families to make the forts a pleasant garrison for all. Now he was being warned by the treaty commissioners, his guides, and friendly Indians that the Powder River tribes had no intention of allowing whites to travel through their country. Carrington was clearly concerned about his circumstances but was equally determined to succeed on his first field assignment. So, on June

17, 1866, Carrington followed orders and proceeded north on the Bozeman Trail, directly into the heart of Red Cloud and his followers' treasured hunting ground.

Immediately after he left Fort Laramie Red Cloud launched a campaign to mobilize Indians of any tribe to make a stand against white invasion on the Bozeman Trail. He even personally visited his avowed enemies, the Crows, to seek an alliance. The Crow chiefs, still hoping to convince the United States of their friendship and to obtain recognition for their title to Absaroka, politely declined.[9] Within a few months, Red Cloud had assembled a camp of more than five hundred lodges representing as many as two thousand warriors and their families, stretching forty miles along the Tongue River, a tributary of the Missouri that runs through Absaroka and the middle of Carrington's Mountain District.[10] This camp was more populous than the city of Omaha at the time and was perfectly situated to feed and support its inhabitants and their horses through the coming winter. Meanwhile, Carrington and his entourage, "splendidly furnished with everything except arms, ammunition, and horses," as an early writer of the event aptly stated, continued his march directly toward them.[11]

After two weeks, Carrington arrived at Fort Connor, about 150 miles north of Fort Laramie in central Wyoming. Named for the general of the previous year's unsuccessful military campaign to castigate the Lakota, this post had been manned by two companies of volunteer "Galvanized Yankees"—former Confederate prisoners released to fight Indians. Carrington moved the fort a few miles north, renamed it Fort Reno, and relieved the volunteers who were understandably eager to return home. After assigning two companies to garrison this post as his southernmost link on the trail, Carrington and his remaining troops, now less than four hundred men, moved out to locate the Mountain Division headquarters. From this point north on the trail, the Lakota launched a campaign of harassment against the regiment and any other non-Indians attempting to travel the route. The alliance attacked army and emigrant trains, stealing live-

5. The photographer-journalist Ridgeway Glover penciled this view of Fort Phil Kearny early in the fort's construction long before the stockade was erected. Glover was killed and scalped shortly after this sketch was drawn. No photographs of the fort or surroundings survived the artist; his equipment was apparently destroyed when he was attacked as he explored the area outside the fort on his own. From the collections of the American Heritage Center, University of Wyoming.

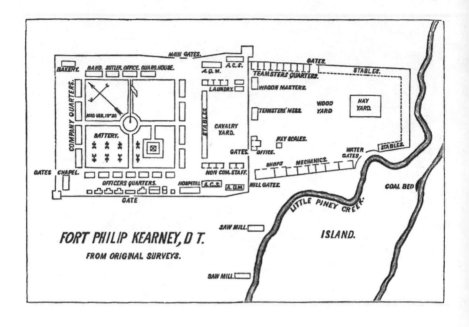

FORT PHILIP KEARNEY, D.T.
FROM ORIGINAL SURVEYS.

6. Henry Carrington was meticulous in designing Fort Phil Kearny, as can be discerned by his diagram of the post's layout. From *Absaraka* by Margaret Carrington.

stock and killing hapless travelers that strayed too far from their contingents. Carrington's response was to increase security and press on.

On July 15 Carrington selected the site of the new fort and Mountain Division headquarters on a slightly elevated plateau between two branches of Piney Creek. The site was named in honor of Gen. Philip Kearny, a famous one-armed general killed in action in the Civil War in 1862. Kearny was known throughout the army as "Fighting Phil," hence the name Fort Phil Kearny. Kearny was also the nephew of Gen. Stephen Watts Kearny, the namesake of Fort Kearney, Nebraska.[12] Carrington immediately set his men to constructing the fort. Civilian crews left in the predawn hours to cut wood for the post's stockade and buildings in a "pinery" five miles to the west of the fort. Employing a brilliant hit-and-run guerrilla war strategy, Indians attacked the crews so frequently that military escorts were required for all wood trains between the fort and the pinery and every civilian and soldier became expert in "corralling" the wagons in defense. By the end of September, Indians had stolen hundreds of cattle, oxen, and mules and killed several dozen emigrants, soldiers, and civilian employees on the Bozeman Trail. Most attacks were within a mile or two of the fort—some even within view—but Carrington took only defensive measures. His initial orders were to defend the trail and "protect the peace," and even if he wanted to attack the Lakota, Carrington had many grave problems to solve before he could put together any kind of offensive strategy. He had to focus all his energy on constructing and supplying the post before winter in order to protect his regiment as well as the women, children, and civilians under his charge. On top of these problems, Carrington also had serious personnel issues.

The enlisted men were in vigorous good health after months of marching and hard labor building the fort. The weak and disreputable had been weeded out—more than 150 had deserted since the start of the expedition—leaving the hardiest and most dependable men. They were "tough and willing workers," but two-thirds were new recruits who had never seen battle or even fired a weapon. Many had to be trained how to ride a horse.[13] Carrington could not afford the time away from construction to train them how to be soldiers, nor could he waste his limited ammunition on shooting practice. Only the thirty musicians of the band, specially armed for the expedition, had new Spencer carbines and enough ammunition. Still armed with the now-obsolete, muzzle-loading Springfield rifles, the main force had less than fifty rounds of ammunition per man.[14]

According to Alson Ostrander, a clerk in General Cooke's department during this time, Cooke approved and forwarded to Sherman every request from Carrington for more soldiers, horses, weapons, and ammunition.[15] However, Sherman appears to have stalled the reallocation of soldiers to fortify the Bozeman Trail posts. During a late summer tour of the western portion of his command, Sherman went as far as Fort Laramie—he was there just six weeks after Carrington's arrival had upset Red Cloud—and had traveled the entire route with barely a sign of Indian activity. Though he did not go north on the Bozeman Trail from Fort Laramie, Sherman concluded from the reports he heard that the few depredations that the Indians had carried out did not represent a major opposition to the army troops.[16] The general did ask Grant for more troops to defend the mail and telegraph routes on the long, exposed roads of the plains and mountains, but the army's recruitment efforts were not filling regiments fast enough to meet his requisitions. Compared to his first tour of the region in May, Sherman observed a dramatic increase in the length of the working rail line west of Omaha. He was convinced that if Cooke and Carrington's Mountain Division could make do with its assigned companies through the winter, the completion of the rail to the forts just south of Fort Laramie would solve their logistical and manpower problems. Like Cooke, Sherman assumed the regiment of infantry and company of cavalry that had been detached to Carrington was fully staffed and sufficient to accomplish their short-term goals.

Carrington's chain of command was never completely sympathetic to his claims of shortages of men, weapons, ammunition, horses, and forage and the impact these deficiencies had on the day-to-day protection of the Bozeman Trail. This is partially because of Carrington's mixed-message reports and their infrequency due to the length of time it took for mail to reach the East. The lack of understanding on the part of Carrington's superiors can also be explained by Sherman's and Cooke's opinions of Indian warfare—both believed that their army was easily up to the task of defending themselves against marauding Indians even if they couldn't protect an entire road filled with emigrants. Also, Sherman and Cooke both assumed that Carrington's orders for horses, weapons, and ammunition had been fulfilled, but army administration was still reeling from the rapid postwar reorganization and could not keep up with the demands of the field. Once the bureaucracy was surmounted, requisitions took months to fulfill because of the transit time to get to the remote post. Cooke and Sherman also mistakenly believed that cavalry and infantry companies that were assigned to Carrington months earlier had reported for duty. This misunderstanding coupled with Carrington's reports of needs for even more men and supplies led both Sherman and Cooke to the opinion that Carrington was excitable and reactionary.

In July 1866 Congress finally passed the Army Reorganization Act—it had taken the politicians more than a year after the Civil War to agree on the mission, size, and scope of operations of the army. The reorganization eliminated the three-battalion regiments, making each battalion a regiment itself. In the reorganization, the First Battalion of the Eighteenth was retained as the Eighteenth Regiment, the Second Battalion was converted into a new Twenty-seventh Regiment, and the Third Battalion into a new Thirty-sixth Regiment.[17] Carrington had immediately requested that he stay with the new Eighteenth after the reorganization, but he had yet to receive orders confirming where the Eighteenth and the two newly formed regiments would be assigned.[18] By early fall, Sherman and Cooke had decided to use the army reorganization, which would go into effect on January 1, 1867, to move Carrington out of the danger zone and replace him with someone who had combat experience. The army was ignorant of the magnitude of immediate danger Carrington's ill-equipped little fort was in, although the colonel and his men were becoming more enlightened every day.

While Carrington fought army and government bureaucracy to bring Fort Phil Kearny up to strength, Red Cloud and his leaders planned its complete destruction. Carrington was not fully aware of the strength and determination of Red Cloud's huge army of well-trained, well-fed, and well-equipped warriors camped a few miles north. Though he was alarmed by the frequent raids and attacks on the fort, Carrington had to wait for reinforcements and his requisitions to be filled before his troops could take the offensive. The women, children, and unarmed civilians who accompanied the army on this so-called peaceful mission had become virtual hostages, for no one was safe from attack outside the stockade of the fort. Carrington's worst problem, however, was that he was desperately short of officers. The commander and his fort eagerly awaited the arrival of Bvt. Lt. Col. William J. Fetterman, one of the Eighteenth Regiment's most revered and experienced officers, who was due to report for duty any day.

On September 21, 1866, Fetterman received orders to leave his recruiting assignment in Ohio and join his regiment at Fort Phil Kearny.[19] During his six-week journey Fetterman had plenty of time to contemplate his future. As the senior officer of the Second Battalion, Fetterman could expect to take command of the new Twenty-seventh Infantry Regiment, including the Twenty-seventh's official headquarters, Fort Phil Kearny, when the reorganization went into effect on January 1, 1867. Word of Fetterman's imminent promotion and arrival was met with delight by the many officers and enlisted men at Fort Phil Kearny who had fought under his command in the war. Fetterman's spirits must have risen with the altitude as he reconnected with comrades-in-arms during layovers at forts along the long jour-

ney to his mountain post. In the summer of 1866, army personnel traveled from Ohio and points east to the frontier posts of
the Department of the Platte by taking a network of train lines
to St. Louis, where they boarded a Missouri River steamboat.
After a ten-to seventeen-day trip—depending on the water level
and the current—they arrived in Omaha, the eastern terminus
of the Union Pacific Railroad. Then the soldiers rode the train
to the end of its line where construction crews were installing
more than two miles of rail a day.[20]

During the spring and summer of 1866, as Cooke was setting
up operations in Omaha and Carrington was making his way
west to the Bozeman Trail, the Union Pacific laid more than
two hundred miles of track westward from Omaha. Frances
Grummond was told she was the first female passenger on the
Union Pacific when she accompanied her husband to Fort Phil
Kearny from Omaha in August. They switched to horse-drawn
ambulances at the end of the track one hundred miles west of
Omaha.[21] When Fetterman came through a little over a month
later, he was able to ride a train one hundred miles farther, all
the way to Fort Kearney, Nebraska. Silas Seymour, an engineer
and Union Pacific executive, took the train from Omaha to Fort
Kearney on September 11, 1866—ten days before Fetterman was
to begin his trip west—and was thrilled that it took only eight
hours.[22] The train had averaged twenty-five miles an hour, the
distance a wagon train could make on a good day. Sherman
eagerly observed the Union Pacific's progress, as the problems
of transportation and communication that plagued his frontier posts improved dramatically with each completed stretch
of track.

From Fort Kearney, Fetterman accompanied military expeditions between posts on the overland trail. Forts McPherson,
Sedgwick, Laramie, and Reno guarded the trails between Fort
Kearney, Nebraska, and Fort Phil Kearny. At each of these
posts, Fetterman was required to report to the post adjutant
who located a place for him to stay while waiting for the next
detachment heading west. Generally, officers were placed as

guests at the homes of other officers. Fetterman described his trip as a "very long one," saying that "had it not been for the politeness and hospitality of the officers at the different posts along the route [it] would have been very tedious."[23] War veterans of the Eighteenth Regiment who had served with and under Fetterman were posted at every one of these forts, where he had many reunions and opportunities to hear first- and secondhand news about Carrington's expedition.

Lt. Frederick Phisterer and Capt. Henry Haymond, two officers who fought closely with Fetterman in the Atlanta campaign, had accompanied Carrington all the way to Fort Phil Kearny only to be reassigned to eastern posts one month later. As they picked their way east along the same trail Fetterman would follow west in a few weeks, they left in their wake many officers who were aware of what was transpiring on the Bozeman Trail. As post adjutant at Fort Phil Kearny, Lieutenant Phisterer had written and logged all of his commander's reports. He had intimate knowledge of the strengths and weaknesses of Carrington's operations—including the severe shortage of weapons and ammunition. Both men had experienced the ferocity of the Lakota alliance. In fact, Captain Haymond was the first of Carrington's officers to command a unit during an all-out attack. He and a small group were lured into an ambush when they pursued Indians who had raided a nearby emigrant train—arrows killed two and wounded five of his men before relief arrived. Soldiers and emigrants were killed almost every day Haymond and Phisterer were on the Bozeman Trail. Their brief sojourn was long enough for the two officers to appreciate Indian military prowess and the clear and present danger of the remote forts. Fetterman surely considered and registered the opinions of his respected friends as he was told of their experiences.

Undoubtedly, Haymond and Phisterer also shared their opinion of Carrington with their counterparts. In sworn testimony after the Fetterman incident both men stated they had no confidence in Carrington's military ability based on the common knowledge that Carrington had no field experience and their own observations of his "easy excitability." Haymond testified that although Carrington was unpopular with the regiment because of this sentiment, "socially, he was well-liked."[24] The transferred officers' stories and opinions, along with Carrington's official reports and telegraphs that necessarily passed through Fort Laramie on their way to Omaha, furnished a plethora of information for Fetterman to consider on his way to his assignment. Years later, in conceding he failed to have the confidence of some officers, Carrington said, "Few came from Omaha or Laramie without prejudice, believing I was not doing enough fighting."[25] The informal "officers' grapevine" on the long route from the east formed many of their opinions—including Fetterman's—about Carrington before they ever reached the fort.

At Fort Laramie Fetterman joined a cavalry company of sixty-three new recruits bound for Fort Phil Kearny under the command of Lt. Horatio S. Bingham. Also joining the detachment was Capt. James W. Powell, a former lieutenant Fetterman commanded at the battle of Jonesboro where Powell was severely wounded in heavy fighting. Fetterman later commended Powell, who received a second brevet because of it. Now the veterans were on horseback, reminiscing and speculating about the situation ahead as they rode north to their new post. On this last leg of his long journey Fetterman described a "very exciting Buffalo chase" where he "wounded three, but they are very tenacious of life and would not die."[26] The 236-mile trip from Fort Laramie to Fort Phil Kearny also gave Fetterman an opportunity to observe the problems of using fresh recruits on the frontier. According to Carrington, many of the cavalrymen who accompanied Fetterman could scarcely mount their horses without help, let alone shoot the muzzle-loading weapons they were issued.[27] Fetterman's long trek from the east was very enlightening; he knew the many problems Carrington faced, the prejudices of his fellow officers, and the dangers of Indian warfare before he set one foot in Fort Phil Kearny.

The highly politicized and overwhelmed postwar military

machine placed Fort Phil Kearny's officers in their life-threatening situation. The journey from the east to their remote post, coupled with the imminent army reorganization, shaped the men's expectations about frontier army life and played a role in their subsequent decisions and actions. The frontier environment was completely foreign to most of the soldiers, and their adaptation to Indian warfare and the changing face of the army that had been their home through the war also influenced their conduct. Another factor that affected the behavior and demeanor of the officers was the presence of ladies at the outpost. The social and cultural values of this era—particularly Victorian sensibilities governing an officer's chivalrous and gentlemanly nature—ultimately enabled women to write the history of Fort Phil Kearny.

Ladies of the Regiment

The population of Fort Phil Kearney fluctuated greatly during the first six months of operations on the Bozeman Trail. At its peak, nearly seven hundred soldiers and civilians lived and worked in the immediate vicinity, but as units were detailed to other posts or sent on mail and other duties, the number of soldiers averaged far fewer than the four hundred and fifty who marched up the trail with Carrington. The number of women at the fort would fluctuate as wagon trains with families passed through on their way to Montana, but from the records and manuscripts available, it appears that there were rarely more than a dozen women living at the post at any given time. From October to December there were five officers' wives, two or three female servants, and a couple of enlisted men's wives who also served as camp laundresses. Nineteen-year-old Elisabeth Wheatley and her husband, James, ran a civilian mess and boarding house just outside the gates of the stockade. The Sioux wife of Pierre "French Pete" Gazeau, a trader who had been in the region for several years, moved to the fort following an Indian attack that killed her husband and his business partner less than a month after the fort was established.[1]

Scholars agree with contemporary writers that women—particularly the ladies of "officer's row"—changed the character of society in a regiment. Army wife Frances Roe wrote in her memoirs that women's "very presence has often a refining and restraining influence over the entire garrison, from the commanding officer down to the last recruit." Roe also asserted that the least developed, most dreadful postings were "where the plucky army wife is most needed."[2] Roe drew a distinction between her fellow ladies and the other women of the army, a distinction that historians agree was not artificial, but "the result of different upbringings and outlooks. Officers' wives raised with education, refinement, and a strong sense of reserve considered the other women on the frontier to be brawlers—tempestuous and uncouth—but necessary for their comfort."[3]

In her seminal work on the dependents of the frontier army, Patricia Y. Stallard captured the essence of the "microcosm of the western military post," where the inhabitants of such a small community could have no secrets. Citing an officer's wife who lamented that "Gossip, malicious and otherwise, throve," Stallard positions an officer's wife as "the most outstanding asset to [his] career," as long as she "could adroitly maintain her own personal honor while diplomatically advancing his career."[4] In *Life and Manners in the Frontier Army*, Oliver Knight describes a "rigid caste system" among the women of frontier army posts where "at the top sat the commanding officer's wife—known to the Army as the K.O.W., because the literal abbreviation would not do." Citing frontier army novelist and former soldier Charles King's works, Knight wrote that "the tone of garrison life depends immeasurably upon its social leader, the wife of the commanding officer."[5] The commanding officer's wife "was expected to set the standards of conduct on the post, function as the official hostess, and receive all civilian and military guests with equal courtesy."[6] Though Fort Phil Kearny was Margaret Carrington's first garrison, she seems to have been ideally suited for the task of shaping the community into a proper Victorian settlement. Margaret was well liked by the other officers' wives and was respected by the soldiers of the fort. At age thirty-four,

7. Margaret Irvin Sullivant Carrington. After General Sherman advised her to keep a journal of her adventures in a new land where "all would be peace," Carrington was able to quickly publish a memoir from her notes and sketches. Her personal notes have not surfaced, nor have any photographs of her other than this one. From the Collections of American Heritage Center, University of Wyoming.

she was a mature and wise woman described as "commanding in presence" and "dignified in deportment."[7]

Like most officers' wives, she came from "a class level where household labor was performed by hand—a servant's hands."[8] For many of these women, adapting to a life without servants was their greatest challenge. Hinting at her own lack of experience in domestic labor Margaret wrote, "Fortunate were those who in earlier days had been advised that other rooms than the parlor have their uses. . . . Primitive ways are to be learned; but the tent becomes neat and genteel, and the taste of its arrangement and adornment gives capital hints to the mind of the beauty of patience."[9] However, the colonel's wife may have been referring to some of her less fortunate subordinates, for the Carringtons were served by George, described by another wife at the fort as "a colored man-servant, who when dressed at his best, looked not unlike a head-waiter in a more pretentious hotel capacity."[10]

Born at Danville, Kentucky, on May 10, 1831, to Joseph Sullivant and Margaret Irvin McDowell Sullivant, Margaret came from a wealthy, influential family. Margaret's great-grandfather, Lucas Sullivant, a Virginian of Irish descent, is credited with being the founder of Columbus, Ohio. Born in 1765, Lucas Sullivant moved to Kentucky as a young orphan, where he learned surveying in the field. As a deputy surveyor under Gen. Richard C. Anderson, surveyor general of the Virginia Military District of Ohio, Lucas led a surveying expedition into the Scioto valley in 1797, where he surveyed and platted and became proprietor of the town of Franklinton, which was eventually annexed into Columbus, Ohio.[11] Franklinton was one of the first villages in the Northwest Territory and the oldest in central Ohio. To encourage settlers, Sullivant gave away land to families along the main thoroughfare, now called Gift Street in his honor.[12] Sullivant was one of the town's most prominent men for decades. He was the first president of the first bank, owned a lucrative toll bridge erected across the Scioto River on the road leading from Columbus to Franklinton, and was a county clerk.[13] Sullivant built the first

Ladies of the Regiment

brick home in the town and married Sarah Starling, "a Kentucky girl of royal English lineage, who through her generosity and kindliness in Franklinton, was called 'Lady Bountiful.'" The Sullivants had three sons, William, Michael, and Margaret's father, Joseph, who inherited his father's love of literature and learning and "more than any one person, was to be a factor in the broad development of the Ohio State University and public schools of Columbus."[14] As a respected and renowned scientist and scholar, he was later immortalized at Ohio State where the Joseph Sullivant Medal, one of the university's highest honors, is awarded every five years to this day.[15]

In June of 1830 Joseph married Margaret Irvin McDowell Sullivant, a first cousin of Irvin McDowell, a future well-known general in the Civil War. One year later, at the age of twenty, Margaret died after giving birth to their first child, Margaret Irvin Sullivant. When Margaret was eighteen months old, Joseph married Mary Eliza Brashear, a relative of Pres. James Madison, who raised Margaret along with six other children born from 1833 to 1847.[16] Margaret's stepmother was described as "a devoted wife and mother, and of a most unselfish and uncomplaining disposition" who "fulfilled her duties in a most cheerful and commendable manner." When Margaret was nineteen, Mary died of an apparently protracted illness. Joseph wrote that in the latter part of her life Mary had suffered "great pain and prostration from the malady which finally terminated her useful existence," and that as a pious Christian "in the hour of death . . . [she] quietly passed away in triumph of faith, without a fear or a doubt."[17]

As the oldest of seven children with an invalid mother, Margaret was thrust into the role of matron of the house at an early age. Her youngest brother was not quite three when their mother died. For the next two years, Margaret was head of the Sullivant home, leaving only after she married Henry Carrington. Though her father wrote that he was an "impracticable person, who has spent much of his life with books, bugs, weeks, stones, and 'sich like' when he should have been

MARGARET IRVIN SULLIVANT,
WIFE OF
COL. HENRY BEEBEE CARRINGTON, U. S. ARMY,
BORN MAY 27, 1831,
DIED MAY 11, 1870.

CARRINGTON

8. and 9. Margaret Carrington had six children but only two survived to young adulthood. It is likely that Henry Carrington was an inactive or latent tuberculosis carrier, as Margaret and all of his children, from both Margaret and Frances, died of "consumption." Frances died at an older age, but apparently of the same symptoms. Henry was not admitted to the Military Academy due to "recurring lung problems." Photograph courtesy of Leona L. Gustafson, Franklin County, Ohio, Gravestone Photos, http://homepages.rootsweb.com/~rocky/Franklin_Cemeteries/index.html.

OF THEIR CHILDREN

MARY McDOWELL
BORN OCTOBER 5, 1852, DIED APRIL 7, 1854.

MARGARET IRVIN
BORN NOVEMBER 22, 1855, DIED JULY 25, 1856.

JOSEPH SULLIVANT
BORN JUNE 9, 1859, DIED SEPTEMBER 29, 1859.

MORTON
BORN JANUARY 23, 1864, DIED AUGUST 23, 1864.

engaged in more important matters—that is, making money," the Sullivants doubtlessly had servants all through Margaret's childhood and young adult life with her father.[18] Years later, as she struggled to adapt to life on the frontier, she wrote that it was a blessing for a woman to know how to cook and clean and that she eventually learned these "primitive" skills.

Her father and grandfather's penchant for education and reading ensured Margaret was very well educated. Her father described Margaret as cultivated and commanding of respect, a compliment to both his daughter and himself, the self-avowed academic, intellectual, and scholar. Her writing is that of a well-read and sophisticated author and is peppered with citations of classic literature and historical events. Margaret and her family were prominent members of the Presbyterian church, where Henry Carrington taught Sunday school and helped raise funds to expand the church. Neither of the Carringtons wrote of their courtship, but it is likely Margaret first met Henry at church—though they could also have been introduced through Carrington's law partner who had connections to her father.[19]

Margaret married Henry, who was seven years her senior, in December 1851. The next twelve years of her life were marked by tragedy. She bore six children, four of whom died between the ages of six months and two years. Only two boys, James and Henry, survived beyond early childhood. The trauma of the deaths of their children seems to have strengthened their relationship, for Margaret and Henry were seldom apart. During the Civil War, she and the boys moved with the colonel to Indiana and, according to Margaret, lived with him in camp as he established operations and commanded the recruitment of the Eighteenth Infantry Regiment.[20] It was this experience, camping in an army base a few miles from a city, that Margaret cited as preparation for her family's challenging assignment and her new domestic responsibilities on the frontier. Frances Courtney Grummond, the young army wife who became Margaret's charge a few short months after she arrived at Fort Phil Kearny, had even less experience camping and keeping house.

Ladies of the Regiment

Frances P. Courtney was born in 1845 into an affluent family in Franklin, Tennessee, a major center of the antebellum South's plantation economy. Her father, Robert T. Courtney, was a tradesman whose family moved from Virginia in 1825 and her mother, Eliza J. Haynes Courtney, was from one of Franklin's founding families.[21] The 1850 census listed Robert's occupation as "House Carpenter," a trade that afforded the Courtney family a comfortable life, including having several domestic slaves.

Frances wrote that although her father was a slave owner, he was "an ideal one," and Henry Carrington—a fervent abolitionist—later rationalized her father's slave ownership by saying Robert Courtney "was sure that the system was wrong, and that the nation would never realize its highest prosperity until freedom became general."[22] Having been raised in a home with slaves, Frances, like Margaret, lamented in her book about the ever-present "servant problem" of the frontier army officer's wife. Describing her first days in the West, Frances elaborated on her futile attempts at darning and mending, and her ineptitude in the kitchen was so well known that, upon settling in at Fort Phil Kearny, she and her husband ended up eating in the unmarried officers' mess.[23]

Frances was the fourth of seven Courtney children. They grew up in town and were educated in local schools. Her oldest sister, Florence Octavia (Octie), wrote that the family had generous means during those years and that the family owned at least two other homes in addition to their residence. Older brother William wrote that his father owned several houses and lots in town along with six slaves. Even so, Frances's adolescence was not without tragedy. In 1857, when she was eleven, her nine-year-old brother, Robert (Bobbie), died, and eighteen months later, on December 1, 1859, her father passed away.[24] But her greatest challenge came when she was fifteen and the Civil War raged into Franklin, forever altering the course of Frances's life. The national conflict divided Tennessee—voters narrowly ratified the legislative act to secede, and there remained considerable support for the Union throughout the state. The North-South fracture extended to the community of Franklin and many Tennessee families, including the Courtneys. The family was weakened by the death of their patriarch less than two years before the war, and their allegiances eventually split. Frances, her mother, and two younger brothers, nine-year-old John and five-year-old Phillip, ultimately joined Octie's ardent support of the North's cause, while her older brother and sister, William and Virginia (Jennie), allied with the secessionists.[25]

Because of Tennessee's economic resources and location, the state held enormous strategic importance during the war. Middle Tennessee, including Franklin, was viewed as the corridor to the South as well as the region's breadbasket, so northern troops moved quickly to occupy the area. For the first months after the war began, the area shifted between Union and rebel occupation. Tensions were high throughout the region as many residents maintained their allegiance with the Confederacy. Guerrilla attacks and espionage against the Union were rampant and most northern sympathizers tended to keep their sentiments to themselves.

It is not clear what motivated the five members of the Courtney family to ally with the North, but Octie claimed that "for a time I was the only member of my family devoted to the Union cause." In a memoir written as a tribute to Union general George H. Thomas, Octie maintained she was arrested and tried for treason toward the Confederacy, "because of innate patriotism and fearless expression of loyal sentiment, when my position was asked." Octie wrote that she escaped her captors and fled behind the Union army lines to the headquarters of the regional post where she remained until early 1862.[26] During this time, Octie married Lt. James H. Cochnower of the Seventy-fourth Ohio Infantry whom she apparently met while the Seventy-fourth was stationed in middle Tennessee.[27]

The two Courtneys with southern allegiance were actively involved with the Confederate army: brother William enlisted in the Thirty-second Tennessee Volunteer Infantry Regiment

Ladies of the Regiment

10. Frances Courtney Grummond Carrington. When she applied to the army for her slain husband's pension, she discovered George Grummond had another wife who had already claimed it. After writing a letter of condolence to Carrington when Margaret died, a correspondence ensued and Henry and Frances were married shortly thereafter. From the collections of the American Heritage Center, University of Wyoming.

and sister Jennie, who lived in Augusta, Georgia, had married a Confederate officer.[28]

In February 1862 the Union captured the region from the Confederacy and Franklin was garrisoned with federal troops that soon built Fort Granger on a bluff above the Harpeth River at the edge of town. With the Union army in control of the town, and Octie married to one of their officers, it is safe to conclude that the four Courtneys who still lived in Franklin were more openly supportive of the Union. However, skirmishes continued to erupt and several times in 1863 fighting moved from street to street and house to house, obligating federal officers and Union supporters like the Courtneys to retreat to the safety of Fort Granger. In her book, Frances compares her treacherous crossing of the North Platte River with one such "emergency" during the Civil War where she was forced to cross the swollen Harpeth River clinging tenaciously to the neck of a blind mare to keep from drowning.[29]

During this period of Union occupation, Frances met Lt. Col. George W. Grummond of the Fourteenth Michigan Infantry. Grummond was stationed at Fort Granger in early 1863 and was promoted to lieutenant colonel in October, serving briefly as temporary commander of the fort. The handsome colonel was soon courting Frances, who was ten years his junior. In January 1864 Grummond's regiment was assigned to support Sherman's march on Atlanta, thus interrupting Frances's budding relationship with the dashing officer. Grummond spent the next year—the rest of the war—in campaigns in the Carolinas and Georgia where his record indicates he served with distinction in the battle of Bentonville.[30]

Six months after Grummond left for Georgia, the Courtney family lived through one of the war's bloodiest confrontations. The battle of Franklin has been called "the Gettysburg of the West," with both sides suffering frightening casualties during five hours of furious combat in a rare nighttime conflict. The Union lost nearly twenty-five hundred men and the South lost more than seven thousand—including six generals. The next

11. Lt. Col. George W. Grummond, Fourteenth Michigan Infantry, ca. 1864, about the time he met Frances Courtney after leaving his wife, Delia, in Michigan. Courtney did not find out Grummond was married until she filed for his pension following Grummond's death. Library of Congress Prints and Photographs Division, Civil War glass negative collection no. LC-USZ61-2033.

morning, the community found that both armies had moved north to prepare for another major confrontation in Nashville, and Franklin was left to deal with the horrific casualties. Forty-four homes and buildings were converted into field hospitals for both Union and Confederate soldiers. The Courtneys opened their three homes, feeding and caring for two hundred Union wounded from their own supplies while everyone waited to hear the results of the fighting to the north. Two weeks later Frances and her family and their Union charges were thrilled to hear that Gen. George Henry Thomas's troops had decimated the remaining Confederate Army of Tennessee in the battle of Nashville. In a few months the war was over and General Thomas, the newly appointed military leader of Tennessee during Reconstruction, invited Frances and her family to the Chicago Sanitary Fair in May where they were recognized for their care of the Union wounded. The family maintained a relationship with General Thomas over the years, and Octie was apparently invited to an unveiling of a statue dedicated to him in Washington DC but was unable to attend the ceremony and instead sent the afore-mentioned tribute describing her family's experiences during the Civil War and her appreciation for the general. Her tribute was later published as a small pamphlet titled "Recollections Awakened by the Unveiling of the Thomas Statue!"[31]

Frances "renewed her acquaintance" with Lieutenant Colonel Grummond at the end of the war, possibly even meeting in Chicago through a mutual connection with General Thomas, and they were married on September 3, 1865. Her brother William, who served in the Confederate army throughout the war, signed the bond uniting his sister with the Union officer. Grummond opted to stay in the military, and Frances must have been eager to leave the war-ravaged South to accompany her new husband on an exciting adventure. The newlyweds left Tennessee bound for New York at the end of 1865, and shortly thereafter Frances was traveling with her husband to his assignment at Fort Phil Kearney.[32]

Frances was three months' pregnant when the Grummonds

Ladies of the Regiment

arrived at the post on the Bozeman Trail in October. Hinting at her condition and acknowledging the authority of the commanding officer's wife, Frances described how a large double bedstead was made by the fort carpenters "through the kind consideration of Mrs. Carrington." This was a luxury indeed—and indicates just how much the presence of women influenced activities and priorities at the fort—for the soldiers and laborers were working against time to complete the stockade and all of the post's buildings prior to the onset of winter, and most of the men were still living in tents.

From the start the Grummonds were popular, especially the gracious and spirited southern lady who had so bravely supported the Union soldiers during the war. Frances was young, pretty, and friendly, and unlike the handful of other army wives at the fort, she had absolutely no domestic skills and very little desire or capability to learn them. Having been raised in a slave-owning family, Frances never learned how to sew, mend, cook, or clean. But the fort community rallied behind Frances, who was not only domestically challenged but also in the "delicate condition" of early pregnancy. A soldier was assigned to perform light domestic duties, and the other wives endeavored to teach her basic cooking skills—to little avail. For the most part, the Grummonds dined with other families and in the single officers' mess tents.

Margaret and Frances strove to be the epitome of a nineteenth-century Victorian lady: a pious, submissive, pure woman dedicated to making a good home. But the dangers and challenges that the small, isolated military community faced together, along with the close proximity and inevitable interaction with people from all walks, enabled officers' wives to occasionally skirt the traditional Victorian cultural values that normally divide army post's residents into distinct social classes.

Frances wrote of her interaction with a wide range of men: "As our world revolved in a very small space there were no happenings that were unrelated, and the stories of miners, trappers, and guides were more intensely interesting as told by word of mouth than when filtered through the printed page."[33]

Margaret described the personal traits of several civilian men, including the mail runners and miners, hinting at friendships, or at the very least, acquaintances, with men of varied social status and backgrounds. For instance, she wrote of the "experience and quiet coolness, [and previous life] in Oregon and Washington Territories" of Mr. Van Volzpah, and the "sound sense and solid honesty" of "miner Phillips" and another miner, Captain Bailey, who, "after seventeen years in frontier explorations retained the manners and habits of a pleasant gentleman, full of intrinsic worth and steady courage."[34] Both Margaret and Frances described their familiarity with the famous scout James Bridger, a sagacious man described as "peculiarly quaint and sensible" and a "sterling friend" whose "genial manners and simplicity of bearing commanded respect as well as the attachment and confidence of all who knew him well."[35]

Margaret also explicates the unusual and untraditional position she and the other women were placed in by being embedded in the day-to-day efforts of an army at war. For instance, Margaret devoted a chapter of her book, "Indian Warfare: Things a Woman Can Learn When She Has Seen Them Tried," to the decidedly male topic of Indian warfare. Much of her work is obviously ghost-written by the colonel, but her detailed description of Indian military tactics juxtaposed against the army's futile, though gallant, response bespeaks a woman forced out of her traditional role. "When even a woman shares the contingencies of entering a new country with troops, she must learn something besides the lessons of house-wifery, endurance, and patience. . . . Yes, even a woman, after several hundred miles of journey alternately in the ambulance or side saddle, sometimes in corral . . . will draw conclusions for friends to consider, even if they only elicit a smile at her timidity, simplicity, or weakness."[36]

Despite these subtle deviations from the norm, Margaret's age, experience, and position as the wife of the commanding officer—especially one who was seeking to confirm his leadership capabilities by keeping a solid grip on all goings-on at the fort—ensured she seldom strayed from the traditional role of a proper lady. Though forced to learn a few more domestic chores than the typical middle-class woman of the era, Margaret had a black man-servant and was able to call on soldiers, known as "strikers," to perform any duty required so that she was not forced to compromise her standing by performing many of the duties that fell to other wives. Frances exemplified the traditional Victorian woman's role in her unabashed incompetence at domesticity. Admitting that "the servant question" was an issue that arose throughout her entire married life, she wrote of regular clashes with her husband about obtaining a servant so as to avoid "the risk involved in cooking."

Reading between the lines near the beginning of Frances's book, *My Army Life and the Fort Phil. Kearney Massacre*, affords a glimpse of her personality at this time and a perfect example of contemporary Victorian womanhood. Her fear and discomfort in her new position pushed her frequently to the brink of hysteria, reaching the "extreme limit of endurance" and "threatening to end it all." In many places, her story reads like the trials of Job as she suffers the lowly life of a lieutenant's wife with an ever-present feeling of foreboding.[37]

Margaret, Frances, and the other ladies of the regiment came to the frontier with mixed feelings; their trepidation was assuaged by encouragement from Sherman and other senior officers who assured them they were embarking on a mission where all would be peace. Their rosy visions of domesticating the wilderness soon gave way to the reality of a level of deprivation and danger that exceeded the fears of even the most timorous among them. It is difficult to postulate how different daily life would have been if the officers' wives were not present at Fort Phil Kearny. But even without ladies to protect, defend, and respect, the men of the post aspired to distinguish themselves in battle and hoped for the dangers they would soon encounter. They too got more than they bargained for.

Officers and Gentlemen

Carrington entered the Mountain District in June 1866 with twelve officers and anticipated another half dozen to be attached to his command within a few weeks. One month later, he was down to six officers at Fort Phil Kearny, the district's headquarters. Carrington assigned two officers to remain at Fort Reno, the southern post on the trail, and after establishing Fort Phil Kearny, he sent two of his officers ninety miles north to the Yellowstone River to build and garrison Fort C. F. Smith, the district's northern station.

In a devastating blow to his command—clearly reflecting the army's postwar disarray and headquarters' ignorance of circumstances in the field—Carrington's superiors notified him that his two most senior officers were reassigned to recruiting duty in the East immediately upon arrival at Fort Phil Kearny. The two officers, his assistant adjutant general Captain Phisterer and his battalion commander Captain Haymond, had been intimately involved with the expedition since its inception and were an integral part of Carrington's organization. The experience of these two officers, after spending months planning and two full months on the road with the mission, was indispensable and Carrington could scarcely believe the absurdity of the order. Though he formally objected to the reassignment, Carrington was commanded to comply and on August 1, thirteen days after they placed the first stake in the ground marking the location of the new fort, the two men departed, leaving Carrington with six officers.

This number would soon change, for a small party led by five lieutenants was en route from Fort Laramie to report to Carrington at Fort Phil Kearny. After a brief layover at Fort Reno, the group—consisting of ten enlisted men, a surgeon, a chaplain, and six civilians—was ambushed by a Lakota war party at Crazy Woman's Creek. During this fight, Lt. Napoleon H. Daniels became the first officer killed on the Bozeman Trail.[1] Days after the four officers reported for duty, Carrington assigned one, Lt. George Templeton, to Fort C. F. Smith and another, Lt. James Bradley, to escort Inspector General William Hazen who came to conduct a tour of the Mountain District. Carrington could ill afford to release Bradley and the twenty-six soldiers and horses Hazen required—this was almost half of the horses Carrington had at his post—but, again, he had to comply with orders issued by an oblivious central command. Bradley and the rest of Hazen's escort would not return until the end of October. The two remaining officers of this expedition, Lieutenants William Wands and Prescott Skinner, brought Carrington's contingent of officers at Fort Phil Kearny up to eight.

These eight men, the group of officers who actually managed to stay at Fort Phil Kearny for more than a few weeks, were a diverse lot. They all had Civil War service, but few had been west of Ohio before this assignment. Frontier duty at a desolate post in hostile Indian territory was a difficult transition for many veteran soldiers. They had experienced hardship in the field during the war, but Civil War officers were used to operating within a short distance of towns and cities and being part of a network of units supported by a comparatively reliable supply chain. The isolation and stress of Indian-fighting service intensified communication, supply, and morale problems at these posts. On top of these issues, frontier army officers held commissions several grades lower than they enjoyed just a few months earlier and

12. Capt. Fred Brown. Brown was a popular man at the fort and known for his jovial personality. Brown, Fetterman, and Ten Eyck spent the most time with the Carringtons and appear to have had the same cultivated tastes and interests. Wyoming State Archives, Department of State Parks and Cultural Resources.

were adjusting to lower pay and prestige in an environment that was more costly and far less comfortable than any previous assignment. This adjustment was more than some could bear. At Fort Phil Kearny, Lt. John J. Adair resigned his commission in order to return to civilian life shortly after arrival, although he agreed to stay until Lieutenant Bradley returned from escort duty.

On the other hand, despite the hardships, some men thrived in this rugged and challenging environment. Two of the eight officers at Fort Phil Kearny at the end of August, Dr. Samuel Horton and Dr. C. M. Hines, were surgeons and did not command troops. This left six officers to command six companies of soldiers as well as perform battalion, regimental, and district administrative duties. Carrington was forced to assign all of them multiple commands and to use noncommissioned officers in positions of greater authority.[2] Most of these overworked and underpaid officers yearned for a chance to distinguish themselves and secure a promotion. To them, the strike-and-retreat Indian harassment going on just outside their post offered just such an opportunity.

Capt. Fred Brown, the post quartermaster, was responsible for the army's herds of livestock and horses—the primary target of the frequent Indian raids around the fort. Brown took his duty seriously and was the first officer out of the stockade when pickets signaled a raid on his stock. Brown was a friendly, sociable man who was well liked by all; even though he was a hard drinker, the teetotal Carringtons were exceptionally fond of him. On September 23, after Indians raided the post's beef herd, Brown led a victorious counterattack in which his unit recovered all the stock and killed half a dozen warriors. From this point on, Brown seemed to be addicted to the thrill of Indian fighting. He kept his horse saddled at all times and dashed out of the fort at the first sign of trouble. Brown did not seek Carrington's permission to chase the Indian attackers; his responsibility for the post's livestock gave him the authority to participate in every skirmish within sight of the fort—which

13. Capt. William H. Bisbee, Fourth U.S. Infantry, in 1880. Bisbee was devoted to Fetterman and became Carrington's greatest detractor, wielding great influence after transferring to the office of Carrington's superior, General Cooke. Bisbee went on to serve a long military career and published his own memoirs, *Through Four American Wars: The Impressions and Experiences of Brigadier General William Henry Bisbee*, in 1931. Wyoming State Archives, Department of State Parks and Cultural Resources.

was nearly every conflict. By many accounts, Brown was an outstanding quartermaster throughout the Civil War and he was unfairly excluded from the postwar brevet list. When Brown received orders to return to Fort Laramie to join his company in late September, he was devastated. To return to the safety of quartermaster duties at Fort Laramie would end all hope of a promotion or brevet in recognition for bravery. He stalled his transfer, with Carrington's tacit support, by claiming he had to complete inventory and paperwork, and three months later he had yet to report to his new post, prompting Fort Laramie's commander to complain to department headquarters. Brown had standing orders from Carrington to use his judgment to protect army property including livestock, wagons, and equipment, as well as the personnel of the woodcutting trains. As Brown had the first, and only, success against an Indian attack during Carrington's command at Fort Phil Kearny, Carrington was being logical in giving Brown the discretion to defend the fort's property.[3]

Lt. William Bisbee became the post adjutant after Lieutenant Adair announced his resignation. Bisbee brought his wife with him on the expedition from Fort Kearny, Nebraska, but this was the only thing he had in common with Colonel Carrington. Of all the officers, Bisbee was Carrington's greatest detractor—most likely because of the significant difference in their personalities and backgrounds. Bisbee was not very well educated and was frequently abusive to his men—a personality trait that Carrington found especially appalling.[4] Bisbee, along with Lieutenants Wands and Adair, frequently accompanied Brown on retaliatory attacks against their Indian adversaries, although most of their attempts were in vain. During the late summer and fall, these four officers acquired a significant amount of Indian-fighting experience. Of the core group of officers stationed at Fort Phil Kearny during Carrington's tenure, Capt. Tenodor Ten Eyck, Carrington's second in command, was the only man who did not appear to have a desperate desire to fight Indians.

Ten Eyck was an engineer who had just returned from trying

14. Capt. Tenodor Ten Eyck commanded the detail sent to relieve Fetterman after news of the battle reached the fort. Hints of cowardice followed Ten Eyck for the rest of his army career, and when a historian suggested Ten Eyck could have saved the Fetterman contingent, Ten Eyck's daughter Frances launched a mission to restore his name. Wyoming State Archives, Department of State Parks and Cultural Resources.

his luck in the Colorado goldfields when he enlisted as a private in the Wisconsin Volunteers at the beginning of the Civil War. His commanders soon recognized he was officer material because of his education and age—Ten Eyck was over fifty years old at this time—and after six months he was commissioned in the regular army as captain of H Company in the Eighteenth Infantry Regiment. Ten Eyck was captured in 1863 and spent more than a year in a Confederate prison camp where he contracted dysentery and nearly died. His wife gained an audience with President Lincoln and secured Ten Eyck's release from prison, after which he spent the rest of the war at various camps in Ohio and Indiana performing administrative duties under Carrington's command. Ten Eyck was selected as a guard of honor when Lincoln's body lay in state in Indianapolis.[5] The connection to the president is unclear; however, Ten Eyck's father, Conrad, was a signer of the Constitution of the State of Michigan and appointed by Pres. Andrew Jackson to be the first U.S. marshal of the state, and it is possible that his political connections opened doors at the state and federal level for his children.

After the war, Ten Eyck, by now in his midfifties, left his wife and five children in Wisconsin and traveled with the Eighteenth Regiment from Ohio to the frontier. While at Fort Kearney, Nebraska, Ten Eyck hired Susan Fitsgerald, simply known as "Black Susan," to be his maid and laundress for Company H. Fitsgerald accompanied Ten Eyck to Fort Phil Kearny and became quite well known for her cooking.[6] Ten Eyck was an excellent engineer and supervised the initial surveying and construction of Fort Phil Kearny. He was an introspective and exceptionally well-read man—his personality and background was the most similar to Carrington's out of all the post officers. However, Ten Eyck had a serious drinking problem that eventually destroyed his career. Both Ten Eyck and Fitsgerald ran into difficulties a few months after Fort Phil Kearny was established, Fitsgerald for selling pies made from government supplies and Ten Eyck for public intoxication. Ten Eyck kept a diary throughout the three years of his frontier service. His laconic entries provide some of the best primary source material on the history of Fort Phil Kearny and the Fetterman incident.[7]

In the autumn of 1866 several officers arrived to augment Carrington's weary command. On October 6, Lt. George Washington Grummond, one of the most controversial officers involved in the Fetterman affair, reported for duty. Grummond had what appeared on the surface to be a stellar Civil War career, rising from sergeant to lieutenant colonel in the first two years of the conflict. However, closer scrutiny reveals an unseemly background of aggression, cruelty, and ungentlemanly conduct. His rapid promotions were based on near-reckless bravery in battle. In August 1864, after several incidents in which his irrational zeal for conflict and acts of brutality—all while intoxicated—imperiled his troops, a group of his junior officers petitioned the adjutant general to investigate whether Grummond was fit to command. Citing numerous instances of Grummond's drunkenness while on duty, as well as several cases of physical abuse of his men, the petition resulted in Grummond's appearing before a general court-martial. He was found guilty of "threatening to shoot a junior officer and of shooting an unarmed civilian," and received a public reprimand.[8]

Less than a month later, in the first few days of September 1864, Grummond botched a mission with Brig. Gen. Robert Granger in Tennessee. Granger ordered Grummond to bring his unit to a designated location at a specific time to coincide with Granger's in order to launch a coordinated attack on Confederate forces under Gen. Joseph Wheeler, but Grummond rushed his unit into the theater of operations three hours early. Granger did not mince words when he filed his report on the incident: "This movement of [Colonel Grummond's] I consider unfortunate, as it unquestionably hastened the movement of Wheeler from Lawrenceburg." Not only did Grummond alert his enemy to the planned operation, but he was also engaged in battle before Granger's units arrived and had to send an emergency courier to his commander asking for support. Granger was livid and immediately relieved Grummond from the operation.[9] Grummond's superiors accused him of overzealousness several more times in 1865, describing his actions with phrases such as "pushing hastily forward," "obliged to retire, not without loss," "not even a semblance of a company organization," and "compelled to retire somewhat in confusion."[10]

Grummond managed his personal affairs with equal imprudence. At the outbreak of the war, the twenty-six-year-old sailor took a three-month enlistment as a sergeant in Company A of the First Michigan Infantry Regiment, leaving his twenty-year-old wife, Delia, and their young son in Detroit.[11] Grummond reenlisted on May 1, 1861, as a captain, but in less than a year he contracted a serious illness and was forced to resign his commission and return to Detroit to recuperate. After about six months at home, Grummond signed up as a major with the newly reorganized Fourteenth Michigan Infantry in March of 1863, leaving Delia, who was six months pregnant, and their five-year-old son, George.

Grummond spent the rest of 1863 on active duty in middle Tennessee. Under Col. Henry Mizner, the Fourteenth was tasked with clearing the region of guerrilla bands of Confederate sympathizers, and Mizner, who mounted his entire regiment with horses secured from local farms, pursued the lawless bands so relentlessly that the area was cleared by the end of the summer. Grummond, who grew up on ships sailing between the urban centers of the Great Lakes, must have developed his passion for horses and the romance of the cavalry during this time. With Mizner's troops in firm control of the region, they garrisoned at Fort Granger and spent the better part of a year in and around Franklin where Grummond met the beautiful young southern belle Frances Courtney. In October 1863 Grummond, recently promoted by Mizner to lieutenant colonel, served briefly as temporary commander of Fort Granger. He was also courting Frances, who was ten years his junior.

In January 1864, Grummond and four hundred other men in his regiment reenlisted with the understanding that they would continue their service as mounted infantry or cavalry. After four months of rotating detachments on furlough, the men returned to Nashville to find their regiment had been reverted to infantry and were assigned to support Sherman's march on Atlanta, thus interrupting Frances's budding relationship with the dashing officer. Grummond spent the next year—the rest of the war—in campaigns in the Carolinas and Georgia where he was noted to have served with distinction in the battle of Bentonville. [12]

Meanwhile, back in Detroit, Grummond's wife, Delia, delivered their second child, Mary, on June 26, 1863, a few months after he left for Tennessee. Grummond apparently discontinued supporting his family through the remainder of the war and on September 23, 1865, Delia was granted a divorce on the grounds that her husband, "being of sufficient ability to provide a suitable maintenance for her, hath grossly, wantonly, and cruelly refused and neglected so to do." Delia Grummond was awarded custody of their two children and George Grummond was ordered to pay his wife two thousand dollars in alimony in one-quarter installments over the next year, though the sum was substantially higher than his annual salary. This did not seem to disturb Grummond, for on September 3, 1865—twenty days before his divorce was decreed—he married Frances Courtney in Tennessee. The two Mrs. Grummonds did not find out about each other until after his death.[13]

Lieutenant Colonel Grummond was mustered out of the Michigan Volunteers at the end of the war and enlisted in the regular army as a second lieutenant. This was a huge demotion in pay and prestige, even for the postwar officer corps. Grummond told his naïve young wife that he was recommended for a brevet of brigadier general, and Margaret Carrington commented in her book that he was "understood" to have been breveted brigadier general.[14] However, there is no record of Grummond receiving a brevet of any grade. It seemed the lieutenant colonel wanted to get as far away from his obligations as possible, thus he accepted a commission as a second lieutenant expecting to be assigned duty on the remote frontier. The newlyweds left Tennessee at the end of 1865 and, after a few interim assignments on recruiting detail, arrived at Fort Phil Kearny on October 6, 1866. Although Grummond's past did not have a chance to catch up with him—he had less than three months to live—his actions on the frontier were driven by the same recklessness and ambition that got him into trouble during the war.

One month later, on November 3, 1866, the final group of officers involved in this drama arrived at Fort Phil Kearny. Fetterman and his detachment crested Pilot Hill and saw their new home spread out below. A solid-looking stockade encircled a small rise located in a magnificent valley at the foot of the Bighorn Mountains. Inside the stockade were dozens of buildings in various degrees of completion, but the fort appeared to be quite far along in construction. As Fetterman rode in, the soldiers and citizens of the fort must have breathed a collective sigh of relief. The constant attacks of the previous three months had the entire community on edge and the arrival of nearly seventy men and horses, led by one of their best and bravest officers, was a welcome sight. Before Fetterman dismounted he spotted many of his old friends and subordinates. Fred Brown, William Bisbee, and John Adair reported to him in Georgia—Brown and Bisbee had been his quartermaster and adjutant throughout the entire Atlanta campaign.[15] Dozens of sergeants and privates who remembered Fetterman in his finest hour came out to greet their old commander. For those who believed Carrington was an inferior officer because he had no battle experience, here was a man who had led hundreds of men through some of the Civil War's worst battles and could compensate for the commander's weaknesses. This was just what the post needed to build the confidence of the recruits and join the officers into a cooperative team.

Fetterman found the climate to be delightful and was pleased with the location. Within a few days he described himself as "pleasantly domiciled in an excellent log house which my company hastened to build me on my arrival, and feel perfectly contented with the country, and the life I am to lead."[16] His first night must have resembled a family reunion, as Fetterman was popular with officers and enlisted men alike. The war veterans of the Eighteenth, the men who had survived the physical and mental test of battle, formed a club of sorts. In describing the psychology of the Union soldier on the battle line, historian Earl Hess writes that the struggle for survival in a deadly and dangerous environment forged a special relationship between veterans: "The spirit of comradeship created a sense of belonging in the regiment that resembled the sense of family but went beyond it as well. The members were tied together by something different from blood. . . . They depended on one another for survival."[17] Within this close-knit "family" a good officer was looked up to like a father. Men developed attachments to their favorite officers who looked out for their well-being and inspired them with enthusiasm for duty. Fetterman's arrival strengthened the bond that already existed between the many veteran soldiers at the fort. Pvt. F. M. Fessenden, a war veteran and member of the regimental band, remembered Fetterman as a friendly and jovial man. Fetterman played with Fessenden's infant daughter and jokingly suggested she be named "Sedgwick" after the fort where she was born on the march out from Nebraska.[18] Charles Wilson, a private in Company H, described Fetterman as a father figure to his men, "always looking out for them, seeing to their needs, and saving all unnecessary suffering."[19]

Meanwhile, Carrington was a lame duck commander during the seven weeks Fetterman reported to him at Fort Phil Kearny. Carrington knew that he had failed to instill confidence in his leadership with many of his officers, but he also knew that the imminent army reorganization would relieve him of the supervision of this fort and its officers, as he would move on to another post with the First Battalion, which was to become the new Eighteenth Infantry Regiment. The Eighteenth's Second Battalion would become the Twenty-seventh Infantry Regiment and remain at Fort Phil Kearny, most likely under senior officer Fetterman's command. Although Carrington and his officers may have been less than happy to work with each other, the group knew they had less than two months to tolerate each other because the reorganization would take effect on January 1, 1867. If any of the officers really believed that Carrington's cowardice and lack of experience was the only thing preventing them from attacking the Lakota, they could see this predicament was nearly over. However, even if Carrington's officers were as contemptuous of him as their testimony indicated after Fetterman's death, the presence of ladies prevented them from being openly insubordinate.

Carrington, Fetterman, and most of the officers at Fort Phil Kearny were properly chivalric gentlemen. Three weeks after he arrived, Fetterman wrote to a friend that the fort was "favored with the presence of four ladies."[20] The officers were always conscious of the ladies' presence. During the day, the wives could be found out on the parade grounds enjoying a game of croquette, walking to the sutler's store, or casually strolling within the confines of the stockade. In the evenings, officers with wives entertained guests for dinner and frequently the entire command gathered to enjoy concerts by the regimental band. On Sundays the officers attended church services and spent the day socializing. The officers of the post were not openly disrespectful and disobedient to the commander in front of women, who were nearly always present, because they were culturally indoctrinated with a Victorian code of conduct. This code dictated that the officers be gentle, courteous, respectful, and kind to all. A good deal of testimony describes a relationship of congeniality and civility between Carrington and his officers. As Captain Haymond testified, the men at the post had no confidence in Carrington but in a social setting, "he was well-liked."[21] Lt. William F. Arnold testified, "Some of [the officers] were not on the most friendly terms, but never clashed at all. The feeling was not harmonious but there was no open rupture."[22] Capt. William H. Bisbee, the most caustic of Carrington's critics, was uncharacteristically reserved in his description of the state of feeling among the officers. "Almost without exception it was harmonious, except a general feeling of disgust towards Colonel Carrington in command of the troops."[23]

Behind closed doors, out of view of the women, military protocol and ambition prevented an officer such as Fetterman from being openly defiant. Fetterman's work as an assistant adjutant general during the height of the Civil War exposed him to the complex bureaucracy that Carrington faced. He was fully aware that the officer corps—especially at the staff level in Washington—had plenty of men with little or no field experience. To an officer with Fetterman's experience, Carrington was simply one of the many commanders, some competent and some inept, whom he would report to on his way to the top. On November 26, 1866, Fetterman wrote to a friend in Ohio, "We are afflicted with an incompetent commanding officer viz. Carrington, but shall be relieved of him in the reorganization, he going to the 18th and we becoming the 27th Infantry."[24] This letter confirms his opinion of Carrington, but it also confirms that Fetterman knew their days together were numbered, as this letter was written thirty-five days before the reorganization was to go into effect. Fetterman was a military man who would think twice before he jeopardized his career by being insubordinate to his commander—no matter how incompetent he felt him to be—particularly when he would be reporting to him for such a short amount of time. Also, it is unlikely that Fetterman displayed an unprofessional demeanor in front of his men because he was so thoroughly indoctrinated with the military code of conduct.

Carrington was equally as conscious of military procedure and the necessity to maintain discipline and professional relationships with his officers. Even though he was going to be leaving in a matter of weeks and likely handing control over to Fetterman, Carrington assumed full responsibility for his operation and continued to command the post. There may have been a subtle contempt for Carrington, but the professional military men at the post would not commit—or tolerate—insubordination. Carrington continued to issue orders and supervise all activities of the district, and the officers followed his orders.

There is no question that the last two months of 1866 at Fort Phil Kearny were filled with conflict. The Indians attacked with maddening regularity while Carrington, Fetterman, and the other officers flailed, desperately trying to figure out how to respond. These were the first soldiers out of the Civil War to come up against the strike-and-retreat warfare of the Plains Indians, and they were getting their heads handed to them. It is easy to see how frustrating the situation was for a successful soldier and to assume that Fetterman simply got mad and wanted to retaliate at all costs, but that requires suspending all confidence in his military bearing. It is inconceivable that Fetterman, with his experience at the battalion and corps level, did not appreciate the significance of the many difficulties Carrington faced in trying to launch an offense. There were not enough horses to mount more than a few dozen men, and the animals they did have were weak from a lack of grain and forage. On his trek from Laramie, Fetterman had witnessed just how inexperienced the post's recruits were; he began drilling them for the first time shortly after he arrived. His soldiers' weapons were obsolete and there were less than fifty rounds of ammunition per man. The stark reality of the situation was that they had to follow Carrington's strategy of cautious defense until the mind-numbing bureaucracy of the War Department—still reeling from postwar reorganization—acted on their requests for more horses, men, weapons, and ammunition.

Most historians point to the conflict between Carrington and his officers as the primary cause of the Fetterman disaster. Claiming the discord was palpable throughout the post, they portray Fetterman as immediately disagreeing with Carrington and forming a coalition against him. Carrington is described as having no control over his officers. These accounts do not evaluate the officers' relationships and the post's discipline within the context of Victorian cultural values of the era. Traditional accounts of this story also underestimate the significance of the military indoctrination of the officers involved and the impact the imminent army reorganization had on their interactions. In assuming that Fetterman believed eighty soldiers could ride through, and conquer, "the entire Sioux Nation," historians position Fetterman as thoroughly unable to see his enemy's strategic superiority. There is evidence that Carrington and Fetterman worked together better than has been previously presented and that, in the few weeks that remained of his life, Fetterman experienced enough Indian warfare to come to respect his opponents, even if he did not fear them.

Hard Lessons Learned

The first three months in Absaroka were filled with hard work and adventure for the soldiers and civilians who formed the community in and around Fort Phil Kearny. In addition to about 450 soldiers, there were nearly 200 civilian employees of the government during the peak of activity at the Mountain District headquarters. They were skilled tradesmen, general laborers, teamsters, clerks, interpreters, and guides. Many were young men working their way to the goldfields of Montana who signed on for a few months of employment to fund the rest of their journey. The guides, scouts, mail carriers, and interpreters were seasoned veterans of the West, remnants of the fur-trapping and trading era. Several of these men were famous in their day—Jim Bridger, James Beckwourth, Jack Stead, and Mitch Boyer—and their presence provided no small comfort to the men and women who were new to the frontier.

The vast majority of the soldiers at Fort Phil Kearny had never been west of Ohio before they came to Absaroka. The grandeur of the location was nearly overwhelming to the newcomers. The fort was situated on a plateau and provided an extraordinary view in every direction. The snow-capped mountain peaks to the west sloped to tree-filled foothills where the men cut wood for the fort about five miles away. Just to the north of the fort was a low rise named Sullivant Hills, presumably to honor of the family name of Carrington's wife Margaret Sullivant Carrington. North and east of Sullivant Hills was a ridge of about the same height, called Lodge Trail Ridge. Big Piney Creek ran through the valley formed between Sullivant Hills and Lodge Trail Ridge, passing a few hundred feet to the east of the fort. They could see for more than twenty miles to the east in a panorama featuring plains, badlands, rolling hills, and the deep blue water of Lake DeSmet. Less than a mile south of the fort was a high hill, appropriately named Pilot Hill, where pickets maintained watch over the post and the entire valley. The clear, dry climate with temperatures in the eighties during the day moderating to the low sixties at night was invigorating. Margaret Carrington wrote, "Sickness is so rare, that for days in succession, during the constant labor and exposure of 1866, no soldiers attended the stated daily sick call, and the hospital itself was monopolized by cases of surgery only."[1]

The construction of the fort, the laying in of supplies and forage for the winter, and the establishment of formal military operations in the area occupied nearly every waking hour for the members of the post community. Occasionally, the monotony of hard labor and military bureaucracy was interrupted by an exciting event. A few times buffalo came so close to the fort that Carrington allowed a small group of mounted men to hunt them. The entire fort stopped to watch the thrilling chase, although it ended in failure more often than not. Of course, the main source of excitement was the ever-present prospect of an attack by groups of warriors from Red Cloud's large camp.

From July 15 to September 30, Captain Ten Eyck recorded twenty-one entries in his diary describing raids and assaults made on the army by the Lakota alliance. Seven of the last ten days of September he recounted skirmishes in his pithy, matter-of-fact way. Although the fort was taking shape and operations approached a semblance of routine, the constant threat of attack kept tensions high throughout the post. Carrington, as district commander, was supposed to leave the day-to-day man-

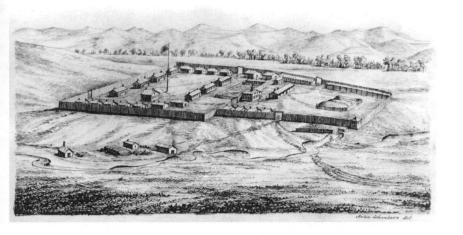

15. This sketch of Fort Phil Kearny was drawn by 2nd Lt. Jacob Paulus, who served at the fort after the Fetterman battle. From the collections of the American Heritage Center, University of Wyoming.

agement of the fort to Ten Eyck, the post commander. Inevitably, conflicts arose between the two as Carrington became increasingly obsessed with security and issued orders that undermined Ten Eyck's authority. Finally, on October 8, Carrington relieved Ten Eyck and assumed the role of post commander. Five days later, General Cooke notified Carrington of the dissolution of the Mountain District—eliminating a layer of bureaucracy for many of the officers but changing little in the military operations in Absaroka. Until the army reorganization was scheduled to take effect, Carrington remained in command of the three battalions of the Eighteenth Regiment and the three posts along the Bozeman Trail.

Carrington put Ten Eyck in command of the Second Battalion and Ten Eyck's home company, Company H. Three weeks later, Fetterman's arrival moved Ten Eyck down another level in authority. Fetterman outranked Ten Eyck and assumed command of the Second Battalion relegating Ten Eyck to the command of his one small company. Around this time, Ten Eyck appears to have demonstrated a drinking problem. His diary entries record many bouts of illness and on November 18, Carrington arrested Ten Eyck for "a mistake made at Dress Parade," presumably a euphuism for being drunk.[2] A few days later Ten Eyck recorded he had a satisfactory interview with Carrington regarding their difficulties, but he was not released from arrest until November 24. In the first three weeks of December, while Fetterman, Powell, and Grummond were busy drilling and training the soldiers for the first time, Ten Eyck was relieved of command of the mounted infantry and was required to turn over the horses, saddles, and ordinance that were in his custody.[3] It is difficult to determine whether Ten Eyck's drinking problems were a result of his career misfortunes or whether his decline in authority was a result of his drinking. In either case, by mid-December Ten Eyck was excluded from nearly all command responsibilities even though Carrington was desperately short of officers. Ten Eyck's entry on December 13 hints at his frustration: "Fine day. Relieved by Lt Powell. This has been a bad day for me."[4]

Hard Lessons Learned

The month of October was exceptionally stressful for Carrington. The pressure of managing the construction of the post while under the constant threat of attack was bad enough, but he could not seem to convince his superiors of his difficulties. Cooke sent a telegram via Fort Laramie saying Carrington could "probably dispense with your ninety-four horses, after mounting all the cavalrymen. They could be used for cavalry at Laramie. The same as to any useless horses at C. F. Smith and Reno."[5] Carrington surely stared at the message in disbelief. His promised cavalry units had yet to arrive, more than half of his horses (thirty-three in one day) had been lost to successful Indian raids, and the twenty-seven horses he was forced to relinquish to General Hazen's inspection tour were still away. Carrington had just reported to Cooke that he could not chase his enemy with the three dozen horses he had left, as they were too weak from lack of forage because his orders for grain had not been filled.[6] The companies at his two other forts were in even worse shape—Carrington could only spare three horses for the two companies that went north to open Fort C. F. Smith.

A few weeks later, Cooke sent Carrington a telegram threatening a general court-martial if monthly and tri-monthly reports for the previous three months were not immediately forwarded. The courier bringing the telegram was overtaken fifty-five miles outside of Fort Laramie with an updated telegram stating Carrington's reports—diligently and punctually filed—had just been received at Cooke's headquarters. In this message Cooke indignantly ordered Carrington to keep up a weekly mail delivery with couriers covering not less than fifty miles per day. Carrington explained to Cooke, once again, that he could not spare the horses nor were they in good enough shape to cover that much distance in a day.

Carrington must have been near his wit's end by the last week of October. Then, to his great relief, Lieutenant Bradley and his detachment of two dozen mounted infantry—Carrington's best horsemen—returned from escort duty on October 27. Also, a large shipment of corn had finally been delivered and the horses were gradually regaining their strength. Carrington declared a holiday for the post to celebrate the completion of the stockade and most of the buildings on October 31. Three days later, Fetterman, Powell, Bingham, and the sixty-three mounted soldiers arrived. Carrington was aware of Fetterman's excellent reputation as a leader and his experience under fire, and his arrival along with the addition of Bradley, Bingham, and Powell gave him the greatest depth in officers he had had since he established Fort Phil Kearny. Carrington wrote to department headquarters on November 5, "I look for this month to determine [the Indians'] purpose, and hope yet to be able to strike a blow which they will feel more than the last, and not risk a single post on the line in the attempt."[7]

Carrington trusted Fetterman to take the offensive immediately. Two days after he reported for duty, Fetterman came to Carrington with a proposal to set a trap for the hostile bands of Lakota alliance warriors who harassed the post on a daily basis. Carrington authorized the plan, this being the very day he wrote to Cooke that he hoped "to strike a blow." That night Fetterman and his men hobbled some mules next to a stand of cottonwoods where the soldiers waited to ambush the warriors who would inevitably come to steal the livestock. Fetterman—and the entire post community—waited all night for his prey to come and attempt to steal his "bait" so that he could strike a blow for the army. Instead, a Lakota raiding party stampeded a small herd of cattle on the other side of the fort. Two days later, Fetterman experienced the other end of a failed ambush attempt. Accompanying a wood party to the pinery, Ten Eyck, Fetterman, and Bisbee avoided a potential disaster when several warriors prematurely sprang from their hiding place, warning the soldiers of their enemy's intent.

Carrington's wealth of officers and mounted soldiers was short-lived. By the second week of November, fifty of the sixty-three cavalrymen—and their horses—had left the fort on mail and wagon train escort duty. The week of November 11,

Hard Lessons Learned

Lieutenant Adair made his resignation official and Lieutenant Bradley transferred to a unit in Utah. Carrington also had some personnel management problems with a few officers. First, Ten Eyck's drinking problem had become apparent to the other officers.[8] Then, on Sunday, November 11, one of the most misrepresented events in the Fetterman story occurred.

Company E, under the command of Lieutenant Bisbee, was forming for guard duty when Pvt. John Burke showed up late. In a profanity-filled rant, Bisbee ordered his sergeant, Garrett, to discipline Burke. Burke responded with an epithet and Garrett struck him with the butt of a musket and fractured Burke's skull. The Carringtons and several other couples were walking to church and witnessed the entire incident. Carrington was appalled at the violence and profanity, especially on the Sabbath and in front of ladies. After church services, Carrington returned to his office and issued General Order No. 38, a lengthy diatribe calling for all commissioned and noncommissioned officers to obey regulations and practice humane discipline. Saying in one part that "vulgar, profane, abusive language [can never] command respect," the order was a direct censure of Bisbee's actions. Ironically, Bisbee was the post adjutant and had to write out, sign, and post the order on the headquarters' bulletin board. The order became known as "Bully 38" by Bisbee's friends and supporters.[9]

Most historians have attributed this incident of violence to Fetterman. Dee Brown, author of several books on the subject, describes the incident as being between Sergeant Garrett and Private Burke of Company A, saying "the commanding officer of Company A interceded, resorting to violent profanity himself." Brown then points out that Fetterman was the commanding officer of Company A.[10] Brown's conclusion was likely drawn from the fact that a Private Burke from Company A was one of the soldiers killed in the Fetterman debacle. This was Pvt. Thomas Burke, not the aggrieved Pvt. John Burke from Company E. Historian Robert A. Murray, in a detailed analysis of this incident, uncovered records and testimony from Pvt. John Burke's formal petition for redress of grievance proving unequivocally that it was Lieutenant Bisbee and Company E.[11]

More evidence pointed to Lieutenant Bisbee than Fetterman. Frances Carrington described the event as "the brutal striking of a soldier by his sergeant and some profane endorsement of the sergeant by his own lieutenant." Fetterman was a captain, not a lieutenant. In Carrington's published testimony, from which much of the story of the Fetterman Massacre is derived, Carrington states, "[Bisbee] differed from my views of discipline in physical and verbal abuse of soldiers, requiring my issue of General Order No. 38, already cited."[12] Yet, Brown and nearly every historian of this event were so convinced of Fetterman's arrogant demeanor that they jumped to the conclusion that this was an excellent demonstration of his violent personality and of the animosity that was building between Fetterman and Carrington. Fetterman should be given more credit than this, because a considerable record substantiates that he was a gallant and chivalrous gentleman with impeccable military demeanor—the violence and profanity of this incident do not agree with the available descriptions of Fetterman's character.

Instead, this incident should be emphasized to explain the huge rift between Carrington and the two officers who became his most vocal critics—Lieutenant Bisbee and Captain Powell. Bisbee and Powell were singled out by Carrington in his description of the "Bully 38" order when he said, "[I] invariably supported [my] officers, each and all, who conformed to Order No. 38, before given in evidence. . . . Order No. 38 was enforced, although not according to the acceptance of Bt. Maj. Powell and Capt. Bisbee." Carrington went on to point out that only Powell and Bisbee objected to his disciplinary rules: "No others complained of this discipline. Striking, cursing, and other such modes of brutal departure from Order No. 38 were not supported, but reprehended, and Bvt. Maj. Powell's theory was most obnoxious to the spirit of that Order; while another officer, when absent, boasted that he 'broke out a soldier's teeth with the heel of his boot'—out of pure respect for [my] discipline."

Drawn from photograph taken in the year 1867

Captain James W. Powell

16. Capt. James Powell. Powell rose from the enlisted ranks during the Civil War and was considered uneducated and crude by Carrington and other officers. Powell was also devoted to Fetterman, who had recommended him for promotion during the war. Wyoming State Archives, Department of State Parks and Cultural Resources.

The "other officer" in Carrington's statement was likely the man most embarrassed and offended by "Bully 38," Lieutenant Bisbee, who left the post in December.[13]

Victorian cultural values divided Fort Phil Kearny's officers' row into two distinct social classes. Although military protocol placed Bisbee and Powell, as commissioned officers, above the noncommissioned officers and enlisted men in the post's society, they were considerably less educated and were not from the "better class society" that other senior officers and their families represented. The Carringtons were most intimately involved with the well-educated and well-mannered Wands, Horton, and Grummond families as well as Ten Eyck and the bachelors Brown and Fetterman. Carrington later described Powell's lack of social graces—and enmity—saying that Powell was the Carringtons' guest for dinner the first night he arrived at the post but did not ever visit their house again socially, "either on invitation, or on his own promptings." Carrington pointed out that Powell did not even come out to say good-bye to the Carringtons when they left the fort in January, "when his former host and hostess started eastward on a stormy winter's day of uncertain risk and exposure." Carrington also wrote that Powell's "illiterateness, profanity and coarseness were over-looked on account of his antecedents as a soldier, and those mistakes which made mirth for others were never repeated, or harshly judged by his colonel." According to Carrington, Powell "repeatedly subjected himself to the kind but positive rebuke of the Colonel for his scoffing at the Chaplain, Lieut. Adair, and religion generally, [and] his style of treating soldiers and general methods, with the men." Many years later Carrington wrote that he "pitied Powell, who married a barefooted camp laundress."[14]

Bisbee and his wife may not have been as obviously dissociated from the other officers and their families, although evidence suggests the Bisbees were not considered to be of the upper ranks of post society. Frances Carrington subtly refers to Mrs. Bisbee's talents in the kitchen as distinguishing her from the other ladies who were used to servants providing the family

Hard Lessons Learned

meals. On September 6 Judge J. T. Kinney, the post sutler, hosted a picnic described by Margaret Carrington as an elegant dinner "that would not have dishonored a city restaurant." According to Captain Ten Eyck, all the officers and their ladies—except the Bisbees—attended the event. Ten Eyck did not elaborate on why the Bisbees did not attend the soiree, but from the writings of both Margaret and Frances Carrington it appears that the Bisbees were not involved in the Carringtons' social circle. Both women wrote of the kindness and generosity of Mrs. Wands and Mrs. Horton, but Mrs. Bisbee—who had a small son and would seem to have had much in common with Margaret Carrington and Frances Grummond—is barely mentioned and then only in passing references to significant events.[15] After Lieutenant Bisbee was publicly humiliated by Carrington's "Bully 38" order, the Bisbees probably felt separated from the society of the other officers.

Carrington's New England accent and his pious and pedantic mannerisms underscored the differences between his rank and social class and that of Bisbee and Powell. These differences—highlighted by the "Bully 38" order—fueled Bisbee's and Powell's resentment of their commander and drove their personal vendetta to ensure Carrington was cast as incompetent during the government investigations in the wake of the Fetterman disaster. Bisbee left Fort Phil Kearny in early December to become Cooke's personal aide-de-camp and, with Powell as his source, furnished Cooke with copious amounts of damaging information about Carrington's management of Fort Phil Kearny in an attempt to destroy Carrington's career. Powell later provided some of the most damning testimony against Carrington.

Late in November Carrington received a telegram from Cooke ordering him to take the offensive. "You are hereby instructed that so soon as the troops and stores are covered from the weather, to turn your earnest attention to the possibility of striking the hostile band of Indians by surprise in their winter camps." In 1857, as a cavalry commander, Cooke had led a unit of soldiers in a midwinter crossing of the Rocky Mountains that nearly devastated his entire force. All but 10 of the 144 horses on his mission starved to death and in a period of thirty-six hours fifty mules died. Three men froze to death and almost all suffered from frostbite. At one point the situation was so grave that the men were described as "too stunned to complain."[16] Having survived such a mission, Cooke must have felt justified in explaining, "An extraordinary effort in winter, when the Indian horses are unserviceable, it is believed, should be followed by more success than can be accomplished by very large expeditions in the summer, when the Indians can so easily scatter . . . beyond pursuit." In a not-so-subtle allusion to his view of Carrington's timidity, Cooke pointed out that Maj. James Van Voast of Fort Laramie had volunteered and was authorized to lead just such a mission in a few weeks. Cooke chastised Carrington, telling him he had plenty of men and "a large arrear of murderous and insulting attacks by the savages upon emigrant trains and troops to settle." Cooke concluded his stern message with "you are ordered, if there prove to be any promise of success, to conduct or to send under another officer such an expedition."[17]

Along with this message, Carrington received an order to cease employment of citizen mail carriers and guides and to use only mounted troops or Indian scouts. These communications surely seemed surreal to the exhausted and frustrated colonel. He had at that time barely four companies of men and three dozen serviceable horses. No new weapons were ever delivered while Carrington commanded Fort Phil Kearny, nor was his desperate ammunition shortage ever resolved during this time. However, it was Cooke's order to release Bridger and the other guides that Carrington found most ludicrous and unenforceable. Frances Carrington wrote that Carrington endorsed on the back of this order "Impossible of execution" and kept Bridger and the other guides on duty.[18]

At this point Carrington probably looked forward to the upcoming army reorganization and letting Fetterman take over this nightmare. However, the colonel could not let a failure at

Hard Lessons Learned

this, his first field duty, go on his record—future assignments and his own honor were at stake. Carrington had to prove himself as a strong leader in battle as well as a capable administrator. He responded to Cooke, "I will, in person, command expeditions when severe weather confines them to their villages, and make the winter one of active operations in different directions, as best affords chance of punishment."[19] Carrington's best weapon—considering his shortages of men, horses, weapons, and ammunition—was the military acumen of Captain Fetterman. By now, Fetterman had been involved in several skirmishes with Red Cloud's warriors and, although they were frustrating in their consistent lack of success, each one taught the professional soldier a new lesson about the tactics of his enemy. In anticipation of an order to go on the offensive, Fetterman drilled the soldiers of the fort in infantry maneuvers daily.

The first opportunity for Carrington to engage in "active operations" came on December 6 when pickets on Pilot Hill signaled that a large force of Indians was attacking the wood-cutting party at the pinery. With Fetterman and three other officers, Carrington planned and directed the relief effort, the first of only two large-scale offensive engagements ever to be taken by the colonel. Fetterman led Lieutenant Bingham and thirty cavalrymen who just returned from escort duty while Carrington commanded Lieutenants Grummond and Wands and twenty-one mounted infantry soldiers. Fetterman's group was to ride directly west to the corralled wood train and push the enemy north of Sullivant Hills toward Peno Creek. Meanwhile Carrington's party would circle north and then west around Lodge Trail Ridge to meet the Lakota attackers in the valley of Peno Creek when they retreated—trapping the Indians between the two forces. The mission was an error-filled disaster almost from the beginning.[20]

After he was delayed by a broken saddle, Wands was directed to the wrong party by soldiers outside the fort and ended up joining Fetterman's group. As was the case with every Indian alarm, Quartermaster Brown and several of his men also came racing up to join the attack. Fetterman's group—now including Wands, Brown, and Bingham—encountered more than one hundred warriors when they reached the corralled wood train. The Lakota quickly retreated with the soldiers pursuing them north of Sullivant Hills—right in the direction of Carrington's waiting force. The trap appeared to be working. Wands and Brown had far more experience in these skirmishes and tried to persuade Fetterman, Bingham, and the cavalrymen to slow down and stop wasting ammunition as they shot at the out-of-range Indians. The weak army horses quickly grew tired and began to stumble in the rugged terrain, distracting the soldiers from the fact that they had ridden into a trap themselves. Suddenly, at the foot of a steep hill they had just descended, the cavalry was nearly surrounded by hundreds of warriors rushing from their hiding places in bushes and ravines.

Fetterman immediately ordered his men to halt and dismount—he had already learned that a full retreat from attacking Indians would lead to a massacre. In a move that startled his fellow officers, Lieutenant Bingham shouted "come on" and led about three-fourths of his cavalrymen through an opening left by their attackers—apparently toward the fort in a panicked retreat. Fetterman, Brown, and Wands had to point their guns at the ten remaining cavalrymen to force them to stay and fight. For twenty minutes Fetterman's soldiers and the Lakota alliance warriors engaged in a pitched battle; Bingham and the other cavalrymen did not return. The fighting stopped momentarily when Carrington's party appeared at the crest of a ridge a few miles north and the combatants on both sides assumed it was a relief mission. Unfortunately, Carrington's unit had not seen the battle and continued to the prearranged location for the ambush.

For his part, Carrington had encountered his own difficulties. A few minutes out of the fort, his horse crashed through the ice of Big Piney Creek and Carrington fell into three feet of freezing water. Grummond urged Carrington to return to the post because of the danger to his health, but Carrington told him the men would think him a coward. Instead Carrington led his horse through the ice, breaking the way for his men. Shortly after crossing the creek a few Lakota horsemen appeared on the hills ahead of them, and Grummond and three of the soldiers raced off in pursuit. Carrington yelled at Grummond to halt several times and finally had to send an orderly with a command to obey his orders or return to the fort. When Grummond returned Carrington had to remind him of the plan at hand. They had to cross Big Piney again and Grummond, who had apparently spotted Bingham after he had abandoned Fetterman's group, claimed his horse could not cross at that point and feigned to look for a better crossing. Carrington was already across with several of his men and assumed that Grummond would catch up to him after he found an alternate ford. Carrington did not notice the three other soldiers, including Sgt. Gideon Bowers, who followed Grummond. A few minutes later, Carrington and the six remaining men of his command found themselves surrounded by a small group of warriors. In the twenty minutes Carrington spent fending off his attackers, the Lakota band that was skirmishing with Fetterman's group retreated. Fetterman and his men mounted their remaining horses and vainly attempted to chase the enemy, but they quickly realized they could not keep up. Fetterman rode toward the designated meeting place, where Carrington was engaged. When Carrington's attackers saw Fetterman's column they withdrew and the two groups of army soldiers finally united. The carefully laid trap had failed.

Carrington, Fetterman, Wands, and Brown quickly discovered that Grummond and Bingham were both still missing. Two of the soldiers from Carrington's group said they thought they had seen Bingham up ahead, so the group rode to the top of a hill to look for him. A lone Indian horseman was spotted about a half a mile away and Fetterman and Brown asked for permission to pursue, but Carrington refused. As they scanned the horizon to the west, where they expected to see Bingham or groups of Lakota alliance warriors, shots were fired on the Montana Road, just behind and below them. Suddenly, they heard, "For God's sake, come down here quick!" A small party of well-mounted warriors was hotly pursuing Grummond and three soldiers down on the Bozeman Trail. Seeing the larger body of soldiers above them, Grummond's attackers quickly retreated. A few seconds later, a near-hysterical Grummond rode up to Carrington and the officers. According to Lieutenant Wands, Grummond was "foaming at the mouth" and "swore a great deal and was very incoherent." When he was finally able to communicate, Grummond's news shocked the soldiers: Bingham and Sergeant Bowers were dead.

In the thirty minutes since Grummond had snuck away from Carrington, he and Sergeant Bowers and two privates had joined Bingham and one other soldier in pursuit of about forty of Red Cloud's fighters who appeared to be retreating along the Bozeman Trail. In an obvious decoy maneuver that completely duped Grummond and Bingham, one warrior dropped behind and the two officers closed in on him. Bingham used his last two bullets to bring down the Indian's horse, threw his revolver away, and pulled out his saber. Grummond had left the fort in such a rush he forgot his revolver and was already brandishing a saber—his only weapon. The two officers were so busy swinging their blades at the dismounted warrior who was artfully dodging their blows by running under their horses that they failed to notice they had ridden into an ambush. Bingham was the first to grasp their situation when he looked up and shouted, "We are surrounded!" With sabers swinging, the two officers made a dash through an opening in their enemy's line and raced for the other four soldiers in their group, who were on a hill about a half mile back. Grummond miraculously made it through but found about twenty warriors racing behind him. The soldiers fired on Grummond's pursuers, buying him enough time to join them on the hill. Bingham had not made it through the line and was swarmed by his attackers. Grummond and the four soldiers had no time to contemplate Bingham's horrible situation as they were immediately encircled themselves.

Hard Lessons Learned

Grummond ordered the men to dismount and fire their weapons. The circle of Indians dismounted and began to close in. In a few seconds, two of the four soldiers and one horse were badly wounded with arrows. Realizing they could not hold this position until reinforcements arrived, Grummond ordered the men to mount and try a headlong rush—just as he and Bingham had done a minute earlier—through the enemy's ranks. Sergeant Bowers's horse was too weak to make the dash and the other three soldiers looked behind to see him dragged off his dying horse. They were about to meet the same fate when they spotted the Carrington-Fetterman contingent.

Much has been made of the "blunders, disobedience of orders, misunderstandings, recklessness, and cowardice" of this day's engagements,[21] but few historians have pointed out the cooperation between Carrington and Fetterman. Of all the officers, Fetterman was the one who followed orders explicitly and was always in place where he was expected. Fetterman also followed protocol and submitted a report of the incident the next day, whereas Carrington was forced to issue a written Special Order to force Grummond and Brown to report the details of their actions.[22]

Fetterman's report was addressed to Lieutenant Bisbee, as post adjutant, and contained some thinly veiled accusations of cowardice and ineptitude against Carrington.[23] To his credit, Carrington attached Fetterman's report to his own lengthy report and forwarded them to department headquarters. Later, when the army scrambled to affix blame on someone for the Fetterman disaster, Fetterman's report was published but Carrington's report, of which Fetterman's was an official attachment, somehow never made it into the public record. Lieutenant Bisbee, by now Carrington's worst enemy among the officers, later claimed that Fetterman blamed the fiasco on Carrington. Bisbee was promoted to captain and departed for his new assignment as aide-de-camp to General Cooke at department headquarters in Omaha on December 9. In this capacity, Bisbee exerted an enormous amount of influence on Cooke and his superiors in the immediate aftermath of the Fetterman incident. Bisbee's animosity for Carrington, and his influence on the army's perception of Carrington in the investigation of the disaster, played a major role in the later histories of the event.

With Bingham's death, Bisbee's departure, and Brown's delayed but looming reassignment to Fort Laramie, Carrington was back down to six officers for six companies. Though he was surely inclined to reprimand Grummond, Brown, or Wands for mistakes and insubordination during the fight on December 6, he could not afford to place them on arrest or relieve them from duty. In his own report, Carrington was charitable to his officers, again wanting to show his own strength of leadership. He wrote, "Brevet Lieutenant Colonel Fetterman, Captain Brown, and Lieutenant Wands . . . acquitted themselves with great credit." Carrington did not include Grummond in this list, but neither did he document Grummond's embarrassing performance. Carrington even defended the fifteen insubordinate cavalrymen, saying, "It is due to the cavalry to say that they were mostly recruits and are all ready to take the next chance."[24]

The events of December 6 are often portrayed as a foretelling of Fetterman's final skirmish on December 21. Citing the confusion, panic, and disobedience of the soldiers and the many traps and ambushes Red Cloud's forces successfully deployed on this day, historians present Fetterman's final showdown as a repeat of the December 6 fiasco. The Lakota alliance is given credit for learning from the event—the warriors determined that the soldiers could be easily lured into a trap—but Fetterman is positioned as not learning a thing.

Fetterman had been at Fort Phil Kearny for one month. In that time he had been involved in a half dozen skirmishes and nearly twice that many had occurred in and around the fort. Not one of the army's offensive or defensive attacks had proven successful. Jim Bridger reported that Crow Indians told him it took more than half a day to ride through the camp of the hostile Lakota alliance and that the number of warriors was growing every day.[25] Fetterman had seen the fear and panic in the eyes of his raw cavalry recruits as they fled their first encounter with the enemy—and they had been on horses. As he trained his foot soldiers in the basics of infantry maneuvers, he had to have realized that an unmounted infantry unit was an even weaker force against the prowess of the Indian fighters and their ponies. It is difficult to believe that, after all this, Fetterman still arrogantly assumed he and eighty men could "ride through the whole Sioux Nation."

The night they buried Bingham and Bowers—the latter a much-beloved sergeant who had been through the worst of the Civil War with Fetterman, Brown, and Bisbee—Margaret Carrington quoted Fetterman as having learned a lesson. Saying to Carrington when he handed in his report of the day's catastrophe, "This Indian war has become a hand-to-hand fight, requiring the utmost caution," Mrs. Carrington wrote that Fetterman said he wanted no more such risks.[26] Yet the well-worn story of the Fetterman Massacre contends that Fetterman, rather than being chastened by his experiences, was angered and frustrated to the point of irrationality. Dee Brown wrote of Fetterman's comments, "Unfortunately, Fetterman forgot this lesson, the last he would learn from the Indians."[27] Analysis of Fetterman's final battle and the information that has been used to reconstruct it show that, contrary to this popular conception, Fetterman was very aware of the dangers of Plains Indian warfare and the inferiority of his fort's military strength.

‡ CHAPTER ‡

The Battle of the Hundred-in-the-Hands

Accarding to Colonel Carrington, between December 6 and December 19, 1866, Indian parties appeared almost daily around the wood party or near the fort, but they did not attack. Inside the compound the residents understood the severity of their situation. By all indications, morale was low and tensions were high. Frances Carrington wrote, "All of us were apprised frankly of the exact state of affairs and assured that there was no immediate danger at the post if all were prudent and avoided gossip and nervous agitation."[1] Capt. Tenodor Ten Eyck's entries during this two-week period were punctuated with comments such as "all quiet," "day passed quietly," and "no Indians." Despite the danger and vulnerability, teams continued to the pinery, as the post needed to stockpile as much wood as possible before the onset of the harshest months of winter. Carrington doubled the strength of military escorts with the wood trains and attempted to make the best use of his few officers. On December 13, in a decision that illustrates the colonel's desperate shortage of officers and his obvious disappointment in Ten Eyck's job performance, Carrington assigned Grummond—who had so egregiously disregarded military protocol just a few days earlier—to replace Ten Eyck as commander of mounted infantry. Fetterman was now in charge of the infantry—the largest number of soldiers at the fort—while Grummond led the mounted infantry and Powell replaced Bingham as commander of the cavalry. The three officers drilled their units daily, and the soldiers slept in their clothes, ever ready for a raid or an all-out assault. Everyone at the fort watched Pilot Hill for a sign from the lookouts indicating the arrival of expected reinforcements, but instead the sentry's flags constantly warned of hostile Indian activity nearby.

On December 19, the Pilot Hill pickets signaled that the wood train was corralled and under attack on the way to the pinery. Carrington ordered Captain Powell to take command of a unit to relieve and secure the stranded workers and either bring them back to the fort or escort them on to the pinery. Powell quickly went to the corralled train, relieved it, and brought the workers back without incident, but this day's events increased in significance after Fetterman's contingent was annihilated two days later. After the train was safely returned, Carrington sent a telegram to department headquarters stating, "No special news since last report. Indians appeared to-day and fired on wood train but were repulsed. They are accomplishing nothing, while I am perfecting all details of the post and preparing for active movements."[2] This cavalier dispatch, typical of Carrington's messages focusing on any minor success, would come back to haunt Carrington during the weeks after the Fetterman incident when the colonel sought to prove the lack of support he received from army headquarters. Cooke used this telegram to prove to Sherman and Grant that "two days before the massacre . . . [Carrington] felt strong enough to take the offensive."[3]

Two days later, when the Fetterman disaster unfolded, Carrington had not yet submitted an official report on the events of December 19. It is not clear whether Carrington even planned to write a detailed report on Powell's mission or to elaborate on the telegraph that was meant to assure his superiors that he was under control and about to take offensive action. However, in his report on the Fetterman fight, Carrington went into great detail about the incident of December 19, claiming Powell's successful return was the result of strict adherence to Carrington's orders and implying that Fetterman disobeyed this same command two days later. In his testimony before the investigating commission after the Fetterman Massacre, Carrington testified that "[Powell] did his work—pressed the Indians towards Lodge Trail Ridge, but having peremptory orders not to cross it, he returned with the train, reporting the Indians in large force, and that if he had crossed the ridge he never would have come back with his command."[4]

Powell was subsequently interrogated about the events of December 19 when he testified before the Fetterman investigation commission. He did not mention Carrington's supposed order but did say his decision to return with the train after he saw large parties of hostile Indians saved the lives of his command. Powell's testimony does not support Carrington's claim that he "pressed the Indians towards Lodge Trail Ridge, but having peremptory orders not to cross it, he returned." Powell's account makes it clear that he did not "press" his Lakota alliance antagonists at all—his detail did not come close to, or even head in the direction of, Lodge Trail Ridge. This engagement was significant because infantrymen marched to a skirmish on foot with a small supporting detachment of cavalry. Every previous encounter involved mounted infantry and cavalry participating in "running attacks" on horses. But, with only thirty-seven serviceable horses, Carrington and his officers had to employ new tactics. Powell's mission put weeks of drilling the soldiers in infantry maneuvers to their first real test. Lieutenant Brown, ready to go as always, reported to Powell that he could command the small supporting detachment of cavalry and Powell approved. Powell, riding alongside the marching infantry, told Brown and the cavalry to go ahead to the corralled train and not to engage the enemy if the force was too large. When Brown got to the train, the Indian attackers retreated—obviously trying to lure the soldiers over Sullivant Hills into a trap—so Brown escorted the train the rest of the way to the pinery. When Powell caught up with the train and Brown, the workers were

The Battle of the Hundred-in-the-Hands

already loading logs into the wagons. Powell observed so many parties of Lakota warriors on the hills around the area that he decided to withdraw the entire train and his command back to the fort—which was accomplished without incident.[5] Pressing his enemy toward Lodge Trail Ridge would have entailed turning his unit to the northeast and marching, not riding, through some of the same valleys and defiles that enabled the ambush of Fetterman's party on December 6. Powell clearly did not press the enemy; he marched straight west to the pinery and straight back to the fort. There was no venturing sharply north and then east around Sullivant Hills to chase or press the Indians to Lodge Trail Ridge. It seems even the brash Lieutenant Brown, described as desperate for Red Cloud's scalp, figured out this was a trap. Carrington's testimony describes a completely different story, obviously trying to imply Powell was given the exact same orders as Fetterman to "press the enemy" but not cross Lodge Trail Ridge. This also supported Carrington's claim that if Fetterman had obeyed his orders as Powell had, he too would have survived.

After a week of unseasonably warm and pleasant days, Friday, December 21, dawned quite cold with heavy clouds portending snow. At about 11:00 a.m., pickets indicated the wood train was again corralled and under attack. According to Carrington, he ordered Powell—based on his success two days earlier—to take a detachment of cavalry and relieve the train, but Fetterman "claimed by rank to go out." Carrington "acquiesced," giving Fetterman and his infantry the duty.[6] No witnesses or testimony corroborate this claim. Lieutenant Wands was officer of the day and assisted Carrington in communicating orders and preparing the detachments for the relief effort. Wands did not mention in his testimony that Carrington offered the command to Powell; he stated that Carrington ordered a detachment of fifty men from four different infantry companies under command of Fetterman to proceed to the wood train. Nor did Powell testify that Carrington had "tendered him the command" of the relief party—something that would have surely stuck in the officer's mind after the entire command he would have led was wiped out a few hours later.

Pvt. F. M. Fessenden, who was detailed as a headquarters orderly the day of the disaster and claimed to have been in the office and heard the transaction between Carrington and Fetterman, said that Fetterman simply asked for the command. Fessenden wrote, "I was there when Major Powell and Colonel Fetterman came in and heard Fetterman ask for command of the relief party and when that was settled Colonel Carrington turned towards Colonel Fetterman and said, 'Colonel, go out and bring in that wood train,' and not a word was said about how, or route, or where not to go."[7] Fessenden does not assert that Fetterman "insisted" or "claimed by rank," but his choice of words in saying "when that was settled" could be construed to imply there was a dispute between Powell and Fetterman over the command. However, circumstantial evidence does not support Fetterman's claiming the command by rank over Powell.

For instance, while Fetterman's infantry detachment formed outside of Fetterman's company quarters, Lieutenant Grummond asked Lieutenant Wands for permission to lead a party of cavalrymen in support of Fetterman. After clearing it with Carrington, Wands gave Grummond the detail. If it was possible to coerce Carrington into assigning a relief command based on rank, Powell could have insisted on taking the cavalry because he outranked Grummond and Powell had been placed in command of the cavalry company after Bingham's death.

It is also possible that Carrington gave the mission to Powell, who refused or declined to assume the command, in which case Carrington would have had to turn to Fetterman to lead the detachment. Powell had refused to take field commands on several occasions and Carrington later testified that, as opposed to the other officers under his command, Powell never once "volunteered a movement toward Indian aggression." Most notably, on December 6 Carrington had ordered Powell to come from the fort with an ambulance for the bodies of Bingham and Bowers, but Powell sent Lieutenant Arnold in his place.[8]

The Battle of the Hundred-in-the-Hands

One other piece of circumstantial evidence refutes Carrington's claim that Fetterman begged for the command: why had Fetterman not claimed by rank to assume Powell's relief mission two days earlier? If Fetterman was as desperate to fight Indians as Carrington portrayed him, it seems logical that he would have insisted on taking command of the December 19 relief effort. There is a plausible reason for Fetterman's taking the command on December 21 but not December 19. It could be that Carrington's orders were different on December 19. Perhaps on December 21, emboldened by Powell's success two days earlier and what appeared to be his officers' newly found self-discipline, Carrington decided to make one of the "active movements" he promised his superiors. If so, he would want his most experienced officer and military tactician in charge of this mission, not a man as disinclined to take orders and fight Indians as Powell seemed to be.

Regardless of the circumstances that placed Fetterman in command of the mission, Carrington later went to extraordinary measures to prove that Fetterman forced his hand. Carrington also claimed that he gave explicit orders, strictly defensive in their purpose, to both Fetterman and Grummond and that their flagrant disobedience of these orders caused the deaths of Fetterman's entire command.

According to Carrington, he was so concerned about the two officers' ambition to win honor that he went to considerable effort to make sure that they understood his specific orders, which were, "Support the wood train, relieve it, and report to me. Do not engage or pursue Indians at its expense. Under no circumstances pursue over the ridge, viz., Lodge Trail Ridge." Carrington testified he first gave this order to Fetterman as the infantry detachment formed outside Company A quarters. Fetterman then inspected men from companies A, C, E, and H, approved forty-nine for the detail, and immediately marched with the unit out of the fort. As a condition of approving Grummond's request to command the cavalry, Carrington ordered the reckless soldier to report to Fetterman and "implicitly obey orders, and not leave him." As Grummond was preparing, Carrington sent Wands to repeat the orders to Grummond and then, as Grummond and his twenty-seven cavalrymen rode out of the fort, Carrington climbed the sentry platform and halted them so he could repeat his "precise orders" one more time.[9] Wands's testimony supports Carrington's detailed and repeated orders to Grummond, but no one heard the orders given to Fetterman. In fact, Wands stated that the orders he passed on to Grummond were to "tell Fetterman"—not remind him—not to cross the ridge.[10] Powell said he saw Carrington in conversation with Fetterman as he prepared his infantry detachment, but he did not hear what orders or instructions were given.[11]

If Carrington's orders were, as he claimed, to go directly to the wood train to support and relieve it, Fetterman immediately disobeyed them. Witnesses are uncharacteristically unanimous about the fact that Fetterman did not proceed due west to the wood train as Powell did two days earlier. Instead, Fetterman went northeast directly toward the southern end of Lodge Trail Ridge. Grummond caught up to Fetterman's marching unit about a half mile out. The contingent was soon joined by Quartermaster Brown and two of his civilian employees, James Wheatley and Isaac Fisher. The three men were mounted; Brown had borrowed Carrington's sons' pony because horses were at such a premium, and the two civilians were eager to try out their new Henry sixteen-shot rifles. Fetterman now had eighty men in his relief command—exactly the number that the Carringtons later claimed Fetterman had once said could ride through the entire Sioux nation. Anyone who was outside at the time could observe the detachment's progress, and it was clear to all that Fetterman's intention was to cut off the retreat of the wood train's attackers. The relief party had been gone less than thirty minutes when the pickets on Pilot Hill indicated that the wood train was no longer engaged and had broken corral formation and moved on to the pinery. Fetterman was about a mile away from the fort at this time. If Fetterman's assignment was

17. First published in New York in December 1855, *Frank Leslie's Illustrated Newspaper* provided illustrations and reports of wars from the Civil War to World War I. Known for its patriotic stance, the paper frequently featured cover pictures of soldiers and heroic battle stories. Less than a month after the Fetterman battle, the paper published this drawing, titled, "The Massacre of United States Troops by the Sioux and Cheyenne Indians, near Fort Philip Kearney, Dakotah Territory, December 22nd, 1866." From *Frank Leslie's Illustrated Newspaper*, January 19, 1867; Library of Congress Prints and Photographs Division, no. LC-USZ62-108153.

purely defensive, as Carrington maintains, why was he allowed to continue on toward Lodge Trail Ridge after the wood train was safely on its way to the pinery?

Clearly, Carrington understood Fetterman's intentions as he watched him from the lookout post on the top of his house. If Carrington did not approve of Fetterman's strategy—to intercept the Indians—he could have easily sent an orderly to call the contingent back. Carrington testified that after he understood the wood train had broken corral and moved on he "entertained no apprehensions of further danger." Yet, Fetterman's party was allowed to march on toward Lodge Trail Ridge. About this time Carrington sent surgeon C. M. Hines, along with two soldiers and two quartermaster employees in wagons, to the wood train to make sure they had no injuries and, if none, to cross over to Fetterman's party. This indicates Carrington knew Fetterman was not at, or going to, the wood train and that Carrington thought Fetterman's mission might eventually require the services of a surgeon and wagons. Carrington later claimed he noted that Fetterman was "evidently moving wisely up the creek and along the southern slope on Lodge Trail Ridge, with good promise of cutting off the Indians." He said that although the usual course was to follow the wood road west to the train, "the course adopted was not an error, unless there was then a purpose to disobey orders." According to Carrington, when Fetterman's command was lost from sight at the fort it was moving west along the slope of Lodge Trail Ridge and giving no indication that it would cross over the crest.[12]

For a brief time the post went about its daily routine—except for Frances Grummond. She was "dazed" when she heard her husband insist on taking command of the cavalry and going out to engage in another battle with the Lakota after his close encounter on December 6. She ran back to her little cabin and slammed the door, but her husband disregarded her distress. The ladies of the fort spent the rest of the day trying to calm her fears.[13] Carrington returned to his office but was presently alerted by his orderly that the sentry reported firing from the

The Battle of the Hundred-in-the-Hands

direction of Fetterman's detachment. Carrington raced up to his lookout post and heard the gunfire but could see no Indians or soldiers. A few minutes later, Surgeon Hines rode back into the post reporting to Carrington that he could not make his way to Fetterman because a large force of hostile warriors blocked his way. By now the firing was intense and it was clear a heated battle was under way. Carrington ordered Captain Ten Eyck to assemble a relief command and called Wands to come up to the lookout and report any activity. Less than forty men passed Carrington and Ten Eyck's quick inspection—this was every available soldier left at the fort with a working weapon. Along with Surgeon Hines and Lieutenant Matson, Ten Eyck's unit marched out of the fort on the "double quick." Carrington ordered the quartermasters and wagon masters to muster every armed man in their employ for immediate duty and sent about forty of them with three wagons, an ambulance, and some extra ammunition to catch up to Ten Eyck.[14]

As Ten Eyck's command scrambled across Piney Creek, removing their boots and stockings to wade across the icy stream, they heard scattered shots of gunfire. There had been a brief lull in the shooting as they prepared to leave the fort, and after this series of intermittent firing there followed a very rapid and regular volley that gradually died out to a few scattered shots. Ten Eyck's detachment raced east from the fort past the southernmost hill of Lodge Trail Ridge and frantically scaled the summit of a peak that overlooked the ridge, moving so fast "they straggled on the ascending slope, from the speed they made." When they crested the hill, they could see for several miles—and the spectacle was beyond their wildest imagination and their darkest fears.[15]

Below them, the Bozeman Trail followed Lodge Trail Ridge for about a mile and then descended down into the valley of Peno Creek. Ten Eyck and Hines estimated there were between 1,500 and 3,000 Lakota alliance warriors gathered on the road and down into the valley—both men based their estimates on the large groups of soldiers they had seen during the Civil War.

Many of the warriors were mounted, racing back and forth taunting Ten Eyck to come down the road. A group of about a hundred were clustered around some boulders a half a mile away. Ten Eyck could see no sign of Fetterman's command.

Expecting an attack at any moment, Ten Eyck sent an orderly back to the post requesting reinforcements and artillery. Then he moved his unit closer while staying at their vantage atop the hill, and the party of Lakota fighters around the boulders began to retreat. It was at this point that the quartermaster's wagons Carrington sent from the fort caught up with Ten Eyck. The Lakota alliance's army apparently thought the wagons contained the big mountain howitzer—the "gun that shoots twice" that had successfully awed them in the few skirmishes that were close enough to the fort for it to be of use—so they slowly retreated as Ten Eyck advanced. Meanwhile, the orderly Ten Eyck sent to the fort, Pvt. Archibald Sample, raced straight to Carrington, who was watching from his rooftop lookout. The breathless horseman told Carrington that Ten Eyck could see nothing of Fetterman but the road was filled with Indian war parties challenging the soldiers to come down. Ten Eyck wanted to know if Carrington could send the howitzer and more men. Sample lowered his voice and said, "Captain was afraid Fetterman's party was all gone up." That thought had to have crossed Carrington's mind while he wrote out a quick response to Ten Eyck: "CAPTAIN: Forty well-armed men, with 3,000 rounds, ambulance, etc., left before your courier came in. You must unite with Fetterman, fire slowly, and keep men in hand; you could have saved two miles towards the scene of action if you had taken Lodge Trail Ridge. I order the wood train in, which will give fifty more men to spare."[16]

Carrington was referring to Ten Eyck's decision to pass the southern edge of Lodge Trail Ridge rather than follow the route that Fetterman had taken to the north and then east directly over the ridge. Ten Eyck chose his route so his command could reach a small peak that overlooked the surrounding country before dashing over the ridge into the unknown. This practical

The Battle of the Hundred-in-the-Hands

decision probably saved the lives of Ten Eyck's command, but Carrington's message—with its implication that Ten Eyck took too long—cast a cloud of suspicion that followed Ten Eyck for the rest of his life. Sample brought Carrington's message to Ten Eyck who, now bolstered with the forty well-armed citizens, was proceeding down the Bozeman Trail looking for Fetterman's detachment. Suddenly, a soldier yelled, "There they are!"

Fetterman's command had, indeed, gone over Lodge Trail Ridge onto the Bozeman Trail and beyond. Lakota, Arapaho, and Cheyenne decoys, led by the soon-to-be-famous Oglala Lakota warrior Crazy Horse, had taunted Fetterman and his soldiers from the moment they left the fort. Most historical reconstructions of the battle put the infantry and cavalry together, chasing Crazy Horse and the decoys eastward up the west side of Lodge Trail Ridge and over its crest. Continuing down Lodge Trail Ridge's eastern slope, the soldiers marched up the rise of another ridge along which ran the Bozeman Trail. They turned north on the trail as it followed the top of this ridge and slowly descended for nearly a mile to Peno Creek. Hundreds of Lakota alliance warriors hid behind bushes, trees, and large clumps of dried grass down below the marching soldiers on both slopes of the ridge—exhibiting remarkable and uncharacteristic patience as they waited for the signal from the decoys indicating all the army men were in the trap. The front end of the contingent was almost to Peno Creek when Crazy Horse's decoys gave the sign. Thousands of arrows flew through the air from both sides of the road—wounding and killing as many Indian warriors as army soldiers in this initial volley. The war cries of the massive force appearing out of nowhere had to have been terrifying.

Of the mounted men, who were farther into the trap, Wheatley, Fisher, and a small group of the most experienced soldiers—knowing that retreat from an Indian attack spelled disaster—dismounted and took cover behind a small outcropping of rocks. This group launched a formidable defense with a fusillade from the civilian's sixteen-shot lever-action repeating Henry rifles coupled with disciplined gunfire from the accom-

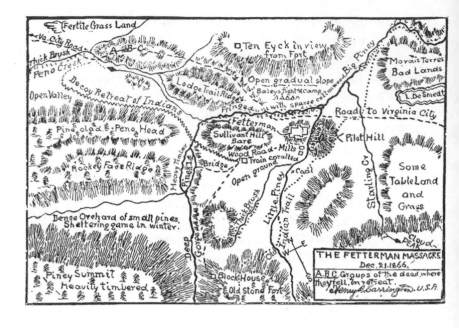

The following labels appear on the map:

Fertile Grass Land
Va. City Road
Thick Brush
Peno Creek
A B C
Ten Eyck in view from Fort
Movais Terres Bad Lands
Big Piney
L. De Smedt
Open gradual slope
Lodge Trail Ridge
Baleys fight camp
Fringed with sparse cottonwood
Decoy Retreat of Indians
Open Valley
Road to Virginia City
Pilot Hill
Pine clad Peno Head
Fetterman
Sullivant Hill Bare
Wood Road - Mills
Train corralled
Starling Cr
Some Table Land and Grass
Rockey Face Ridge
Heavy Timber
Pine R
Bridge
Open ground
Thick Brush
Little Piney
Coal
Old Indian Trail
Red Cloud
Dense Orchard of small pines. Sheltering game in winter.
Deep Gorge
N
W E
S
THE FETTERMAN MASSACRE
Dec. 21. 1866.
A. B. C. Groups of the dead, where they fell, in retreat.
Henry B. Carrington. U.S.A.
Piney Summit
Heavily timbered
Block House
Old Stone Fort

↬ 18. As part of his supporting reports and documentation, Carrington constructed this detailed map of the battle to accompany his description. The map was printed in several of his own publications as well as in Frances's *My Army Life*. From *My Army Life* by Frances Carrington.

panying soldiers. This enabled Fetterman and his officers to regroup the startled soldiers and begin a slow retreat. About a quarter of a mile back from the Wheatley and Fisher fighting force, a group of these soldiers, mostly cavalry with the band's Spencer rifles—lever-action weapons with reloadable seven-round magazines—made a stand. With their backs to each other, facing the onslaught from both the east and the west, they staggered their shooting and kept up a solid line of fire. The soldiers could fire, pump the lever to extract the used shell and feed a new cartridge into the firing chamber, and then manually cock and fire the trigger to get out seven shots from the magazine of the Spencer carbines very quickly, but they were particularly vulnerable when they had to stop to insert another seven-shot magazine. At this point the cavalry released their horses in a group hoping that the prize would prove irresistible to the warriors, but this tactic proved futile against their enemy's overwhelming numbers. The soldiers' ammunition began to run out and the barrage of arrows quickly reduced their ranks. This is when Grummond was killed.

Back another half mile was a formation of large boulders. The infantry—virtually unprotected without horses and carrying outdated single-shot muzzle-loading Springfield muskets—made a dash for this cover during the cavalry's brief resistance. Here, Fetterman managed to get the men into defensive formation and they were able to hold their attackers off for a few minutes. The drills Fetterman instituted must have bought some time as the soldiers staggered their shots, which required manual loading—army studies reported the average soldier could fire the Springfield muzzle loaders about twice a minute. At this point there were three separate engagements, none within view of another. After Grummond was killed, the cavalry panicked and retreated to the infantry's location, although few made it all the way to the rocks. The soldiers began to run out of ammunition and Red Cloud's army could sense their enemy's growing desperation. When Indian spotters signaled that the army's relief party was on its way from the fort, the warriors made their final push and overran the last few surviving soldiers in each of the locations. During the final moments of the battle, the soldiers were locked in frenzied, brutal, hand-to-hand combat with the initial wave of warriors who broke through the defensive lines. At the end, Fetterman and Brown are said to have put their revolvers to each other's heads, counted to three, and fired.

This reconstruction is based primarily on the locations of the three groups of dead soldiers as documented by the relief party. However, J. W. Vaughn's extraordinary analysis of the Fetterman battle site in *Indian Fights: New Facts on Seven Encounters,* published in 1966, offers some interesting alternative hypotheses to the prevailing scenario—especially when combined with the idea that Fetterman was not driven by irrational arrogance. Bringing together aerial photography, metal detectors, and reviews of infantry and cavalry operations, along with the extensive collection of testimony, memoirs, and military records of the event, Vaughn's study postulates that Fetterman most likely knew he was entering a trap. Using a time-versus-distance formula, Vaughn proves that it would have been impossible for Fetterman's foot soldiers to make it all the way to Peno Creek where the ambush began. It is almost certain that the mounted men led by Grummond and Brown raced out more than a mile ahead of the infantry in pursuit of Crazy Horse and the decoys and were met by the first rush of Indians at the far northern stretch of the battlefield. The heavy firing heard at the beginning of the skirmish was the initial barrage of the Wheatley and Fisher group. Fetterman and the infantry were probably still deployed as skirmishers at the crest of Lodge Trail Ridge at this moment. Grummond's cavalry was clearly not within supporting distance of Fetterman's infantry, and vice versa, when Red Cloud's forces sprang their trap.

If Fetterman directed Grummond to charge ahead over the ridge in violation of direct orders given to him personally by Carrington or through Grummond, then he is indeed solely responsible for the annihilation of his troops. However, a considerable

The Battle of the Hundred-in-the-Hands

19. *Harper's Weekly*, launched in 1857, was aimed at the middle and upper classes of the United States. In addition to the importance of illustrations and cartoons by artists like Winslow Homer and Thomas Nast, the paper's editorials played a significant role in shaping and reflecting public opinion from the start of the Civil War to the end of the century. Here they publish "The Indian Battle and Massacre near Fort Philip Kearney, Dacotah Territory, December 21, 1866." From *Harper's Weekly*, March 23, 1867; Library of Congress Prints and Photographs Division, no. LC-USZ62-130184.

body of evidence documents Grummond's impetuous behavior in battle during the Civil War and more recently in the Indian fight on December 6, and it is more than likely that Grummond raced ahead without regard to Fetterman's authority. This leads to three potential scenarios to consider as Fetterman and his infantrymen paused at the top of Lodge Trail Ridge.

First, this was very possibly an offensive mission and Fetterman was following Carrington's orders. If Carrington had really ordered Fetterman to simply relieve the wood train and under no circumstances cross Lodge Trail Ridge, there was no point in Fetterman leading his mission in the direction of the ridge—the opposite direction of the wood train. The only reason to allow Fetterman to position his command in the rear of the Lakota parties attacking the wood train was if Carrington intended to trap the Indians with an offensive or punitive action. Few historians point out that Fetterman was commanding the largest relief force ever sent out by Carrington. Several witnesses saw the commander and his second-in-command talking at length as the detachment formed. If Fetterman were to succeed in an offensive attack it would be a huge coup for both officers. The army, in its typical postwar fashion, had yet to notify the officers of their new assignments in the reorganization that was to take effect in less than ten days. A triumphant victory with their limited resources would help both Carrington and Fetterman secure positions they desired. On a more practical level, the fort was in a precarious situation and impressing Red Cloud's hostile followers with their strength and military abilities might buy them some time until reinforcements arrived.

The primary evidence used to support Carrington's giving the "defend-only" order to Fetterman is Carrington's own testimony. Historians cite Carrington's identical orders to Powell two days earlier as circumstantial evidence of the likelihood he gave this command to Fetterman. Yet, no witnesses ever confirmed that Carrington gave this exact order to Powell, and to date historians have not questioned Carrington's version of Powell's relief of the wood train on December 19. A few Fort Phil Kearny soldiers' memoirs purport to have heard Carrington give his orders to Fetterman. For instance, historian John D. McDermott states that evidence to support Fetterman's disobedience is "overwhelming," pointing to Carrington's "identical orders to Powell two days before," and that "eyewitness documentation exists in abundance."[17] McDermott cites a 1927 article in which a Sgt. Alexander Brown claims to have heard Carrington issue the command to Fetterman, but the veracity of this and many other later memoirs by soldiers from Fort Phil Kearny is weakened by the inclusion of many dubious or flat-out erroneous statements obviously taken directly from the Carringtons' publications. No officer or soldier directly involved with the incident who was called as a witness to testify before the investigating commissions ever stated that he heard Carrington's orders to Fetterman.

On the other hand, an abundance of testimony corroborates Carrington's orders to Grummond. Lieutenant Wands testified that Carrington elaborately delivered his orders to Grummond three times. Wands stated that Grummond's orders were to "report to and receive all his orders from Colonel Fetterman, and also to tell Colonel Fetterman, and to remember himself that this command was to go out and succor or relieve the wood train, bring it back if necessary, or if Colonel Fetterman thought best, take the train to the woods . . . and bring it back, and under no circumstances were they to cross the bluff in pursuit of Indians."[18] As noted earlier, Wands states that Grummond's orders were to "tell" Fetterman, not "remind" him of this order. It is possible that the many soldiers who heard these explicit and elaborate orders given to Grummond assumed they were identical to Carrington's orders to Fetterman and later stated that they heard Fetterman's orders. If Carrington originally authorized Fetterman to execute an offensive maneuver and Grummond did not pass on Carrington's updated orders, Fetterman would have logically directed Grummond to advance a charge and try to flush out or lure Indians back to his waiting infantry.

The remaining scenarios operate under the assumption that

Carrington did give Fetterman this order, either directly or through Grummond. As Grummond and the cavalry raced ahead after Crazy Horse and the other decoys in violation of orders, it would have been impossible for Fetterman or any of his dismounted infantrymen to stop them. In one scenario, Fetterman may have decided to follow Grummond and the army's horsemen over the ridge in order to support them in the highly likely case of an Indian ambush. In this case Fetterman is technically responsible for the disobedience of soldiers under his command, but his actions are justifiable because he advanced to support his men. Based on Vaughn's battlefield analysis, what appears most likely is that Fetterman and his infantry heard the initial salvo of gunfire after Grummond and the mounted men impetuously dashed out of view a mile beyond the crest of Lodge Trail Ridge down the Bozeman Trail to Peno Creek, and Fetterman knowingly led his men into a trap to come to the aid of the cavalry. The courage that this decision required is difficult to imagine: a quarter-mile march over a crest and down into a battle just beyond view, with a group of fifty raw recruits outfitted with nothing more than muzzle-loading rifles, listening to the nonstop fusillade of the Henry rifles and deafening war whoops of the frenzied Indian forces. These may have been the actions of a reckless man, but at that moment Fetterman surely did not think he could easily ride through the entire Sioux nation.

We will never know what went through Fetterman's mind as he stood at the top of the ridge, but it had to have been a gut-wrenching decision to order his men to go forward. He must have known it was a trap based on his previous experience. Fetterman had been ambushed by Lakota alliance war parties several times in the preceding seven weeks and witnessed the terror of hand-to-hand combat of Indian fighting. He also knew just how untested his infantrymen were, and they had obsolete weapons and little ammunition. And his orders from Carrington were surely in his thoughts. He was too good a soldier for all of these concerns not to have crossed his mind.

Fetterman pressed forward with his men, making it to the

The Battle of the Hundred-in-the-Hands

boulders about a quarter of a mile down the trail. There, the freshly drilled infantry formed ranks and defended their position. They could hear the fighting several hundred yards beyond, but they could not see past a point a few hundred feet away where the road dipped below a small rise. Eventually, Brown and a few terror-stricken cavalrymen ran into their midst shouting that Grummond was dead and that there were thousands of Indians on either side of the ridge just below the rise. As the infantry continued their defense at the boulders, the rapid fire of the Henry rifles stopped and a minute later there were no sounds of gunshots coming from below. Their own ammunition was almost exhausted and the number of warriors on all sides suddenly grew beyond their comprehension. With only a couple of soldiers able to shoot at a time, Red Cloud's fighters broke through Fetterman's ranks and in a desperate, every-man-for-himself last stand, the Indians overwhelmed the soldiers. A considerable amount of physical evidence supports Vaughn's scenario, as do several Lakota, Cheyenne, and Arapaho accounts of the battle.[19]

Another controversial and fallacious detail thoroughly ingrained in the story of the battle is the supposed joint suicide of Fetterman and Brown. American Horse, an Oglala warrior who became a famous leader of his people and friend of many prominent white settlers, was one of the decoys who, along with Crazy Horse, lured Fetterman's troops into ambush. Years later, American Horse told Judge Eli Ricker, a recorder of Indian Wars history, that he had knocked Fetterman down with his horse and then clubbed him and killed him with his knife. Red Cloud and American Horse both told their friend James Cook, a pioneer rancher in western Nebraska, that American Horse had killed Fetterman. American Horse eventually gave Cook the club he used to hit Fetterman. Cook's historical ranch has since been dedicated a national monument where this "Fetterman Disaster Club" is on display. Fort Phil Kearny's post surgeon, Dr. Samuel Horton, who examined the dead soldiers after the battle, corroborates this story. Horton's report states that most in the

20. Lakota leaders Red Cloud (*right*) and American Horse. In the opening salvo in the war on the Bozeman Trail, Red Cloud stormed out of treaty negotiations with the army at Fort Laramie when Carrington and his huge caravan of soldiers, civilians, and livestock reached the fort in May 1866. American Horse was acknowledged by his fellow warriors as the man who killed Fetterman. Library of Congress Prints and Photographs Division, Civil War glass negative collection, LC-USZ61-2033.

21. James Cook, ca. 1887. Cook worked some of the first cattle drives from Texas to Kansas and Nebraska before settling on a ranch at the head of the Niobrara River in northwest Nebraska. While staying with Baptiste "Little Bat" Garnier at the Red Cloud Agency in the mid-1880s, Cook met Red Cloud, American Horse, Little Wound, and Young-Man-Afraid-of-His-Horses, all of whom became lifelong friends and later visited the Cook ranch near Agate, Nebraska. Nebraska State Historical Society, Photograph Collections, C772-1.

22. James Cook. In their later years Red Cloud and American Horse camped next to the Cook ranch and shared stories of the Fetterman battle with the Cook family. Nebraska State Historical Society, Photograph Collections, c772-3.

23. American Horse told Cook he struck Fetterman down with his club and then slit his throat. He gave Cook the club, which is on display at the national monument erected on Cook's former ranch. Photo courtesy Agate Fossil Beds National Monument, Harrison, Nebraska.

Fetterman party were hit with clubs. The report also stated that Brown had a bullet hole in his left temple, but mentioned no gunshot wound in his description of Fetterman's body. Horton wrote that Fetterman's thorax was cut "crosswise with a knife, deep into the viscera," and the surgeon believed that this was the cause of his death. When asked if any of the men, other than Brown, were killed by pistol or gunshot, Horton testified that he saw no evidence of gunshot wounds on any other soldiers or officers.[20]

Carrington launched the story of Fetterman's suicide in his first report of the incident: "Fetterman and Brown had each a revolver shot in the left temple. As Brown always declared he would reserve a shot for himself as a last resort, so I am convinced that these two brave men fell each by the other's hand rather than undergo the slow torture inflicted upon others."[21] It is impossible to know whether Carrington innocently assumed or consciously misrepresented this fact—or why he might have been motivated to fabricate it. Perhaps he felt it sounded like a more gallant ending to the life of a valiant and well-regarded officer than being horribly mutilated. It also reinforced the idea that Fetterman was rash, just like Brown, and that when both men recognized their folly they chose to quickly end it all.

After Ten Eyck and his relief mission cautiously moved down the road toward the boulders, they could see the naked bodies of their comrades clustered in grotesque heaps around the rocks. The group of Indians that surrounded the boulders retreated down to the valley and, gradually, the huge Lakota alliance force dispersed and moved north to their camps on the Tongue River. Ten Eyck posted guards around the perimeter of the scene and ordered the men to examine the soldiers for signs of life. It was quickly apparent that there would be no survivors. The carnage was horrifying. All of the men had been mutilated, many were stuck like pincushions with dozens, and even hundreds, of arrows protruding from their naked bodies. At each location where the soldiers fell, the warriors had removed their clothing to take possessions as spoils of war. The Indians also had enough time to prepare the soldiers' bodies in a way they believed would bring humiliation upon entry to the spirit world. The Indians removed eyes and ears and performed other mutilations to signify a particular soldier's actions of cowardice or bravery during the battle. Preparation and arrangement of the soldiers' bodies bore a great amount of significance to the Lakota, Cheyenne, and Arapaho warriors, sending a message to the remaining occupants at the fort as well as sending a message with the bodies as they entered the afterlife. Only one body, that of Corp. Adolph Metzger, a bugler with Company C of the Second Cavalry, was left undesecrated. He was found fully clothed underneath a buffalo robe. The warriors who overcame the young bugler covered and protected his body from depradations out of respect for his bravery. Years later, Northern Cheyenne warriors gave the dented bugle the soldier had swung at his opponents to Jim Gatchell, a store owner in Buffalo, Wyoming, where the bugle is on display at the Jim Gatchell museum.

The hardiest of Ten Eyck's command loaded the bodies into the wagons. It took more than four hours, and then they were forced to return to the post around dusk with only about half of the bodies—all that the wagons could carry. One can only imagine the scene at Fort Phil Kearny that evening. There were only five surviving officers besides Carrington and less than two hundred and fifty soldiers. Nearly everyone witnessed the gruesome sight of the wagonloads of naked and mutilated bodies that had been carted through the post to the hospital—and they all knew that almost half had been left on the field of battle. The post surgeons began the task of preparing the bodies for burial. Two wives, Frances Grummond and James Wheatley's young wife, Elisabeth, were sheltered and consoled by the ladies of the fort. Their husbands' bodies were not among those that were brought in.

The community's shock was quickly replaced with overwhelming fear of a direct attack on the fort. The community was sure that Red Cloud's camp knew how weak and vulnerable the fort was at this point. Carrington ordered every able-bodied soldier and civilian to be armed and put on duty at various positions around the stockade—not a person went to sleep that night. A few of the old-timers probably tried in vain to convince the soldiers that the Lakota alliance would be celebrating their victory that night and the chance of attack was almost nonexistent. No one knew that the Lakota and their allies were too busy tending to their own casualties and preparing for expected bad weather to plan an assault on the fort. A hunter and sometime guide in the employ of the quartermaster, John "Portugee" Phillips, volunteered to take word to Fort Laramie—a four-to five-day ride under the best circumstances. There were probably hostile Indians all along the route and the weather had turned bitterly cold with a storm appearing imminent, making the trip far more treacherous. Yet, this was Carrington's only choice. He gave Phillips the fort's best mount, his own horse, and several quickly written dispatches to be telegraphed from the telegraph station forty miles north of Fort Laramie. Carrington then escorted Phillips to the back gate and let the horse and rider out personally, wishing them Godspeed. Much has been made of Phillips's ride. Years later, his wife petitioned Congress for reimbursement for stolen livestock and property as well as recognition and compensation for this extraordinary service to the post. Mari Sandoz, the renowned western historian, wrote that Phillips had traveling partners during the entire route and, because he was married to an Indian woman, the danger to him from Indians was overrated. Regardless of the potential for danger from attack, the danger from succumbing to the weather was very real.[22]

Meanwhile, the Lakota and their allies celebrated their spectacular victory and also mourned the loss of a great number of their warriors. Years later, Red Cloud told James Cook eleven warriors died at the battle, but many more were wounded so badly that they died in their camps. The night before, a highly regarded seer had predicted that the warriors would kill more soldiers than could be held in both hands—one hundred sol-

The Battle of the Hundred-in-the-Hands

24. John "Portugee" Phillips was a Portuguese immigrant who came to California as an eighteen-year-old and followed the goldfields for the next fifteen years. While mining in Montana in 1865 he wintered at Fort Phil Kearny as a civilian contractor. Though frequently credited as having solely braved the perilous ride to Fort Laramie to bring news of the massacre to the world, he was in fact accompanied during the entire ride. Wyoming State Archives, Department of State Parks and Cultural Resources.

diers. To the warriors of the Lakota alliance this battle became known as the Battle of the Hundred-in-the-Hands.[23]

The next morning the officers of Fort Phil Kearny held a meeting. There were thirty to forty bodies left at the scene of the battle and they had to decide how to retrieve them, if they retrieved them at all. Margaret Carrington wrote that there was "universal disinclination" among the other officers to return to the field, but Carrington stood his ground, telling them that he would not let the Indians, who risk life and limb to retrieve their own, think that the army did not have the courage to do the same.[24] Carrington and Ten Eyck led a party of eighty civilians and soldiers—all volunteers—to gather the remaining bodies. James Bridger supervised a line of pickets between the fort and the group at the battle site, both parties being exceptionably vulnerable to attack. The remaining forty-one bodies, including Grummond's, were retrieved and brought to the fort at the end of a long, tense day.

For the next three weeks, Fort Phil Kearny was completely isolated from the rest of the world by a series of raging snowstorms. The miserable task of preparing and burying eighty-one soldiers in subzero weather replaced the holiday season. The post's occupants did not know if Phillips had made it to Fort Laramie. On December 27 a small contingent of dedicated soldiers arrived. They had been waiting out the storm at Fort Reno when Phillips rode in on December 23. After hearing of the attack, these brave soldiers pushed on through the deep snow and fierce winds to reinforce Fort Phil Kearny. They brought mail, which contained the official notices of assignments in the reorganization. Carrington and his regimental staff were to transfer to Fort Casper to establish Eighteenth Infantry headquarters while the soldiers of the Second Battalion became the Twenty-seventh Infantry stationed at the three forts on the Bozeman Trail. The commander of the new Twenty-seventh Infantry was Col. John E. Smith; both the lieutenant colonel and the major for this regiment were yet to be assigned. As the highest brevetted rank among the regiment's eight captains, Fetterman would have

The Battle of the Hundred-in-the-Hands

been the second in command and likely a commander at one of the forts on the Bozeman Trail.[25]

Phillips reached the Horse Shoe Creek telegraph station below Fort Reno on Christmas Day. The telegraph operator could not send so long a message as Carrington had dispatched, so a shortened version warned the officers at Fort Laramie of the news of the disaster that would be forthcoming. At eleven o'clock that evening, Phillips arrived at the fort, exhausted and freezing; a short time later, on December 26, 1866, Cooke, Sherman, Grant, and the world found out about the Fetterman Massacre. Carrington insisted that Phillips have the telegram sent not only to Cooke but also directly to General Grant at Army Headquarters in Washington DC. The dramatic message reflected Carrington's anxiety and emotion in the few hours after the massacre. "Do send me re-enforcements forthwith. I risk everything but the post and its store. I venture as much as any one can, but I have had today a fight unexampled in Indian warfare. My loss is ninety-four (94) killed. I have recovered forty-nine bodies, and thirty-five more are to be brought in the morning that have been found." Carrington went on to defend himself and justify his previous requests for men and ammunition; "I hear nothing of my arms that left Leavenworth September 15. Additional cavalry ordered to join have not reported their arrival. Would have saved us much loss today.... I need prompt re-enforcements and repeating arms. I am sure to have, as before reported, an active winter, and must have men and arms." To emphasize the vulnerability and the sense of desperation at the fort, Carrington wrote, "Our killed show that any remissness will result in mutilation and butchery beyond precedent. No such mutilation as that to-day is on record. Depend on it that this post will be held so long as a round or man is left." He concluded with a reiteration of the lack of support he had received: "Promptness is the vital thing. Give me officers and men. Only the new Spencer arms should be sent. The Indians desperate, and they spare none."[26]

Carrington's dispatch caught the attention of his commanders. For a week the three generals telegraphed each other and the commander at Fort Laramie, all demanding information that was held up behind a wall of snow. Grant demanded answers from Sherman who demanded answers from Cooke—Sherman even insisted that Cooke venture a conjecture of what could have happened. Without waiting for Carrington's full report of the incident, Cooke sent a telegram to Gen. I. N. Palmer at Fort Laramie ordering him to detach two companies of cavalry and four companies of infantry to meet Gen. Henry Wessells at Fort Reno and move on to Fort Phil Kearny. Cooke ordered Wessells to assume command of the post, relieving Carrington, who was to move immediately with the Eighteenth Infantry to Fort Casper. This order simply finalized Carrington's assignment after the army reorganization, but Cooke's telegram was intentionally worded as a public rebuke to Carrington. Palmer wired back to Cooke that he would comply but that the weather was too severe to send the men. They were not able to leave Fort Laramie until New Year's Day.

A break in the weather enabled Carrington to send a mail party to Fort Laramie on January 4. In the mailbag was Carrington's lengthy report, dated January 3, on the "fight with Indians on the 21st." The same bag contained a letter from Surgeon Hines to his brother describing the post as being in a state of siege and the details of the massacre. Hines opened his letter with, "Matters in this part of the country do not suit me." Another letter was from a sergeant in Company E to a friend on General Sherman's staff: "The men are sleeping in their clothes, accoutrements on. Indian signals have been seen and we don't know what hour the post may be attacked . . . you can imagine the state of affairs here. . . . Please write soon, and pray God to hasten the day when I shall get out of this horrible place. Goodbye; this may be my last letter; should it reach you, don't forget your friend."[27] Unknown to Carrington, another letter in this delivery was a scathing missive on his management of the affair from one of his officers to the man who would become his greatest detractor, Captain Bisbee, now assigned to Cooke's headquarters in Omaha.

After the mail detachment left, another series of blizzards and frigid weather fell on the region. The weather and the devastation of the massacre left the residents of Fort Phil Kearny feeling especially isolated and vulnerable. They spent twelve more days anxiously waiting for signs from the outside world. On January 16 pickets on Pilot Hill signaled the approach of a large army train. Lieutenant Colonel Wessells and six companies of soldiers finally marched into the besieged little post. It would be hard to say which group was happier to see the other, for the relief column had waded through knee- to waist-deep snow in subzero temperatures since they left Fort Laramie two weeks earlier. Nearly all of the soldiers were frostbitten and one man had frozen to death in his sleep.[28]

The reinforcements brought the mail, including newspaper articles featuring ludicrous depictions of the Fetterman Massacre that would have been laughable if they were not so damaging to Carrington's reputation.[29] The mail also contained Cooke's order for Wessells to relieve Carrington as commander of Fort Phil Kearny and for Carrington to immediately move his headquarters to Fort Casper, about 150 miles southwest of Fort Reno. Even though the weather and the threat of encountering hostile Indian war parties along the route made the trip extremely hazardous, Carrington was forced to leave at once because Fort Phil Kearny was not big enough to house the sudden abundance of soldiers. The Carringtons had taken Frances Grummond, who was more than six months pregnant, into their home since the night of the massacre. Carrington arranged for the young widow and her husband's remains to accompany his regimental headquarters in their move to Fort Casper. Grummond expected her brother to make his way from Tennessee to escort her home, and Fort Casper was easier to reach than Fort Phil Kearny.

After a week of packing and outfitting wagons to accommodate wives and children through the perilous midwinter expedition, Carrington made his good-byes to the men who remained

⌐ 25. Fetterman and the other soldiers who were killed in the December 21 battle were buried on Christmas Eve in a mass grave meticulously documented by Carrington. A month later Frances Grummond requested her husband's body be disinterred and returned with her to Franklin, Tennessee, to be buried in her family's cemetery. His body was apparently moved again, probably after Frances's family (the Courtneys) learned he had been a bigamist. The other soldiers' bodies were disinterred in 1888 and buried on Last Stand Hill at the Little Bighorn Battlefield. Photo courtesy Patricia M. Stallard.

at the post. Only two of his officers stayed: Ten Eyck, who was the sole officer remaining who had been with the Carringtons from the beginning of the expedition, and Captain Powell, who came in November with Fetterman. Wands, Arnold, and Hines and their families were leaving with Carrington. As he rode through the stockade for the last time, Carrington must have felt he was leaving a part of himself behind, for he had put his heart and soul into the creation of Fort Phil Kearny.

Both Frances and Margaret wrote about the harrowing journey to Fort Casper. More than half of the men had severe frostbite before they reached Fort Reno. Many required amputations from which two men died during the three-day layover. The group struggled on, fighting the weather and constantly on the lookout for Lakota war parties. When they finally reached Fort Casper, Carrington was greeted with an order notifying him that the headquarters for the Eighteenth had been changed to Fort McPherson, Nebraska. The group was dumbfounded, for they had to backtrack nearly one hundred miles through the snow and freezing conditions they had endured for more than two weeks. As the unit made its way to Fort McPherson via Fort Laramie, Carrington accidentally shot himself in the thigh. The wound, to his thigh and his ego, was serious. Carrington rode the rest of the trip in his wife's ambulance with his leg hanging in a makeshift sling. He surely wondered if his luck could get any worse. It was not long before Carrington found that his troubles had just begun.[30]

Blazing a Paper Trail

Carrington's full report on the Fetterman catastrophe was written in the days immediately after the massacre while the post was sealed off from the world by two weeks of blizzards and subzero weather. Christmas came and went with little notice, as the entire community was on edge as they fought the storms and somberly prepared the dead for interment—it took days to build the pine coffins and when it came time to dig a grave the weather was so bitter the men had to work in short relayed shifts including a heavy guard. The burial took place on Wednesday, December 26. All the while, the unrelenting snow required constant shoveling to keep a trench around the stockade to prevent the enemy from being able to walk right over it.[1]

On January 1, 1867, the army reorganization went into effect, but a planned ceremony to celebrate the new Twenty-seventh Battalion was replaced with a solemn observance of the dead where Carrington publicly proclaimed his and the entire post's admiration for Fetterman. The vehicle for this tribute was General Order No. 1, an order officially identifying the boundaries of the Fort Phil Kearny Military Reservation. Weeks earlier, Carrington had protested Cooke's insistence that the reservation—land restricted for use by the fort—be limited to five miles square as this would preclude army use of the pinery for wood and most of the grassland used for grazing the post's livestock, leaving the post dependent on contractors for wood and forage. Cooke would hear nothing of Carrington's complaints and insisted that the reservation be kept to twenty-five square miles. Carrington issued the order on the first day of the year as required, and he used it as an opportunity to dedicate the space within the reservation that was used for a burial location for the post's dead and pay homage to Fetterman and the other downed soldiers "in a form doing honor to the dead."[2]

Carrington's portrayal of Fetterman in this proclamation gives no indication that he felt the captain was reckless, undisciplined, or inordinately aggressive. In fact, it paints the picture of an outstanding officer and gentleman who performed his duties with honor and distinction: "Captain Fetterman, son of Captain George Fetterman of the Army, was born in garrison, and was instinct [sic] with the ambition of a soldier. His character was pure and without blemish. He was a refined gentleman and had distinguished his regimental record and honored his own name by duty well done."[3]

As the storms subsided and the shock of the massacre began to wear off, Carrington prepared his official report. Ever conscious of his image as an officer and the perception of his inexperience in command assignments, the colonel was faced with a dilemma. Carrington needed to prove his thorough military control at the post while claiming no responsibility for Fetterman and his command's annihilation. The only way to do this was to prove that Fetterman blatantly disobeyed his orders. To explain why a military man with an unblemished record would suddenly become flagrantly insubordinate, Carrington had to position Fetterman as irrationally overconfident about Indian warfare because he was so new to frontier duty. For days, the lawyer and gifted writer worked on his account of the event.

Carrington's report was dated January 3, 1867—thirteen days after the incident and the first day the storms abated enough for a mail party to depart for Fort Laramie. As the detachment left Fort Phil Kearny, Carrington added a final dispatch to be telegraphed to department headquarters. Since mail deliveries took several weeks, Carrington wanted Cooke and his superiors to know that his formal report was on the way via mail. "The mail takes full report of fight Dec twenty first. . . . All bodies rec'd. . . . the facts disclosed show that the Detachment was several miles from the wood train they were sent to relieve & pushed over lodge trail ridge in order of pursuit after orders three times given not to cross that ridge." Here was Carrington's first written accusation of Fetterman's disobedience. This telegram was dated January 4 and was received at Cooke's headquarters on January 7. It was probably sent from a small telegraph station fifty-five miles north of Fort Laramie. However, somewhere between Cooke's and Sherman's offices this telegram was held up for ten days. Sherman did not forward this telegram to Grant until January 17, stating. "The Subjoined telegram has this moment been recd."[4] Meanwhile, the mail with Carrington's full report and the other letters that had been sent on January 4 took nearly three weeks to arrive at their eastern destinations.

During this time, Grant, Sherman, the Departments of War and the Interior, and Congress were positively frantic for information about the catastrophe. Between December 26, when Carrington's initial telegram notifying headquarters of the disaster was received, and January 17, when Carrington's second dispatch was finally sent from Cooke and Sherman to Grant, dozens of telegrams flew between the three generals' offices. These communiqués left a record of comments that eventually became evidence in a lengthy investigation. The pressure for answers began with Pres. Andrew Johnson. Less than a month earlier, Johnson declared in a public speech that the army was well armed and well supported and the Plains Indians "have unconditionally submitted to our authority and manifested an earnest desire for a renewal of friendly relations."[5] The president wasn't the only official who looked bad. The Department of the Interior, which very publicly proclaimed the peace treaty

Blazing a Paper Trail

of Fort Laramie a success, immediately went on the offensive and sought to push the blame onto the army.

The commissioner of Indian affairs, Lewis V. Bogy, was cited in newspaper articles alleging that the army fired on peaceful, starving Indian women and children. Bogy's analysis of the events was so erroneous that he was ultimately replaced by the president when the investigating committee uncovered the facts. However, his attacks on the army—particularly Carrington and Cooke—were the opening salvo in a vicious political battle over Indian policy. His statements also caused irreparable damage to Cooke's and Carrington's reputations.

Bogy reported that the hostile tribes never came to the fort in a great force and were never really a threat to the army. Bogy wrote that Carrington and his troops fired on Indians who were on a friendly visit to the fort to ask Carrington to rescind an earlier order by Cooke that prevented traders from selling them powder and ammunition. Bogy then asserted that all of the hostilities could be traced to Cooke's order and that the Sioux and other tribes in the area were starving and in "absolute want of guns and ammunition to make their winter hunt." In analyzing the reports of Lakota attacks Bogy proclaimed, "To say that a wagon train was attacked by three hundred Indians, and yet no one killed, is simply ridiculous. There were, perhaps, some five or six men with this train, and if three hundred Indians had really attacked them, it is not doubted that one or more of them would have been killed." As Margaret Carrington wryly observed, "He did not know how slowly six men would have built a post; nor that the timber trains sometimes numbered ninety or more wagons, each drawn by six mules; that each team required a driver; that the work required choppers and loaders and a guard to protect them; and that six men could not do this."[6] Bogy went on to say that reports of three thousand to five thousand warriors were complete exaggerations and that it was physically impossible for that many Indians to support themselves in that region. He concluded, "Although I regret the unfortunate death of so many brave soldiers, yet there can be no doubt that it is owing to the foolish and rash management of the officer in command at that post." In Bogy's opinion the only solution was to move the army away from all hostile Indian areas and give the Department of the Interior the authority to concentrate Indians on reservations and slowly educate and Christianize them.[7]

The president, who looked foolish for prematurely declaring peace on the Plains, harassed Secretary of War Stanton who in turn harassed Grant and Sherman. The two generals then badgered Cooke for information, but the weather did not cooperate. Communications west of Omaha were shut down until mid-January. On December 28, Grant's adjutant general telegraphed Sherman, saying, "Gen'l Grant requests that you will furnish him with any additional information you may receive in reference to the Ft Philip Kearney massacre, and if there has been fault in the matter that you will have it strictly investigated." Sherman immediately responded, "I do not yet understand how the massacre of Col Fettermans party could have been so complete. We must act with vindictive earnestness against the Sioux. . . . nothing less will reach the root of this case." The next day Sherman wired Grant that a heavy snowstorm west of Omaha was preventing communications but he would have the matter fully investigated.[8]

Cooke was clearly concerned about the backlash this incident might have on his career. He sent lengthy telegrams to Sherman and Grant refuting Carrington's claims of shortages of men and ammunition. On December 27, seeking to distance himself from Carrington as much as possible, Cooke wrote, "Col. Carrington is very plausible; an energetic industrious man in garrison: but it is too evident that he has not maintained discipline and that his officers, have no confidence in him."[9] Meanwhile, Sherman was washing his hands of Cooke. On December 30, Sherman wired to Grant that weather was still preventing any news from the West, and that "I am not satisfied with Genl. Cooke—or the two officers now up there, Carrington & Wessells."[10]

The generals waited well beyond the New Year for the weather

Blazing a Paper Trail

to release its grip on the information they so desperately sought. In frustration, they resorted to conjecture and began to take action based on their own assumptions. This led to the first political casualty of the Fetterman affair—Gen. Philip St. George Cooke. On January 7, without consulting Sherman, Grant assigned Gen. C. C. Augur to replace Cooke as commander of the Department of the Platte. Grant wired Sherman at 10:30 in the morning on January 8 letting him know of the decision, stating "you will be much pleased with Augur. He has had long experience among Indians both hostile and peaceable." Sherman wired back that afternoon that the appointment was "most acceptable." When Cooke found out the next day, he was distraught. He viewed his response to the Fetterman incident as an opportunity to repair the damage his ego and reputation suffered during the Civil War. A few days earlier, on January 3, Cooke had submitted a request for reinforcements to the War Department, which Sherman endorsed, and was preparing to launch a highly visible punitive campaign against the Lakota and their allies. Cooke knew that being replaced at this moment implied he was at fault. He immediately wired Grant, "Shall I work on planning what may be all changed or complained of after the disgrace you put upon me? . . . I certainly do not deserve this inconsiderate action in my case." Cooke was even more bitter in his dispatch to Sherman that same day, stating, "You can avert this cruel blow calculated to disgrace me only I fear it may have come from you—I fought and whipped the Sioux and am very nearly equal physically to my best day."[11]

Sherman was sympathetic to Cooke's plight, but his hands were tied. He later wrote to Gen. Grenville M. Dodge, "I had nothing to do with Cooke's removal—the order originated at Washington and came to me complete without my being consulted, and I do not know what influenced Genl Grant, but never supposed Genl Cooke was in the least to blame for the Phil Kearney Massacre."[12] On January 9 Grant told Cooke to follow Sherman's directions regarding any measures taken to launch an Indian campaign and wait for Augur to arrive. Cooke was stunned. For two more weeks he was put through the humiliation of having to respond to Grant's and Sherman's demands for reports and information about his operations and the causes of Fetterman's annihilation while he waited for his replacement. Cooke and his staff—including Carrington's nemesis Lieutenant Bisbee who was now a captain and Cooke's aide-de-camp—were devastated. On January 14 Cooke sent a report to Sherman's office giving his "version of the affair." Cooke wrote that he was still "uninformed," but since he was being called to provide a version based on his "judgement of the probabilities" he used Carrington's reports and his own knowledge of the events to provide the most likely cause of the catastrophe. Cooke went on to say, "Carrington has before December 21, made no expedition against Indians; all his skirmishes have been with war parties attacking his supply trains, or appearing in sight of the fort. I am informed that on these occasions it was the custom of officers and men to sally forth, mounted or afoot, much at their discretion." Cooke then provided Fetterman's report of the December 6 skirmish—without Carrington's own report, of which Fetterman's was an attachment—describing how Brown and Wands joined up with Fetterman without authorization. It is clear that Bisbee was Cooke's informant—he was the only person in Cooke's office who had lived at Fort Phil Kearny. Also, Fetterman originally addressed his report to Bisbee, who was post adjutant, so Bisbee knew it supported his accusations against Carrington.[13]

It was during this time that Carrington's second telegram, claiming the incident was caused by Fetterman's disobedience and notifying Cooke that his full report was en route via mail, arrived. It is not clear whether Cooke's office, after receiving the telegram on January 7, held on to the telegram for ten days and then sent it to Sherman's office or whether the message sat in Sherman's office for ten days. Sherman was justifiably distracted—and probably out of his office for a few days—as his wife delivered a baby the night of January 9 and he had just returned from a mission to Mexico. As Sherman left the office the day of

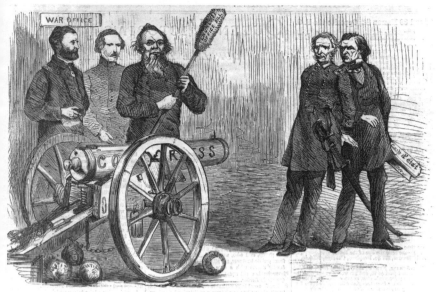

THE SITUATION.

26. After the Civil War, *Harper's Weekly* was a major force in the Andrew Johnson impeachment scandal and Grant's presidential victories of 1868 and 1872. In the immediate aftermath of the Fetterman debacle, Stanton, Grant, and Sherman were caught up in the highly charged political drama of Johnson's impeachment and provided no support to Carrington's frequent appeals. This print shows Ulysses Grant and Edwin Stanton near a cannon, labeled "Congress," aimed at President Johnson and Lorenzo Thomas, whom Johnson appointed secretary of war after suspending Stanton in 1867. Grant subsequently sided with the Radical Republicans in Congress and supported Johnson's impeachment for violation of the Tenure of Office Act. From *Harper's Weekly*, March 7, 1868; Library of Congress Prints and Photographs Division, LC-USZ62-127515.

his son's birth, he endorsed Cooke's January 3 request for reinforcements saying the Fetterman incident demonstrated how strong the Lakota alliance had become and that it was "hard to limit the number of men required to defeat & destroy [the Indians.]"[14] Even though Cooke was soon to be replaced with Augur, Sherman wanted to make sure that his department was appropriated enough men and supplies to launch a punitive campaign. It is clear that Sherman believed at this time that the main cause of the incident was lack of soldiers.

After Commissioner Bogy's public accusations, Grant recognized the Fetterman incident's potential for politically damaging consequences. His quick replacement of Cooke served many purposes. It gave Grant the opportunity to place an old and trusted friend—Augur was one of Grant's classmates at West Point—in a prominent position that required Grant's confidence. Plus this appointment satisfied Sherman, who had not wanted Cooke in the first place. Moreover, this transfer positioned Cooke as a scapegoat and deflected attention away from any potential culpability on the part of the leadership of the War Department. Grant desperately needed to avoid any damaging publicity for himself or his commander, Secretary Edwin M. Stanton.

The Fetterman incident transpired in the middle of a heated political battle between President Johnson and Congress over Reconstruction. As historian Eric Foner points out, the roots of Johnson's impeachment lay in his increasingly hostile relations with a Congress that eventually "enjoined the army to carry out a policy [Johnson] resolutely opposed." The battle ultimately centered on Secretary of War Stanton—an outspoken supporter of Johnson's opponents in Congress. Johnson wanted to replace Stanton with Grant, who would have nothing to do with the plan. In late 1866, after Grant clearly demonstrated his allegiance to Stanton, Johnson asked Grant to escort a delegation of diplomats on a mission to Mexico in order to get Grant out of the way so he could proceed with his plan to depose Stanton. Grant did not budge because his absence would leave Stanton

27. Edwin M. Stanton. Carrington pressed Secretary of War Stanton and General of the Army Ulysses S. Grant to release information that would clear his name, but Stanton was at the center of the battle to impeach and remove Pres. Andrew Johnson from office and Grant was cultivating his own political prospects, so neither politician could afford to have the army appear to be poorly run. They let the blame fall squarely on Carrington's shoulders. On December 20, 1868, exactly two years after the Fetterman Massacre, President Grant appointed Stanton to the Supreme Court and the Senate confirmed that day. Stanton died, however, four days later. Library of Congress Prints and Photographs Division, no. LC-USZ61-985.

vulnerable. Sherman volunteered to go to Mexico in Grant's place, and Johnson acquiesced to the offer. Johnson then wooed Sherman, hoping to lure him to his side and ultimately put him in Stanton's place as secretary of war—something that Sherman, like Grant, steadfastly eschewed.

The very day Sherman found out about the Fetterman massacre, he had just returned from the mission to Mexico. As Sherman and Grant struggled to determine what went wrong in the Mountain District, they fended off Johnson's repeated attempts to get Sherman to come to Washington because they knew Johnson wanted to embroil Sherman in the political situation. The generals and their Department of War had to be very cautious about the presentation of the Fetterman incident to the public and to Congress so as not to give Johnson and his supporters any ammunition against Stanton.[15]

Grant, by now expert in the ways of Washington politics, cleverly anticipated that the Fetterman incident could be used against the army and the Department of War. On January 14 he wrote to Sherman, "Gen. Augur left last evening for Omaha via St. Louis. Are you having an investigation into the Fort Phil Kearny Massacre? A report will probably be called for and it is import that we should know all that can be learned about it as soon as possible."[16] A few days later General Augur arrived in St. Louis and Sherman helped him review all of the letters and dispatches sent from Cooke's office in the past few months. Sherman told Grant, "I feel certain that he can soon master that Department and bring those Sioux into order." However, Sherman was beginning to despair of ever hearing from his western outposts for in this same letter he wrote, "I have failed utterly to get full accounts of the Phil Kearny massacre, but Augur will be instructed to make a thorough investigation & Report."[17]

By now, army officials considered any information about the incident, verified or not, as having merit. A personal letter from a sergeant in Company E at Fort Phil Kearny written to a friend on Sherman's staff suddenly materialized as evidence.

Blazing a Paper Trail

The letter was written in the anxious days immediately after the attack and sent in Carrington's January 4 mail dispatch. It was filled with inaccuracies and conjecture—the writer even admitted he had just been released from confinement so he could not be fully aware of the circumstances. Yet somehow this letter made it into Sherman's hands and was forwarded to Grant and became part of the public record. Stanton somehow obtained a copy of Surgeon C. M. Hines's letter to his brother that was sent in the same mailbag; this letter was forwarded to both Grant and Sherman and also found its way into the public record. Neither letter was particularly damning to Carrington, but they both suggested the desperation of the situation at the fort, and the generals interpreted the letters as demonstrative of Carrington's mismanagement.[18]

Carrington's lengthy report, dated January 3 and sent in the same mail dispatch as Hines's and the anonymous letter, mysteriously remained out of the public's eye. The paper trail of this report, as it was forwarded between offices and eventually "lost," seems to indicate that someone in the offices of Carrington's chain of command wanted to prevent it from coming to light. The fact that the telegram that Carrington sent to Cooke informing him of this report's imminent arrival by mail was held up from Grant by someone in Cooke's or Sherman's office for ten days is further evidence of some type of conspiracy. The report, addressed to General Cooke at the Department of the Platte, arrived in Omaha just as Cooke was being unceremoniously relieved of duty. On January 19, eleven days after being notified of his replacement, Cooke angrily protested to the adjutant general's office and requested a court of inquiry. Grant rejected the request stating, "The application for a Court of Inquiry is disapproved. Gen. Cooke was relieved from command of the Dept. of the Platte solely because it was deemed for the good of the service to do so, and he has no right to question the motives which led to his removal."[19]

Thus ended Gen. Philip St. George Cooke's frontier service. Augur assumed command of Cooke's department on January

23. The day before, in his last official communication as commander of the Department of the Platte, Cooke forwarded Carrington's January 3 report to Sherman with an acrimonious cover letter that followed Carrington for years:

> This report put off for thirteen days, until notice of his being relieved was received. That seems to have given color to it. An officer of high rank, in letter of January 4, from Phil. Kearny, gives the following version: "The men, as usual, when the wood train was known to be corralled by the Indians, rushed out helter-skelter, some leaping over the stockade, which is in no place over eight feet high. What probability there is of their having had with them a proper supply of ammunition you can judge."
>
> No reinforcements ever "assured" to Col. C. failed to be sent. Before the Platte was put formally under my command, two companies of cavalry were ordered from Fort Laramie, but only one turned out to be disposable; an additional company of infantry was afterwards sent. November 25 he wrote he would "make the winter one of active operations in different directions, as best affords chance of punishment." December 19 telegraphed he was "preparing for active movements."[20]

Bisbee, Cooke's right-hand man and Carrington's worst enemy, was surely behind some of the inflammatory information about Carrington in this statement. The letter "from an officer of high rank, in a letter of January 4" was from Captain Powell to Bisbee, sent in the same mail dispatch from Fort Phil Kearny as Carrington's report. Carrington was not aware of this letter or Cooke's quotation from it until many years later, but he was sure that Powell was the author because the words used were the same that Powell used during his subsequent testimony on the Fetterman disaster.[21] The letter was obviously sent in the same mail dispatch as Carrington's report, and it is telling that Cooke had enough time to be made aware of this letter before he forwarded Carrington's report to Sherman. Carrington's report sat in Cooke's office for several days during which time either Cooke and Bisbee conspired or Bisbee took matters into his own hands before showing the full report to Cooke, who was obviously distracted by the disgrace of his imminent replacement. Both men were motivated to portray Carrington as the cause of the catastrophe. Cooke needed to show that it was Carrington, not himself, who was to blame, while Bisbee—who already despised Carrington—was furious with Carrington's portrayal of Fetterman. Carrington's report stated that Fetterman "claimed by rank to go out" on the relief mission and elaborated on the detailed orders that Carrington issued because of his concern over Fetterman's ambition to win honor. Carrington carefully avoided the word "disobey" but made it clear that Fetterman ignored his precise orders.[22]

Bisbee was livid. In his mind Fetterman was a better officer and leader than Carrington would ever be. How could he sit back and let Carrington besmirch his dear friend's good name and honor? Bisbee may have even held up the January 7 telegram from Carrington until this report came into Cooke's office and he was forced to send them both on. Cooke was in the middle of being ousted and was thoroughly embittered about the whole affair; he probably paid little attention to how his staff handled Carrington's telegram and report. In fact, many years later Carrington paid a visit to Cooke, who was very nearly on his deathbed, and asked him how he could have written the damaging words. Cooke replied, "I was in haste to forward your report as the country was greatly excited, and the Government very urgent, so that I endorsed the papers for transmission as prepared by one of my staff but do not remember which."[23] Bisbee, as Cooke's aide-de-camp, was surely the staff person who authored Cooke's devastating remarks and, in all probability, was responsible for the mysterious delays of both the telegram and the full report.

Carrington's report, clearly blaming Fetterman, and Cooke's cover letter, clearly blaming Carrington, both pointed out that the situation would not have occurred if reinforcements and

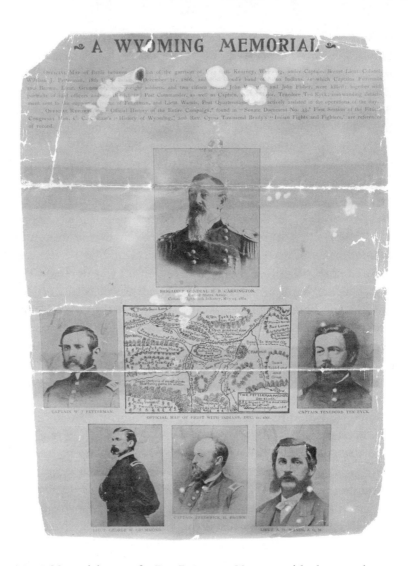

28. Memorial poster for Fort Fetterman Massacre with photos and map. For decades after the battle, tributes were made to the fallen soldiers. Fetterman's comrades were faithful to the officer and protected his reputation. Six months after the battle the army dedicated Fort Fetterman, at the southern end of the Bozeman Trail, in honor of the popular officer. Wyoming State Archives, Department of State Parks and Cultural Resources.

supplies had been sent in a timely manner from the Department of War. Sherman and Grant were faced with a quandary when they finally received the documents. If the report went public, they and the War Department would appear to have culpability for the disaster. If the report remained suppressed, available facts would continue to implicate Carrington and, to a lesser degree, Cooke, and deflect attention from the department. On January 30 the U.S. Senate and House of Representatives issued a joint resolution calling on the secretaries of war and the interior to provide "all of the official reports, papers, and other facts in possession of their respective departments, which may tend to explain the origin, causes, and extent of the late massacre of United States troops by Indians at Fort Phil Kearny."[24] The Fetterman incident then became a vehicle for both departments to publicly accuse each other of negligence, incompetence, and mismanagement in a yearlong paper war over control of the Office of Indian Affairs, which had been transferred from the Department of War to the Department of the Interior in 1849.

On February 2, the War Department forwarded its information and three days later the Department of the Interior followed suit. For reasons that have never been explained, Carrington's report with Cooke's damning attachment was not included in the War Department's submission. The documentary trail of this report confirms that the War Department was in possession of the report at the time it submitted its report to Congress. Cooke's office forwarded Carrington's report to Sherman on January 22 and Sherman forwarded it on to the adjutant general's office in Washington on January 29. The adjutant general's office then sent it to General Grant's office on February 4. This happened to be two days after Grant had submitted his report to Congress, stating, "I send herewith 'all official reports, papers, and other facts,' in possession of these headquarters, bearing upon the subject." Grant could claim that the report was not technically in possession at his headquarters as it was then at the adjutant general's office. It seems rather convenient

HARPER'S WEEKLY.

JOURNAL OF CIVILIZATION

Vol. XXII.—No. 1147.] NEW YORK, SATURDAY, DECEMBER 21, 1878. [WITH A SUPPLEMENT.
PRICE TEN CENTS.

↦ 29. "The Situation." The tension between the Departments of War and the Interior over how to best solve "the Indian problem" dominated the postwar army's strategy for years. Here, a cartoon depicts the renewed fight a dozen years after the end of the Civil War. "The new Indian war now, no sarcastic innuendoes, but let us have a square fight." This constant battle played a major role in Carrington's inability to gain support from either the army or the Office of Indian Affairs—both departments sought to portray the other as less competent and Carrington's version of the Fort Phil Kearny debacle placed culpability at the feet of both departments. From *Harper's Weekly*, December 21, 1878; Library of Congress Prints and Photographs Division, no. LC-USZ62-55403.

that Sherman chose to send this extremely important report to the adjutant's office when every other communication regarding the incident was sent directly to Grant's office—and then the adjutant "officially" forwarded the report to Grant two days after he responded to Congress. Grant's office did not send Carrington's report to Stanton's office until March 9, a full month after Stanton and Grant had provided Congress with "all information," thus exculpating Stanton from any knowledge of the War Department's lack of support of Fort Phil Kearny and the Mountain District.[25]

By then, Congress had already published the information submitted from both departments in a sixty-three-page pamphlet titled *Reports of the Secretaries of War and Interior in Answer to Resolutions of the Senate and House of Representatives in Relation to the Massacre at Fort Phil. Kearney, on December 21, 1866 with the views of Commissioner Lewis V. Bogy, in Relation to the Future Policy to be Pursued by the Government for the Settlement of the Indian Question, also Reports of Gen. John Pope and Col. Eli S. Parker, on Same Subject.*[26] This pamphlet purported to contain all the information from both departments, but clearly contained only what information their administrators wanted the public to see.

The portion of the pamphlet from the Department of the Interior contained Commissioner Bogy's wild claims that Carrington and his troops fired on innocent and starving Indians and blamed the entire episode on Carrington's mismanagement and Cooke's order prohibiting the sale of arms to Indians. The War Department sent its own subset of documents that subtly blamed Carrington. It suspiciously omitted Carrington's report from January 3 and included Fetterman's report of the December 6 battle without Carrington's report, of which Fetterman's was an attachment. The main objective for both departments was to make the other department look incompetent and position itself as the most capable of overseeing the Office of Indian Affairs. Even though it was not their primary goal, both departments cast Carrington as incompetent and clearly to blame for Fetterman and his troops' annihilation.

The Department of the Interior simply wanted the entire army and Department of War to look bad, while the War Department and army needed to show that any problems on their part were individual cases of incompetence and disobedience, not part of an overall flaw in department operations.

In the meantime, Carrington and his entourage were suffering the bitter cold and indignity of being bounced from post to post on the frontier. One of General Augur's first moves as commander of the Department of the Platte was to remove Carrington from any potentially dangerous assignments. Augur wrote, "I am unacquainted, personally, with Colonel Carrington and it is possible that an injustice may be done him, but right, or wrong, his reputation in the upper country is such for inefficiency and unfitness for command that I regard it as unsafe and unjust to leave him in charge of any post in that country. It is for these reasons I have brought him to Fort McPherson where the effects of his incapacity, if it exists, may be readily controlled."[27] Augur had been at the Department of the Platte in Omaha for nearly four weeks and Captain Bisbee, who was now on his staff, surely made his opinion of Carrington known to Augur by this time. Bisbee's behind-the-scenes influence on those who would sit in judgment of Carrington continued for years.

While the government was publishing this incriminating and inflammatory evidence against Carrington, he and his small entourage were on their brutal, and futile, march to Fort Casper. By the time Carrington had spent two weeks recuperating from surgery for his gunshot wound at Fort Laramie and moved eastward on the Platte Road to assume command at Fort McPherson, the pamphlet containing the injurious accusations—minus the deliberately withheld reports—had been published. Before Carrington knew what had been transpiring in the halls of government, he had been publicly set up as a scapegoat for the entire affair. Both the Department of War and the Department of the Interior were so eager to make the other look bad that each had little concern over any injustice done to Carrington. The only thing the two departments agreed on was that further bloodshed and hostilities were assured if something was not done.

As a result, on February 18, 1867, President Johnson appointed a special commission of military officers and civilians to investigate the circumstances of the massacre and to determine the steps necessary to avoid a full-scale war with the Plains Indians. The commission was composed of Gen. John B. Sanborn, Gen. N. B. Buford, Gen. Alfred Sully, Col. Ely S. Parker, Judge J. F. Kinney, and G. P. Beauvais. On March 4 the "Sanborn Commission" met in Omaha, taking testimony from General Cooke, Captain Bisbee, and other army personnel. The commission slowly moved West, stopping at posts along the way to take testimony from soldiers and citizens who had knowledge of the event. Carrington, who had assumed command of Fort McPherson on March 2, was now fully aware of the accusations and rumors that were being published in newspapers and official government reports. He eagerly prepared for the special commission to arrive at his post so that he could set the record straight. Carrington knew that his reports of December 6 and January 3 were not included in the pamphlet the government had published. These omissions logically led Carrington to believe there was a conspiracy or, at the very least, a cover-up of some kind with which he had to contend. It was painfully obvious that he could not accuse Sherman and Grant of placing him in the position of failure; Carrington had to exercise restraint in his allegations so as to avoid casting blame on the nation's top two Civil War heroes. Carrington's best argument was the one he put forward in his carefully crafted report of January 3 that clearly documented Fetterman's disobedience. This evidence had to be brought to the attention of the public to clear Carrington's name. The punctilious administrator drew on his legal and organizational skills to provide a solid, unequivocal case for his defense—a defense based predominantly on the claim that Fetterman disregarded Carrington's logical, clearly delivered orders.

The Sanborn Commission took Carrington's testimony between March 20 and March 27. His statements and support-

☙ 30. Civil War generals Sherman, Thomas, Grant, and Sheridan. Early attempts to obtain support from his superiors convinced Carrington of the futility of claiming army mismanagement. Sherman and Grant were considered national heroes who would be difficult to malign in the press. The commanders were reluctant to help Carrington because they had to protect the reputation of the army, and Grant was being courted to run for president. Library of Congress Prints and Photographs Division, no. LC-USZ62-15621.

31. After the Fetterman Massacre, special commissions ordered by both the army and Congress to investigate the situation on the Bozeman Trail evolved into negotiations with Red Cloud and the Lakota Alliance, and concluded with the Fort Laramie Treaty of 1868. Here Indian Commission members are in council at Fort Laramie: William S. Harney and William T. Sherman (seated to the immediate right of the center pole), Christopher C. Augur, who took command of Fort Phil Kearny after Carrington was relieved (fourth right of pole), and Alfred H. Terry, whose unit came upon the aftermath of Custer's battle at Little Bighorn (fifth right of pole). Photo by Alexander Gardner, 1868. National Archives, Record Group 111: Office of the Chief Signal Officer, 1860-1982, no. NWDNS-111-SC-95986.

ing documentation filled 286 handwritten pages. Carrington addressed in great detail the accusations made by Cooke in his Christmas-week telegrams to Sherman and Grant, and he incorporated his official reports from December 6 and January 3 into the testimony. After taking Carrington's deposition the committee moved west to Fort Laramie to meet with Indian leaders to discuss their issues and the underlying causes for the hostility on the Bozeman Trail. The commission eventually split into three groups to confer with different tribes. Three of the members, including Sanborn, felt they had enough information on the Fetterman incident to submit their joint report, but Judge Kinney, Colonel Parker, and General Sully were not convinced. Kinney was Carrington's sutler at Fort Phil Kearny for a period of time and had a personal grudge against the colonel for not approving several claims for damages he had sought during his residence at the fort.[28] He wanted to return to Fort Phil Kearny under the pretenses of meeting with the Crow Indians, although it appears that his real motive was to gather more incriminating evidence against Carrington. Commissioner N. B. Buford filed his report on June 6, dryly observing, "Two of us, General Sanborn and myself, were of the opinion that we should have made our joint report up to May the 10th, on which day the commission separated. We had long before finished taking testimony as to the massacre. . . . We had written out our report, and agreed upon it, but could not induce Generals Sully and Parker, and Judge Kinney, to give the matter their attention."[29] Kinney eventually obtained testimony from Captain Powell, who, second only to Bisbee in his hatred for Carrington, made some outrageous and spurious claims that Kinney sent through unofficial channels to the secretary of the interior.

Meanwhile, another Sanborn Commission member, Col. Ely S. Parker, who was General Grant's personal aide-de-camp, already formed his opinion about Carrington and forwarded damaging comments in private communiqués to Grant. After hearing testimony in Omaha, before he even heard Carrington's version, Parker wrote to Grant, "Carrington had no sort of discipline in his garrison, and although the Indians had been hostile ever since his arrival there, he took no unusual precautions against them. . . . Fetterman had disobeyed positive orders in going where he did, yet no one was sent out to ascertain why." The commission had just interviewed Bisbee who, obviously, was Parker's informant in Omaha. After Parker interrogated Carrington at Fort McPherson, he wrote to Grant's adjutant, "Not one tenth of the testimony he has given relates to the subject matter of our mission. In my opinion he is not fit to be in this Indian country. He is no fighter and does not understand the Indian character." Parker went on to accuse Carrington of mismanagement and ineptitude: "Many soldiers were killed within sight of the Fort, some within a few hundred feet of it, and yet all attempt at drill & perfect military discipline was neglected. The force was too much occupied in building magnificent quarters for the Col & his family."[30] Ely wrote this without having seen Fort Phil Kearny.

After meeting with the Sanborn Commission, Carrington then became the subject of a military court of inquiry. On February 25 Sherman recommended that the president call for the inquiry to uncover the facts and "report their opinion of what measures if any are necessary by way of punishment."[31] Sherman recommended several officers for the committee, including Gen. John Gibbon and Maj. James Van Voast, whose negative opinion about Carrington had already been made clear to his superiors. Just a few weeks earlier Van Voast's commander at Fort Laramie, Col. I. N. Palmer, wrote to General Cooke at headquarters that he would order Van Voast to lead reinforcement units to Fort Phil Kearny but "he would go very unwillingly if he is obliged to be under Col. C."[32] After hearing the rumors and innuendo being forwarded from his trusted attaché, Colonel Parker, Grant obtained a presidential order to launch the court of inquiry. Gibbon ultimately headed the inquiry and Van Voast was a member. They followed in the footsteps of the Sanborn Commission interviewing most of the same officers and civilians involved in the incident. The Sanborn Commission focused its investigation on doctrine, Indian policy, and how to avoid future uprisings by analyzing the causes of the Fetterman incident. The court of inquiry, on the other hand, sought to uncover exactly what happened at the remote post and assign responsibility for the debacle. Carrington faced both inquisitions with the same determination to prove his innocence and protect his honor. Unfortunately, neither investigatory committee operated without prejudice and it is clear that Carrington did not receive the benefit of genuine due process.

The grueling and humiliating interrogations of the two committees lasted from mid-March until the end of May. Anticipating his testimony would refute the public perception of his ineptitude and culpability, Carrington attempted to return to the responsibilities of his day-to-day command of Fort McPherson. However, instead of clearing his name, leaks from his detractors on the two investigations added to the growing public sentiment that Carrington was at fault. Carrington recognized the futility of trying to continue to command on the frontier under these circumstances and sought a medical leave of absence. On June 8, 1867, Augur and Sherman authorized a six-month medical leave for Carrington to return to the East to recuperate from his gunshot wound. Both generals were happy to have Carrington out of the way. Augur was convinced that, justified or not, Carrington's reputation prevented him from being able to command. Sherman hoped Carrington would quietly return to an administrative role back East while the investigations developed the evidence he and Grant needed to prove that the Office of Indian Affairs should be moved to the Department of War. It was necessary to point blame at the Department of the Interior for allowing traders to supply Indians with guns and ammunition and to prove that the military was capable but underfunded.

The Carringtons returned to the colonel's hometown of Wallingford, Connecticut. He did not, however, quietly accept whatever fate the investigations were destined to hand him. Carrington was absolutely convinced that publishing his report of January 3 would prove once and for all that Fetterman's disobedience caused the December 21 tragedy and that Carrington's management of the post was as good as could be expected considering the lack of support he received from Cooke. During the summer of 1867 Carrington wrote to Sanborn several times to find out when his report might be published. On July 17 Sanborn wrote, "Congress is doing but little and your report, if it has not already been published will not be likely to be at this meeting of Congress." Sanborn went on to say that his committee had not yet reconvened at Fort Laramie to make their final report, so the evidence they had collected — including Carrington's official report and testimony — could not be published yet either. However, Sanborn shared that a lengthy debate over Indian matters was ensuing in Congress and that he had sent a preliminary report to Washington that was scheduled to be printed with a report from the commissioner of Indian affairs in a few days. Though this preliminary report would not contain Carrington's official documents, Sanborn assured Carrington that it painted him in a positive light. Referring to the other investigation, Sanborn concluded, "The Court of Inquiry will not be heard of again I imagine and if you receive no censure you of course stand all right."[33]

Unknown to Carrington, Sherman had terminated the court of inquiry at the end of June before it could finish gathering evidence and testimony. Supposedly, Sherman could no longer spare Gibbon and the other officers during a summer of heated Indian battles. Saying, "Whatever seeming injustice may result by the present adjournment of the Court, can be rectified at some future more leisure period," Sherman told the court to submit the facts so far as they knew them to that point. He said the court could submit a "qualified opinion" or no opinion at all and that Grant would then form his own decision and "apply a remedy, if any is called for, in his own way."[34] The incomplete transcript gradually made its way to Grant's office and on September 10, he made his decision. "In my opinion further action is necessary and respectfully recommend that the Judge

Advocate General be directed to prepare charges against Col. H. B. Carrington." However, a few days later the judge advocate general told Grant that after examining the testimony himself he could find no basis for the charges.[35]

The circumstances surrounding Sherman's sudden adjournment of the court of inquiry "Sine die, without a statement of conclusions," in June and Grant's decision to prosecute Carrington three months later are very suspicious. Sherman's excuse, that the immediate services of the officers of the court were so necessary that they could no longer be spared, contradicts his earlier communications indicating that he would not be pursuing any military actions against hostile Indians until the Indian Bureau was transferred to the Department of War.[36] Continuing to tacitly allow Carrington to be portrayed as incompetent and culpable for the Fetterman disaster was politically expedient for Grant because it continued to deflect blame from the War Department's own mismanagement of the situation—and Grant and Stanton had enough political problems without being implicated in this scandal. President Johnson—with information provided by Stanton, Grant, and Sherman—had proclaimed that the Plains had been pacified and the army was in complete control of the western routes the very month that Fetterman and his men were killed. An in-depth investigation, publishing all of Carrington's reports—including the report of the killing of Lieutenant Bingham and Sergeant Bowers on December 6, the very day President Johnson declared peace on the Plains—would be politically devastating to the War Department. Carrington's January 3 report would also be problematic for Grant and the War Department because Carrington emphasized that he had repeatedly notified his superiors that the Fort Laramie treaty was an absolute failure and that his region was in a state of war—not absolute peace as declared in Washington. By this time Grant was being entreated to run for president and this incident—especially Carrington's two mysteriously hidden reports—would provide effective ammunition for his opponents.

32. Journalists complained of Grant's inscrutability, for which he was frequently compared to a Sphynx. *Harper's* published this cartoon, reflecting the idea that little was known about Grant's political views, but he was revered, especially by Union military supporters. It was during this sensitive time in the fall of 1867 that Carrington visited Grant, who rebuffed the maligned colonel. From *Harper's Weekly*, September 7, 1867; Library of Congress Prints & Photographs Division, no. LC-USZ62-127513.

About the time Carrington found out that the court of inquiry had been adjourned without publishing his testimony, the secretary of the interior published the report Sanborn referred to in his July 16 letter to Carrington. Responding to a resolution of the Senate on July 8, 1867, the document was titled *Letter of the Secretary of the Interior Communicating Information Touching the Origin and Progress of Indian Hostilities on the Frontier,* and became familiarly known as Senate Document 13. The military and civilian members of the Sanborn Commission never agreed on a unified report, so individual members eventually submitted their own assessments. Sanborn's and fellow member Buford's reports were included in this publication. Both focused primarily on Indian policy; however, Sanborn went to great effort to correct misinformation about Carrington's performance, saying he performed his duties with promptness and zeal and did the best he could with the inadequate support received from his superiors. Sanborn observed that Carrington's orders and operations were based on opening the Bozeman Trail via a compact or treaty—not by conquest or force. In discussing the events of December 21, Sanborn cited Carrington's specific and emphatic orders to Fetterman not to cross Lodge Trail Ridge but did not speculate on Fetterman's disobedience. Stopping short of implicating Fetterman, Sanborn wrote, "In the critical examination we have given this painful and horrible affair, we do not find of the immediate participants any officer living deserving of censure; and even if evidence justifies it, it would ill become us to speak evil of or censure those dead." Sanborn's final conclusion was that "the difficulty 'in a nutshell' was that [Carrington] was furnished no more troops or supplies for this state of war than had been provided and furnished him for a state of profound peace."[37]

Sanborn's support was a small victory for Carrington, but Senate Document 13 reprinted many of the damaging documents from the original pamphlet of information from the Departments of War and the Interior—and his reports of December 6 and January 3 were still omitted. Carrington was beginning to despair that his own testimony and evidence emphasizing Fetterman's disobedience would never see the light of day. Without this evidence, the Carringtons believed that the public perception would continue to hold that Carrington was responsible for the deaths of the eighty-one soldiers in what had become known as the Fetterman Massacre. With Grant calling for his court-martial and his friends in power—all radical Republicans locked in a ferocious battle with President Johnson—unable to come to his aid, Carrington was clearly losing the fight to protect his honor.

If the only documents available to re-create the history of Fort Phil Kearny and the Fetterman fight were the published records up to this point, the story would have developed along a different path. The single published report of Carrington's that stated unequivocally that Fetterman had disobeyed orders was his brief telegram of January 4 notifying his superiors that the full report was en route via mail. Sanborn concluded in the just published Senate Document 13 that Carrington issued clear, direct commands repeatedly to Fetterman and Grummond but also pointed out that the detachment did not go directly to the wood train as ordered. Sanborn did not speculate on Fetterman's immediate and obvious departure from the orders nor did he use the word *disobey*. Sanborn also cast a cloud of suspicion over Ten Eyck's performance in moving to the relief of Fetterman's detachment. Based on Carrington's testimony and evidence, Sanborn stated that he was "unable to determine" if Ten Eyck could have reached the scene of action in time to save Fetterman by marching over the shortest route. In the same publication, Fetterman's own report of December 6 was again published without Carrington's covering report. In fact, at this point the record presented Fetterman in a more favorable light than Carrington. On July 19, 1867, a new fort at the southern end of the Bozeman Trail was named Fort Fetterman in honor of the fallen hero.

By the fall of 1867 Carrington was desperate for a venue to publish his report, or at least his own version of the story. Then, one of Carrington's old friends, Gov. William Dennison of Ohio, suggested that Margaret write of her experiences on the frontier, and the Carringtons seized upon the idea as an answer to their prayers.[38] As an impeccable model of Victorian womanhood, Margaret Carrington was able to accomplish what Henry Carrington could not do: influence the American public. Her work also affected future historians' perceptions enough to alter significantly the present understanding of the event.

⊱ CHAPTER ⊰

Women's Work

I t is not clear exactly when Margaret Carrington started to convert her journal into a book. Henry Carrington secured a second six-month medical leave, enabling the Carringtons to remain in Connecticut until the summer of 1868. After a brief return to the frontier, the Carringtons moved to Indiana, and in the fall, Philadelphia publishers J. B. Lippincott published Margaret Carrington's *Absaraka, Home of the Crows: Being the Experience of an Officer's Wife on the Plains.* Less than eighteen months had passed since Henry and Margaret ended their journey to Absaroka. Considering the amount of time to typeset and produce a 284-page edition in 1868, it is safe to assume that Margaret began writing at the first sign of her husband's difficulties while he was being interrogated at Fort McPherson in May of 1867.

Prior to the publication of *Absaraka* in 1868, only two other army officers' wives had published their memoirs, but the reading public had already demonstrated a great interest in the exciting, exotic, and titillating stories of a Victorian woman in dangerous Indian country.[1] *Absaraka* was marketed to take advantage of the growing interest in these women's stories of western adventures as the phenomenon of ladies "writing their way out" of the private sphere—Victorian women's traditional domestic role—was in full swing.[2]

Since before the Civil War, the literary marketplace had been what historian Alice Fans has called "strikingly feminized." So-called domestic novels about home and family were the dominant form of fiction and the huge demand for these books opened the market for a flood of popular literature by and about women's domestic participation in the nation's internal conflict. Literary critics have observed that a "gendered nationalism" held sway in the publishing arena during this era as "streams of novels and omnibus volumes explored Northern women's contributions to the war."[3] Margaret's story about her life with the Civil War heroes of the Eighteenth Infantry Regiment and their role in advancing America's "manifest destiny" took advantage of the market for this gendered nationalism.[4] As Shirley Leckie points out in her biography of Elizabeth Custer, contrasting the culturally correct relations between army officers and their wives with unfavorable depictions of Native American family life served as "ideological justification for the conquest of the Plains tribes."[5] To justify the army's mission to the Bozeman Trail, Margaret championed the Crow Indians, who had "lost possession by robbery" of their homelands through the "occupation by the Sioux and their allies." Juxtaposing the "friendly" Crows against the aggression, violence, and "unrelenting hatred" of the Sioux, Margaret wrote that the Crows' enemies "have become the white man's enemy."[6]

Though Mrs. Carrington framed the book as a personal guide for western travelers, Lippincott billed *Absaraka* as the dramatic story of Margaret and her children accompanying her husband on the highly publicized disastrous mission to the frontier. Predictably, she painted Henry Carrington as a dutiful leader, military hero, and dedicated husband and father. *Absaraka* gave Henry the platform he needed to defend himself through the irrefutable writing of his moral, loyal, and devoted wife. The book reinforced the key facts of Henry Carrington's version of the story. Margaret Carrington was the first to publicly write that Fetterman frequently claimed that "a company of regulars could whip a thousand, and a regiment could whip the whole array of hostile tribes." She also wrote that Fetterman "was impatient because Indians were not summarily punished, and permitted this feeling and contempt of the enemy to drive him to hopeless ruin, where a simple deference to the orders and known policy of his commander . . . would have brought no loss of life whatever." Mrs. Carrington's description of the disaster of December 21 emphasized Henry's clear and specific orders to Fetterman and cited the supposed identical order Carrington gave to Captain Powell two days earlier as proof. She also wrote that Fetterman "claimed by rank" to take the relief command that day. Throughout her story, however, Margaret stresses Fetterman's noble spirit and gentlemanly and gracious character. Her main point about Fetterman was that, in spite of his unimpeachable character, he was driven to "reach forth for laurels that were beyond his reach."[7]

In a politically astute move, Margaret dedicated *Absaraka* to "Lieutenant-General Sherman, whose suggestions at Fort Kearney, in the spring of 1866, were adopted, in preserving a daily record of the events of a peculiarly eventful journey, and whose vigorous policy is as promising of the final settlement of Indian troubles and the quick completion of the Union Pacific Railroad as his March to the Sea was signal in crushing the last hope of armed rebellion."[8] Sherman wrote to Margaret in 1868, "I am this moment in receipt of your handsome volume Ab-sa-ra-ka. . . . I had already been attracted to the book from notices which had wide and favorable criticism." Sherman went on to say, "I shall again read the volume with interest secured by the fact that it is derived from a personal acquisition and a knowledge that its contents are real."[9] Sherman's wording implies he read all or part of Margaret Carrington's work before it was published, and Henry Carrington later stated that Sherman approved the publication of Margaret's first edition. *Absaraka* sold quickly and in 1869 the Carringtons released a second edition that included carefully selected excerpts of Sanborn's report from Senate Document 13 — only those portions that were complimentary to Henry Carrington. Apparently, General Sherman also authorized the Carringtons to include these excerpts in this edition.[10]

As early as April 1867 Sherman recognized that Carrington might not be getting a fair deal. On April 3 he wrote to Grant's office, "As to the Sioux north of the Platte it is idle for us to close our eyes to the fact that they are at war. They declare it openly and without reserve. It is hardly fair to attribute the utter annihilation of Colonel Fetterman's party to the misconduct or incapacity of Colonel Carrington."[11]

While the success of *Absaraka* gave the Carringtons a vehicle to promote their exonerative evidence, the Carringtons remained hopeful that the government would soon publish Henry's suppressed reports of December 6 and January 3. In *Absaraka* Margaret concluded optimistically, "At last the United States Senate called for the report of the commanding officer, at the April session, 1867, and again at the July session; and when it appears, some additional light may be furnished by which to confirm or disprove this comedy of errors."[12] Sadly, Margaret Carrington never saw that day.

Henry Carrington spent most of 1869 promoting *Absaraka* while seeking a fully pensioned medical discharge from the army. He decided on a career in academia and tried to secure a military professorship at several different colleges before accepting an appointment at Wabash College in Crawfordsville, Indiana. The family settled into the college town and Carrington began teaching in January 1870. Just a few months later, Margaret Carrington passed away. Her death, attributed to the bad weather she endured on the frontier, added to the poignancy and irrefutability of their book. Henry continued to promote *Absaraka,* citing proof from the book as well as Margaret's untimely death in his successful bid to retire with pension at the end of the year. Carrington's antagonists—Bisbee, Powell, Grant, and to a certain degree Cooke—did not publicly refute Margaret Carrington's writing because she was a lady. At this point, Margaret's word was Henry's only protection and it proved to be extraordinarily successful in accomplishing this objective.

Frances Grummond was one of the many interested readers of *Absaraka*. Back in February 1867 she parted with Henry and Margaret Carrington at Fort Laramie where Grummond's brother met her as she and the Carrington entourage made their midwinter trek from Fort Casper to Fort McPherson. The Carringtons were forced to lay over at Fort Laramie while Henry recovered from his accidental gunshot wound, so Frances's brother escorted her and her husband's remains on to Tennessee. The army granted special transportation consideration to the very pregnant Widow Grummond, including temporarily reassigning Lieutenant Wands so that Mrs. Wands could escort her. The commander of Fort Casper wrote Department of the Platte headquarters that because of her delicate condition it was "dangerous for her to travel without a female companion. . . . [Grummond] deserves Mrs. Wands to accompany her."[13] Headquarters granted the request and when Grummond delivered her baby seven weeks after she returned to Tennessee she christened him William Wands Grummond in honor of her deep friendship and gratitude to the Wands family. When she applied for a widow's pension for herself and her son, Frances was shocked to discover that her husband had been married when she exchanged vows with him. Delia, the first Mrs. Grummond, had already filed for the pension, sending her divorce decree as proof that she was owed $2,000 in support. For several years, Frances's brother acted as her representative in the complicated process of untangling George Grummond's deceits.[14]

Upon learning of Margaret Carrington's death, Frances sent condolences to Henry. She coyly described their courtship as a correspondence that ensued after her sympathy note "that resulted in our marriage in 1871, and my removal to his new home [in Crawfordsville]."[15] Carrington, with his military pension now assured, settled into life as a military professor. Henry adopted Frances's young son, William, and the couple had three more children in the next four years. Throughout this time, Carrington continued to be obsessed with clearing his name and ceaselessly lobbied political contacts to force publication of his suppressed reports and the complete testimony and evidence he provided to the Senate Commission.[16] After the Lakota alliance vanquished George Armstrong Custer and his mission at the battle of Little Bighorn in 1876, the nation turned its interest once again to the so-called Indian Question. This public interest prompted Carrington to issue a third edition of Margaret's *Absaraka*, released in 1879, in which he added more than 120 pages of appendices, including his assessment of "Indian Affairs on the Plains" up to that point. Then, three years later Carrington published his own book, titled *The Indian Question,* containing the text of an address he delivered in England and some of the same extracts printed in the appendices of *Absaraka.*

Still, Carrington pursued the release of his two long-suppressed reports and his complete testimony. Finally, in 1887 his tenacity paid off when Senator Dawes of Massachusetts—where the Carringtons now resided—demanded that the Departments of War and the Interior provide their copies of Carrington's reports and testimony. Senate Document 97, *Letter from the Secretary of War Transmitting in response to Resolution of February 11, 1887, report of Colonel Carrington on the Massacre near Fort Philip Kearny,* was immediately published. It contained Carrington's January 3, 1867, report including Cooke's damaging cover letter accusing Carrington of incompetence by running a post where the undisciplined men rushed out "helter-skelter," over a poorly designed eight-foot-tall stockade carrying little or no ammunition. Carrington's overly confident communiqués came back to haunt him when Cooke cited Carrington's promise to make the winter "one of active operations in different directions, as best affords chance of punishment" and that as late as December 19 Carrington had telegraphed he was "preparing for active movements."[17]

Carrington was astonished to read Cooke's statements; until this moment he had no idea that Cooke had done him so much harm. Suddenly, the conspiracy behind the suppression of his reports became clear to Carrington. Two of his officers, Bisbee and Powell, colluded to ruin his reputation and their successful efforts turned General Grant against him.

Back in 1867, while Carrington was on medical leave of absence in Connecticut, Sanborn apprised Carrington of Captain Powell's incredible testimony that Commissioner Kinney forwarded to the secretary of the interior through unofficial channels. Powell claimed that there was no trace of military discipline at Fort Phil Kearny and that Fetterman and his men had raced out over the top of the stockade, haphazardly and without ammunition. Cooke's cover, prefaced with "An officer of high rank, in letter of January 4, from Phil. Kearny, gives the following version . . . ," stated Powell's testimony nearly verbatim. Powell also testified that Carrington had been so afraid of Indian attack on the fort that he handed command of the post over to Powell when Fetterman was under attack. Kinney sent Powell's affidavit directly to Washington through unofficial channels in an attempt to stop the publication of Sanborn's report exonerating Carrington. When Grant and Stanton received Kinney's report with Powell's testimony, they already had a copy of Carrington's report with Cooke's stinging cover letter, and Powell's assertions clearly corroborated Cooke's claims. There is a logical reason for this concurrence: Cooke's attachment was most certainly manufactured by his aide-de-camp, Bisbee, who provided the letter "from an officer at the fort" that was clearly from Powell. Powell's commanders had just nominated him for a brevet as lieutenant colonel for his successful repulse of a massive attack by Red Cloud and the Lakota alliance in a battle called the Wagon Box Fight outside of Fort Phil Kearny on August 2, 1867. The positive publicity surrounding this desperately needed success story on the frontier positioned Powell as a conquering hero.

Faced with a choice between the word of Carrington, a failure at fighting Indians with a then-tarnished reputation, or the word of the newly popular champion whom he had recently commended, Grant easily sided with Powell. Carrington went to Washington in the fall of 1867 to meet with both Secretary of

War Stanton and General of the Army Grant to discuss Powell's libelous affidavit and to get someone to authorize the publication of his suppressed reports. Both men told Carrington that they could not help him secure publication of his reports, each deferring to the other as having the authority over the decision. In frustration Carrington told Grant that Powell's affidavit was gross perjury and that he wanted to prefer charges against Powell. Grant replied, "[T]hat is a very serious charge, sir," and abruptly closed the discussion. Carrington left the meeting dismayed and convinced that Grant would not publish his reports in order to protect the recent war hero. Grant's reasons were probably more complicated than Carrington assumed. Carrington did not know at the time that Grant had in his possession Carrington's report with Cooke's cover letter—Bisbee and Powell's handiwork—attached. The evidence was so conflicting and confusing that the only thing the heads of the War Department knew for sure was that further investigation would make their entire operation look even worse than they already did. Grant and Stanton withheld Carrington's reports from publication to protect Powell as well as themselves.[18]

Meanwhile, it took the Department of the Interior two months to comply after the Senate called for the release of Carrington's testimony and evidence. Carrington later claimed the documents had been found "among waste material in a government cellar."[19] On April 5, 1887, twenty-one years after the Fetterman catastrophe, Congress issued Senate Document 33, *Letter from the Acting Secretary Of The Interior, Transmitting In Response To Resolution Of February 11, 1887, Papers Relative To Indian Operations On The Plains.* This incredible document runs to more than fifty typewritten legal-sized pages containing Carrington's selection of documents presented to the Sanborn Commission with his explanatory comments interspersed. Carrington covered his orders to Fetterman and Grummond in extraordinary detail and explicitly portrayed Fetterman as inexperienced in Indian fighting and overly eager for glory. Ultimately, Carrington's testimony and evidence was carefully framed to vindicate his

Women's Work

cautious and defensive tactics by contrasting his calm, well-reasoned decision making against the rash, ill-informed actions of Fetterman.

The Carringtons had long hoped that the publication of his report would exonerate his actions and restore his honor and reputation and, finally, bring an end to his epic struggle. Instead, now that he was aware of the damage that Powell and Bisbee had done through Cooke's cover letter and Powell's bizarre testimony, Carrington renewed his vendetta for the "correction" of history. Sherman retired three years prior, in 1884, and Grant died in 1885, so Carrington was now less restrained in his efforts to repair his reputation. Carrington left his professorship in 1878 after developing an international reputation as an author and historian, publishing books on the American Revolution and George Washington and articles on the Civil War. Carrington devoted himself to making sure that history correctly portrayed his actions and began to work on repairing the damage that Bisbee and Powell had inflicted on his reputation. He continued to promote and reissue *Absaraka* and eventually released a second edition of *The Indian Question* to which he was finally able to add his January 3 report—with permission from the Department of War.

Carrington also maintained a careful watch over other historians' depictions of the Fetterman Massacre. In 1899 C. G. Coutant, a journalist and former state librarian of Wyoming, published *The History of Wyoming*, containing several chapters on the history of the Bozeman Trail forts.[20] Coutant and Carrington wrote to each other several times as Coutant developed his work—Carrington directing the author to Senate Document 33 and going to great lengths to discredit the damaging testimony from Captain Powell. Powell's success at the Wagon Box Fight was quickly becoming legend and would be a featured chapter in Coutant's book. Carrington could not stand to see Powell portrayed as a great hero while his devastating testimony still cast a cloud of suspicion over Carrington's own career.[21]

In 1903 Carrington eagerly met with Dr. Cyrus Townsend

Brady, who was compiling a history of the Plains Indian Wars, and provided the historian with copies of his testimony and detailed rebuttals of Powell's claims. Carrington later wrote that he had given Brady access to all of his evidence, including the actions of Judge Kinney and Powell's slanderous affidavit. However, like Coutant, Brady intended to feature Powell and the thrilling drama of his successful Wagon Box Fight and told Carrington he did not think it was advisable to write about the "methods by which the Government had been induced to delay publication" of Carrington's reports.[22] Nevertheless, Brady allowed Carrington to "read and correct" his chapter on the Fetterman incident and Brady's story reiterated the version of the story that Margaret Carrington introduced thirty-five years earlier. The next year, Brady published his histories as a serialization of articles in *Pearson's Magazine* and then collected them in *Indian Fights and Fighters,* still considered by many to be one of the classics of Indian Wars history. The first of Brady's articles was his story of the "Fort Phil Kearny Massacre" featuring all of the key arguments Carrington originally put forward to support his claim that Fetterman arrogantly disobeyed orders. In a statement that was both a nod to Powell's stature and a corroboration of Carrington's claims, Brady wrote that Powell obeyed Carrington's specific commands on December 19, because "he was too good a soldier to disobey orders." He stated that Fetterman "had frequently expressed his contempt for the Indians," and that Fetterman and Brown were chief of a group of malcontents who "offered with eighty men to ride through the whole Sioux Nation!" Brady repeated Carrington's claim that Fetterman "begged for the command of the expedition," and concluded unequivocally that Fetterman disobeyed orders causing the deaths of he and his eighty men, "just the number with which he had agreed to ride through the whole Sioux Nation." Brady also wrote that Fetterman and Brown, "seeing that all was lost," committed joint suicide.[23] Carrington wrote to his son James in September 1903 that he was "profoundly grateful to Dr. Brady" because no one else took the initiative to

Women's Work

33. Kate Graham Cook grew up in Cheyenne, Wyoming, where she met and married James Cook in 1886. The Cook ranch was a gathering place for western travelers as well as Indians. Kate and James were friends with Tenodor Ten Eyck, though records have not confirmed how they met. Around 1904 Kate sent a hand-copied section of C. G. Coutant's *History of Wyoming*, which claimed that Ten Eyck could have saved the Fetterman contingent, to Ten Eyck's daughter, Frances, setting off the chain of events that ended with the Carringtons traveling to Sheridan, Wyoming, in 1908 to speak at a reunion of Fort Phil Kearny soldiers to clear the Ten Eyck name. Photo courtesy Agate Fossil Beds National Monument, Harrison, Nebraska.

help him repair the damage that Powell's accusations had done to his reputation.[24]

In 1906 Carrington was presented with another opportunity to reinforce his version of history with the help of a woman's voice. After reading the chapter on the Fetterman Massacre in C. G. Coutant's *History of Wyoming*, Frances Ten Eyck—Captain Ten Eyck's youngest daughter—was distraught. Coutant concluded that her father was intentionally slow to prepare his relief detachment and chose an indirect route to get to the scene of action. "Alas," wrote Coutant, "procrastination robbed Captain Ten Eyck of a victory and permitted the death of many brave men who died after their ammunition had been exhausted."[25] In the wake of the Fetterman incident, Captain Ten Eyck suffered the same stigma as Carrington. Rumors of cowardice, alcoholism, and unprofessional conduct followed Ten Eyck through the short remainder of his military career. Ten Eyck chose to avoid the public defense of his actions and left the military in 1871. Tenodor Ten Eyck lived for thirty-four more years, until his death in 1905 in Chicago where he lived with his wife, Martha, and extended family including daughters Alice (and husband William Campbell), Frances, and Mary (and husband Frederick Sholes). Not long after her father's death, Frances received a handwritten extract of Coutant's imputation in *The History of Wyoming* from a family friend, Kate G. Cook.

Cook was the wife of James H. Cook, a well-known frontiersman and owner of the Agate Springs Ranch in Crawford, Nebraska. During the late 1800s, their ranch became a second home both for the Oglala Sioux and for paleontologists from around the world who came to excavate the famous Agate Fossil Beds discovered by the Cooks in 1885 along the Niobrara River. James Cook was a close friend of the Sioux Chief Red Cloud.[26] At some point in their lives, James Cook and Tenodor Ten Eyck crossed paths. Both men had roots in Michigan, and Cook's wife's family and the Ten Eycks had roots in Albany, New York. It is also possible they met while Ten Eyck served in the frontier army or even earlier when he tried his luck in the Colorado

34. Author C. G. Coutant's *History of Wyoming*, published in 1899, implied Captain Ten Eyck's slow relief effort was a cause of the massacre of Fetterman's troops. Frances Ten Eyck spent years communicating with Carrington and others to clear her father's name. Coutant did not respond to her, though she wrote him several times. Wyoming State Archives, Department of State Parks and Cultural Resources.

goldfields and Cook drove cattle through the area. In his book, *Fifty Years on the Old Frontier,* published in 1923, Cook talks about Tenodor as a friend. "My dear friend Major Tenedore Ten Eyck, now passed away, but in 1866 a captain at Fort Phil Kearny, was the man sent out with a relief party to bring in the bodies of his comrades whom Red Cloud's warriors had slain. Later, he often sent word to his old enemy, through me, that when he looked back to the conditions that existed at the time of the fight at Fort Phil Kearny, he could think with less enmity of those who had killed his companions-in-arms with such seeming ruthlessness."[27] The Cook–Ten Eyck friendship extended to other family members. The Cook Collection at the Agate Fossil Beds National Monument contains numerous letters from a decades-long correspondence between Frances Ten Eyck and Kate and James Cook.[28] Kate Cook's letter to Frances Ten Eyck enclosing the Coutant statement launched an extraordinary chain of communications between Ten Eyck, Henry Carrington, and Judge Eli S. Ricker, a neighbor of the Cooks in northwest Nebraska.

Eli S. Ricker was a Civil War veteran, writer, and lawyer who moved to Chadron, Nebraska, in 1884. He served one two-year term as county judge and although he never ran for office again he used the title "Judge" throughout the remainder of his life. In the early 1900s he began gathering information for a book he intended to title "The Final Conflict between the Red Men and the Palefaces." Ricker interviewed Indians, Scouts, early settlers, and anyone he could find with firsthand knowledge of the Indian Wars of the Western Plains. He became engrossed in research but never sat down to actually write his planned book. His interviews, transcribed in impeccable penmanship with perfect grammar and spelling on fifty-five ten-cent tablets, fill more than 1,500 pages. Known as the "Ricker Tablets," they are some of the best primary Indian Wars documents available. Ricker's family deposited the tablets, along with an extensive collection of his correspondence, with the Nebraska State Historical Society shortly after his death in 1926. Many original letters

Women's Work

35. Eli S. Ricker was an early settler in Chadron, Nebraska. From 1883 to 1905 he practiced law, served as county judge, and edited the *Chadron Times*. He devoted his remaining years to research for the book he hoped to write, to be titled *The Final Conflict Between the Red Man and the Pale Faces*. He interviewed at least fifty Native Americans about conditions and battles on the Plains, but the book was never written because Ricker became so engrossed in his research. Kate Cook approached Ricker in 1906 to help her friend, Frances Ten Eyck, clear Ten Eyck's name. The Ten Eyck–Ricker–Cook–Carrington correspondence documents a five-year crusade to help both Ten Eyck and Carrington repair their public images. Nebraska State Historical Society, Photograph Collections, RG1227:1-2.

between Frances Ten Eyck, Henry Carrington, and C. G. Coutant are found in the correspondence files from this collection.[29]

Kate Cook showed Ricker a letter from Frances Ten Eyck responding to Coutant's denunciation of her father. In her communiqué, Ten Eyck was "shocked and angered," and claimed "Mr. Coutant's summary of the causes of the disaster are mistaken and cruelly unjust," and that she "did not intend to let this terrible impeachment to rest upon our father's name."[30] Cook asked Ricker if he could help Ten Eyck. His sense of chivalry, and his sense of history, drove him to respond and to come to the rescue of Frances Ten Eyck. Ricker decided to investigate the matter and wrote to Ten Eyck asking her to provide him with more information and offering his assistance in defending her father to Coutant.

In her response a few weeks later, Ten Eyck said she would "be more than glad to give you the evidence which proves him worthy the honor of brave men." She told him that "the most faithful account of that terrible experience at Fort Phil Kearney is contained in the book titled 'Absaraka, the Home of the Crows,' written by the wife of Colonel Carrington. In my copy is an appendix giving the report of the Special Commission sent to investigate the matter. We have also a very detailed document of official evidence published by the United States Senate in 1887. . . . Both state that they 'found no living officer deserving censure.'" She concluded, "Throughout the army, Captain Ten Eyck was looked upon as the hero of that terrible day. . . . Any effort toward taking this cruel stain from my father's memory will be deeply appreciated."[31]

Ten Eyck told Ricker that she had written to Colonel Carrington, asking for his support in refuting Coutant, and enclosed a complete hand-copied duplicate of Carrington's immediate response. Carrington was clever in the wording of this letter to Ten Eyck. He stated, "Mr. Coutant sent me copy of his Vol. 1, and expressed regrets that he had not much earlier been in closer communication with myself. He had 'Absaraka' and the official Report of the Commission and I sent him quite a long letter for future use." Yet, nothing in Carrington's letter to Coutant in 1902 alludes to an erroneous depiction of Ten Eyck's performance on the day of the massacre. Carrington wrote to Ten Eyck that "Mr. Coutant should not have made surmises, and assumed that which it was impossible to determine, absolutely," and included several pages of evidence of her father's faultless decisions and brave and honorable actions in the relief attempt and the next day's decision to retrieve bodies from the field of the massacre. Carrington also stated, "[E]very other officer at the fort, except Ten Eyck, opposed my going out to rescue the dead."[32] However, Margaret Carrington's book stated that there was "universal disinclination" by the officers to go out to the scene of the battle to retrieve the bodies.[33]

Carrington's support of Ten Eyck in the forty years since the disaster had been equivocal, at best, and in fact Carrington had subtly distanced himself from Ten Eyck. He had good reason. In the years immediately following the incident, as Carrington spent his time preparing his defense and testifying in the formal investigations, Ten Eyck was arrested twice for drunkenness and eventually relieved of duties. He was found guilty of "conduct unbecoming an officer and a gentleman" at a general court-martial and sentenced to be dismissed from the army. Ten Eyck zealously appealed this ruling and it was eventually overturned.[34] Carrington needed to prevent speculation that he entrusted the relief of Fetterman to a drunk, and avoided Ten Eyck and his problems.

Furthermore, it was difficult to defend Ten Eyck when Carrington himself placed Ten Eyck under arrest a few months before the massacre for "a mistake made at Dress Parade." This explains why Carrington did not dispute Sanborn's conclusion in Senate Document 13 stating "[Ten Eyck] moved out and advanced rapidly toward the point from which the sound of firing proceeded, but did not move by so short a route as he might have done. . . . Whether he could have reached the scene of action by marching over the shortest route as rapidly as possible in time to have relieved Colonel Fetterman's command, I am unable to determine."[35] Senate Document 33, Carrington's final authority on the matter, included the note Carrington sent to Ten Eyck as he approached the battlefield from which Sanborn drew his conclusions. "You must unite with Fetterman. Fire slowly, and keep men in hand. You would have saved two miles toward the scene of action if you had taken Lodge Trail Ridge."[36] Carrington published the excerpts of both Senate Document 13 and Senate Document 33, including this note, in an appendix in the sixth edition of *Absaraka* in 1905, the year before his communications with Ten Eyck's daughter. Using Carrington's published material and the primary documents available from the multiple government investigations, it is easy to see how Coutant could conclude that Ten Eyck had some culpability in Fetterman's annihilation.

For Frances Ten Eyck, however, Carrington's lengthy and detailed response gave her hope. Carrington had chivalrously promised to write to Coutant to clear her father's name. While she waited for him to respond, she began to gather more ammunition for her father's defense. She established a network of support by connecting Ricker and Carrington, hand-copying and forwarding letters advocating her father's impeccable service. In a letter to Ricker, she appealed to his sense of honor and chivalry: "I sympathize deeply with your cry of longing for the truth. Some day surely that pure white light will shine through the shadows. All honor to those who help to clear the way for its shining!"[37] She also enclosed a hand-copied letter to her from S. S. Peters, a newspaper reporter for the *Omaha Bee* and former enlisted man at Fort Phil Kearny.[38] Peters responded immediately to her letter asking for his support, saying that it recalled "many sad memories of forty years ago, and none are more painful than the intelligence of the death of your father and my old commander Captain T. Ten Eyck." Writing that he shared in her "just indignation of Mr. Coutant's aspersion upon the courage of Captain Ten Eyck," Peters said his reading of Coutant's work detected "many inaccuracies in it bearing on the Indian War of 1865–8." Peters accompanied Captain Ten Eyck on the mission to relieve Fetterman and volunteered to retrieve bodies with Carrington and Ten Eyck the day after the massacre. Peters assured Frances Ten Eyck that "as regards the 'loss of time and the shorter route' there was neither." He further offered, "I only too gladly add this rambling bit of testimony as a tribute to a gallant soldier, a brave, kind and gentle officer, whom to know was but to love and esteem. I trust that it may be of some value to you in the vindication of the character of Captain Ten Eyck from one of his soldiers who is proud to have followed where he led."[39]

Ten Eyck took the time to copy and send Peters's five-page letter to Ricker believing Ricker would eventually publish his own historical work. She wanted the facts from Peters's testimony in favor of her father to be included in Ricker's book. She also hoped to inspire Ricker to help her obtain a public retraction from Coutant. Ricker wrote to Carrington to gather more information. He focused on the damning tone of the note that Carrington sent to Captain Ten Eyck as he proceeded to the massacre site. Citing a copy of the note in the just-published book by Cyrus Townsend Brady, he asked if the statement "You would have saved two miles toward the scene of action if you had taken Lodge Trail Ridge" might have had "some reproachful significance?"[40] Ricker asked Carrington if he felt at the time he wrote the note that it was possible that the captain had been "unfortunate in his choice of routes?" Had Carrington, upon reflection, changed his mind and concluded Ten Eyck "could not have done better by doing differently?"[41]

When he received this letter from Ricker, Carrington must have realized that Frances Ten Eyck was going to be tenacious in her pursuit of vindication for her father. In his usual didactic and meticulous style, Carrington responded to Ricker, carefully tuning—ever so slightly modifying—his previous public statements to demonstrate support of Ten Eyck. He immediately referred Ricker to Senate Document 33, calling it his "detailed history of the entire Indian Campaign of 1866–7, published twenty years after its date." Carrington provided, in impressive detail, a description of Ten Eyck's relief efforts justifying every action Ten Eyck did or did not make. He concluded, "It was right soldierly for him to seek the first commanding view from which to determine further advance. His detailed report shows that he intelligently comprehended and performed his duty. My brief note written and sent, in an instant of time, was no reprimand, but a guide to his action, giving him the lay of the country and an intelligent key to the scene of battle." Carrington's lengthy letter enclosed maps, pamphlets, and "electro-photos" as evidence for Ricker's use.[42]

Much of the letter repudiated aspersions cast on Carrington's own record during the investigations. Carrington, like Frances Ten Eyck, viewed Ricker as a professional historian with an imminent book on Indian Wars history. By now an expert at positioning himself in the historical record and an accomplished writer and historian himself, Carrington wanted to arm Ricker with the correct facts, *his* version, of Fetterman Massacre history. Thus, Carrington spent a significant portion of this letter discrediting his attackers in detail. Carrington was also compelled to support and vindicate Captain Ten Eyck on behalf of his daughter. His role as gallant protector of a dead soldier's daughter was the proper response of a gentleman of character. Carrington, S. S. Peters, and Ricker were operating as part of Frances Ten Eyck's network of honorable, Victorian gentlemen. She appealed to these men's sense of history as well as their sense of chivalry to a woman in distress. Her appeals drew them into her campaign and caused them to take action.

For the next two years, Ten Eyck made very little progress in her mission to erase the stain on her father's name. C. G. Coutant moved to Alaska and did not respond to her or Carrington's letters. Ricker continued to be bogged down in research and was no closer to publishing his book. Then, suddenly, in the summer of 1908 a flurry of activity took place. Frances discovered the perfect opportunity to vindicate her father in public. A Fourth of July celebration in Sheridan, Wyoming, titled "Wyoming Opened," planned to feature a reunion of the few surviving peo-

Women's Work

ple who served at Fort Phil Kearny at a ceremonial dedication of a monument at the Fetterman battle site. The event committee asked Carrington to deliver a speech at the dedication. Ten Eyck aggressively lobbied Carrington and Peters to do what they could to vindicate her father in public. She also set in motion a backup plan, in case the elderly Carrington was too frail to complete the journey from his home in Massachusetts to Wyoming. She sent a rather urgent letter to Ricker on June 27, just one week before the event, asking if she could turn to him should Carrington fall ill or die before he could clear her father's name. A few days earlier she received a letter from Carrington stating he would "undertake this mission" for her as long as his health could bear it. She wrote to Ricker, "So it seems, dear Sir, to be unnecessary for me to solicit your chivalrous aid to break a lance for the cause of truth and right—yet—who knows? That of which [Colonel] Carrington speaks might come to one so aged. On that case might I turn to you . . . to go to Sheridan and defend my father's name?"[43]

She enclosed a letter from Carrington, in which his ego emerged as he called the Sheridan event "the Carrington REUNION." Saying he was "in his 85th year, and must be very careful of over-exertion," Carrington wrote, "but I feel it a duty, to make this trip to the old field, hoping to correct errors while still living." He then informed Ten Eyck that he would be meeting S. S. Peters in Omaha and wrote of several dignitaries who were attending the event to "introduce him," and that he would consult with them as to the best way to redeem her father. Clearly, Carrington was motivated by the desire to protect and enhance his own image, but Frances Ten Eyck gave him an excellent platform to do so by demonstrating his highly moral and chivalrous character. He concluded his letter by saying that her father "could not have possibly prevented or stopped the Fetterman Disaster, and did the part of a good soldier, the best possible under existing conditions. . . . I will watch for the best opportunity that may come under my thoughtly notice and advise you."[44]

36. On July 3, 1908, Henry B. Carrington, Frances Grummond Carrington, and a handful of the surviving veterans of the Fort Phil Kearny garrison attended a memorial ceremony to dedicate this monument to the battle, which had been constructed during the previous two years by local stonemasons.

37. Fetterman Battle monument plaque, which reads: "On this field on the 21st day of December, 1866, three commissioned officers and seventy-six privates of the 18th U.S. Infantry and of the 2nd U.S. Cavalry, and four civilians under the command of Captain Brevet, Lieutenant Colonel William J. Fetterman, were killed by an overwhelming force of Sioux under the command of Red Cloud—There were no survivors." The plaque repeats several inaccuracies in the legend and its language clearly reflects the racial feelings of the times: historical records show that only two civilians were killed, not the four often mentioned, and the statement that "there were no survivors" overlooks the more than one thousand Lakotas, Northern Cheyennes, and Northern Arapahoes that did in fact survive.

Frances Ten Eyck wrote directly to Coutant. Hoping to touch his sense of chivalry, she issued "a heart felt appeal to your honor as an historian, to your humanity as a man, that you make what amend might be in your power to take from an old and honorable name the stigma of dishonor you had placed there."[45] As further insurance that her mission be accomplished in Sheridan, Ten Eyck enlisted her brother-in-law, Lt. Col. W. W. Robinson, a quartermaster general, to write to his old friend Gen. Charles Morton, the current commander of the Department of the Missouri. Morton was scheduled to attend the reunion, and Robinson asked him to "see to it that all is done that can and should be done" to "correct this injustice."[46]

A trip from Boston to Sheridan, Wyoming, in 1908 would be an arduous task for Carrington, who was in his mid-eighties and in frail health. But Carrington's passion to preserve his image drove him to make the journey. He wedded his case to the rescue of Ten Eyck because it served his own purpose by providing a final chance to position his reputation in history. His sense of justice and chivalry for Ten Eyck also played a part in motivating him to go. Carrington was nothing if not devoted to honor and protecting his name and he had to have been truly moved by Ten Eyck's similar struggle. S. S. Peters, another of Frances Ten Eyck's network, joined Carrington in Omaha en route to the "Carrington Reunion" in Sheridan to dedicate the memorial to the Fort Phil Kearny victims. Peters covered the story for his paper and participated as one of the few surviving soldiers from the post. Ten Eyck secured both men's assurances that they would publicly defend her father's name, and also obtained Ricker's promise to go in place of Carrington should the elderly man fall ill or die before reaching Sheridan. She then sent a telegram to Peters at his hotel in Sheridan just to ensure her father's vindication was foremost on the minds of all participants in the reunion. She was apparently too frail herself for an extended journey, so all she could do at this point was wait for news from the reunion.

Frances did not have to wait long before she heard about

38. General and Mrs. Carrington (*center*) with others at the "Wyoming Opened" celebration and Fort Phil Kearny reunion in Sheridan, Wyoming, in July 1908. Wyoming State Archives, Department of State Parks and Cultural Resources.

the success of her lobbying. On July 5, 1908, the day after the reunion, she received a telegram from S. S. Peters informing her of the irrevocable "vindication of her father . . . most opportunely made in a public address by General Carrington, at Massacre Hill Monument Friday morning, and reiterated by myself before 5000 people in this city Saturday afternoon." Peters's two-page telegram, written with a journalistic flair for drama, described Carrington's forty-nine-minute speech in which he said, "In justice to the memory of a gallant officer now dead, I wish here to say on this spot made hallowed by the blood of as gallant and brave men as ever fought for any cause, I wish to and do refute the aspersion upon the bravery of Captain Ten Eyck who hurried with his meagre command to the rescue of these men who fell here. I wish to say that Captain Ten Eyck did all that mortal man could do and did it nobly and well."

Peters went on to tell of his own speech later that afternoon. Just a moment before he rose to speak, he was handed her telegram. It was a copy of the letter she sent to Coutant, who did not attend the event. "I had not time to read it through before I was called upon to speak. Instead of speaking, I read your letter to Mr. Coutant. I commented upon it as I read it, emphatically denouncing the charges implied in Coutant's *History of Wyoming*." Peters wrote that he turned to Carrington and the other soldiers on the platform and said, "General Carrington, from the bottom of my heart, and for the daughter of my old commander I thank you, for your noble vindication of Captain Ten Eyck." Peters went on to say that Carrington was too emotional to speak, but approached the podium and shook Peters's hand. Telling Ten Eyck that her letter's timing was amazingly opportune, "the incident was of the inspiration of Providence, and I only regret that you could not have been present to witness it. It was unpremeditatedly dramatic and was a fitting climax to a most notable event."[47]

Ten Eyck was jubilant. Two months later when she sent a copy of this telegram along with a lengthy letter of thanks to Ricker, her joy was still evident. She apologized for taking so

39. Carrington delivered a lengthy speech at the dedication in which he laboriously described the historical injustices done to both himself and Tenodor Ten Eyck. One of Frances Ten Eyck's supporters telegraphed her immediately after the address to relay the news of the public exoneration. In *My Army Life*, published a little over a year later, Frances Carrington included a full copy of Carrington's speech. Wyoming State Archives, Department of State Parks and Cultural Resources.

long to inform Ricker of the overwhelming success of her mission but she was "not strong enough to bear the strain and was ill for some time."[48] Frances Ten Eyck accomplished a great deal. She changed the historical record by using her position as a "devoted daughter" to enlist the assistance of three chivalrous, gallant, gentlemanly ex-soldiers. Carrington and Peters publicly changed the historical record through their speeches and subsequent publications. Without her strategic intervention, the primary sources used to research the history of the Fetterman Massacre would have likely continued to emphasize that her father "did not move by so short a route as he might have done" and a cloud of suspicion would have remained over her father's performance. Instead, the "Wyoming Opened" celebration, including the detailed vindication of Capt. Tenodor Ten Eyck, was covered extensively in newspaper articles and updated versions of Carrington's publications. Peters filed a full-page story in the *Omaha Bee*.[49]

As a result of the success of their efforts to vindicate Captain Ten Eyck, Henry and Frances Carrington decided to expand Frances's book, a memoir she was writing about her Civil War adventures in Franklin, which was near publication at the time, by adding another one-hundred-page section detailing the event. Three years later, in 1911, Frances Carrington published *My Army Life and the Fort Phil Kearney Massacre, with an Account of the Celebration of "Wyoming Opened."* Like the first Mrs. Carrington, Frances wrote her story, which included the dramatic story of the tragic loss of her first husband, to support Henry's reputation. The Carringtons also included photos and the complete text of both Carrington's and Peters's speeches vindicating Ten Eyck.[50] The Carringtons published *My Army Life,* another female defense of Henry Carrington's frontier command, because Margaret Carrington's *Absaraka* had proven the value of a woman's role in defining history. Henry and Frances Carrington used his valiant support of Captain Ten Eyck's honor on behalf of his daughter to set the record straight one more time. Frances Carrington reinforced all of the claims that Margaret had made on Henry's

Women's Work

behalf four decades earlier. She wrote that Fetterman, "recently arrived from recruiting service, with no antecedent experience on the frontier, expressed the opinion that a 'single company of Regulars could whip a thousand Indians.'" She also wrote of Powell's successful mission—attributed to following her husband's strict orders—on December 19 and that Carrington's orders to Fetterman were "distinctly and peremptorily given within my hearing and were repeated on the parade-ground when the line was formed," a bold and unchallenged statement that does not agree with any other testimony.[51] More than one-third of Frances Carrington's book was dedicated to the story of the reunion and her husband's selfless work in defense of Captain Ten Eyck. The two Franceses, Carrington and Ten Eyck, were able to correct and cement a version of the past that protected and exonerated their men.

In one of his final acts of historical preservation, Carrington deposited a scrapbook in the Fulmer Public Library in Sheridan, Wyoming. In it, he included a significant portion of Senate Document 33, his oft-cited "official record." He taped a note adjacent to the page where his "you could have saved two miles" communication to Ten Eyck was recorded. His addendum stated, "The foregoing message to Captain Ten Eyck, was in no sense a rebuke, as it has been interpreted in many quarters. . . . [Ten Eyck's performance] was grand military art."[52] This addendum to history was published in Frances's *My Army Life* and Henry's 1909 reprint of *The Indian Question*. Since then, historians have cited these documents and proclaimed that the implied cowardice against Ten Eyck was inaccurate and unfortunate.[53]

The Rest of the Story

Since the "Wyoming Opened" celebration, historians have used *Absaraka, My Army Life, The Indian Question,* and Carrington's scrapbook as primary sources for research on the Fetterman Massacre. These sources have greatly influenced the narrative of what the public knows about the incident. When looking for blame, historians have turned their focus where the Carringtons aimed them: on Fetterman's arrogance. Through the efforts of the Carrington wives, the defining statement of the story has become "with eighty men I could ride through the whole Sioux Nation." As historian John McDermott pointed out, Fetterman's "lack of respect for the Indians as a fighting force, and his opinions concerning the ability of the United States Army to deal with them have been much quoted, appearing in practically every piece written about the Fetterman Fight published during [the twentieth] century."[1]

Fetterman's now infamous statements can be traced to Carrington's carefully thought-out report that was suppressed for more than twenty years after the incident. To exonerate himself, Carrington had to demonstrate in his report that Fetterman was disobedient. Therefore Carrington emphasized the clear, specific orders he supposedly gave to Fetterman out of concern that Fetterman's "spirit of ambition might override prudence." Carrington claimed his concern was founded on the fact that Fetterman and Brown had asked for permission to take "60 mounted men and 40 citizens to go for several days down Tongue River Valley after villages," just the night before their final battle. Carrington emphasized that his refusal was "unfavorably regarded" by both men.[2]

It is important to note that no evidence, other than Carrington's testimony and his wives' publications, supports this claim. No memoirs, diaries, or testimony from other soldiers at the fort purport that Fetterman made this statement or even exhibited this attitude. In fact, it appears that the Carringtons purposely blurred the line between their portrayal of their good friend Fred Brown and that of Fetterman. Both Henry and Margaret Carrington originally wrote that it was Brown alone who wanted to take the men and citizens to the Tongue River. The Carringtons' earlier descriptions of the meeting where Brown made this request position Fetterman as simply being present, not actually participating in making the request. It is more likely that this "meeting" was simply a conversation between Carrington, Brown, and Fetterman—who socialized quite frequently—in which the three officers concurred that when reinforcements, horses, weapons, and ammunition finally arrived a fully equipped mission of about one hundred men could be sent to attack the Lakota alliance camps. Both Brown and Fetterman were fully aware of the reasons why such a mission could not be carried out at that point. Any statements about attacking Red Cloud's camp were simply wishful thinking about the future when there might be ample supplies, horses, and men to accomplish such a mission—they were most certainly not formal requests made out of arrogance or ignorance of Plains Indian fighting skills.

Fetterman and Brown—like nearly all officers in the frontier army, including Colonel Carrington—believed that their own skills and equipment were superior to those of the Plains Indians. However, most soldiers quickly came to respect, or even fear, the tactics and capabilities of their opponents. Most knew what they were getting into before taking their assignments. As he left for the frontier, Fetterman is quoted as having told a friend that "it seemed sad after passing through three years of bloody conflicts, he should be sent out amongst the Indians to meet, perhaps, a barbarous and glorious death, inflicted by ruthless savages."[3] In his explanation for why the cavalrymen panicked and abandoned Fetterman when they were attacked on the fight of December 6, historian Dee Brown pointed out that many newcomers to the frontier "attributed near super-human powers to the Indians and dreaded close fighting with them."[4] The scalping, torture, and mutilation of their captured comrades raised no small amount of fear among frontier army soldiers and officers. Fred Brown apparently made it clear to all around him that he would commit suicide before being taken alive by his Plains Indian enemies, and after the catastrophe most people accepted the idea that both Brown and Fetterman did just that. Confidence and courage were necessary character-istics of successful officers in the frontier army, and it is clear that Fetterman, Brown, and Carrington exhibited these traits. Perhaps there is a fine line between confidence and foolish arro-gance, but Fetterman's background and demeanor do not sup-port the premise that he crossed this line.

Unfortunately for Fetterman's reputation, Carrington was backed into a corner and forced to depict Fetterman as ambi-tious for honor and irrationally overconfident in order to sup-port his claims that Fetterman disobeyed direct orders. After carefully crafting this depiction in his initial report, Carrington became extremely frustrated because someone in power kept it hidden while he was being indicted in the court of public opinion. When Carrington discovered Capt. James Powell's damaging testimony against him, he spent two decades trying to disprove the allegations. However, after the success of the Wagon Box Fight, the American public and the army regarded Powell as a hero and a far more successful Indian fighter than Carrington. Believing the publication of his own report and tes-timony before the Sanborn Commission would ultimately refute

Powell's testimony, Carrington aggressively lobbied officials to release the documents. After their meeting in Washington DC Carrington suspected that it was none other than Gen. Ulysses S. Grant who was positioning him as the scapegoat and suppressing his reports. The Carringtons realized that there was a powerful force working against them and that it would take an even stronger authority to trump the country's most beloved war hero. Only the word of a lady could transcend the dominance of Grant, the nation's next president. Thus, *Absaraka* was able to expand on Carrington's depiction of Fetterman without Henry Carrington having to personally put forward accusations that would be subject to challenge. In fact, none of Carrington's critics broke the code of chivalry to refute the story of a well-bred and respected lady from a prominent family such as Margaret Carrington. She portrayed Fetterman as gallant, chivalrous, and gentlemanly while clearly accusing him of gross disobedience caused by naïveté about Indian warfare. Margaret Carrington did not originate the "eighty men" quote; in her version Fetterman frequently claimed that "a company of regulars could whip a thousand, and a regiment could whip the whole array of hostile tribes."[5]

Nearly twenty years later, when Carrington was finally able to get his long-suppressed report and testimony published, he discovered the devastating work of Lt. William Bisbee and Powell through General Cooke's attachment. Instead of realizing his dream of vindication, Carrington was motivated to continue his pursuit of justice. Historians were portraying Powell as the hero of the Wagon Box Fight and Carrington found no one willing to write about Powell's "false affidavit" against him. Once again, the power of a woman's word was used to overcome a seemingly more authoritative adversary when Frances Carrington came to the rescue of her husband's reputation by writing *My Army Life*.

To justify publishing what historian Catherine McKeen appropriately called "another wifely defense of Henry Carrington's frontier command," the Carringtons positioned her book as primarily about his chivalrous rescue of Captain Ten Eyck's honor on behalf of his daughter.[6] *My Army Life* subtly corrected the official Carrington version of the "Fetterman Massacre" to ensure that future historians did not interpret Carrington's damaging note to Ten Eyck while approaching the scene of Fetterman's annihilation as an implication of fault. In fact, Frances Carrington actually included the text of the note in her story but the sentence beginning "you could have saved two miles" is glaringly omitted.[7] Carrington's final act of preservation, the "Carrington Scrapbook" donated to the Fulmer Public Library in Sheridan, Wyoming, includes—in addition to Carrington's detailed rebuttal of Powell's and Bisbee's accusations—an emphatic statement that Carrington's note was not intended to chastise Ten Eyck. No historian since C. G. Coutant has interpreted this note as a reprimand to Ten Eyck nor has anyone explored the possibility that Ten Eyck may have been able to rescue any part of Fetterman's detachment.

Frances Ten Eyck's mission to clear her father's name also gave Carrington his final opportunity to permanently cast Fetterman as blindly arrogant. In his speech at the reunion in Sheridan, Wyoming, in 1908, Carrington fine-tuned Fetterman's alleged boast to "I can take eighty men and go to the Tongue River." Three years later, when Frances Carrington published her book, she included the text of her husband's speech—and this "eighty men" quote—in her report on the reunion.[8] She also added more detail to Fetterman's supposed statements in her description of the events leading up to the massacre, although, like Margaret Carrington, Frances did not use the specific number of "eighty men" in her version of Fetterman's boasts. Implying Fetterman made the grandiose claim right after he arrived at the fort, Frances Carrington wrote, "Brevet Lieutenant Colonel Fetterman, recently arrived from recruiting service, with no antecedent experience on the frontier, expressed the opinion that a 'single company of Regulars could whip a thousand Indians . . . '" Perhaps even more damaging was Frances's claim that she personally heard Henry Carrington deliver his specific orders to Fetterman.[9]

The three Carrington books, along with Carringtons' heavy influence in both C. G. Coutant's *History of Wyoming* in 1896 and Cyrus Townsend Brady's *Indian Fights and Fighters,* shaped the story of the Fetterman Massacre during the Carringtons' lives. With each publication Fetterman's character was cast as more frustrated, antagonistic, and disobedient—and less gentlemanly. With Henry Carrington's guidance, Brady was the first to attribute the "eighty men" statement to Fetterman. However, Brady and Carrington ascribed the opinion to both Brown and Fetterman: "Some of [the officers], including Fetterman and Brown, 'offered with eighty men to ride through the whole Sioux Nation!'"[10] At this point, the Carringtons' original statement where Brown and Fetterman offered to take "60 mounted men and 40 citizens to go for several days down Tongue River Valley after villages" was forever changed to match just the number of soldiers who were killed with Fetterman: "eighty men."[11]

Frances Carrington died in 1911 and Henry died exactly one year later. Since then, the story of the Fetterman fight has been covered in scores of books and articles and the narrative has barely changed. In 1922 Dr. Grace Raymond Hebard of the University of Wyoming and E. A. Brininstool, a well-known author of western histories and poems, published the two-volume seminal history of the region titled *The Bozeman Trail.* Hebard and Brininstool relied on the Carrington family publications, Henry Carrington's Senate Document 33, and Cyrus Townsend Brady's publications to develop the story of the Fetterman Massacre. Hebard and Brininstool cited both Margaret's and Frances's statements verbatim and portrayed Fetterman as "having a profound contempt for the warriors of Red Cloud, underestimating their strength in battle, and never having had any previous experience in fighting the red men." They claimed it was "this spirit of reckless bravado" that brought Fetterman and his *eighty* men—"just the number Captain Fetterman had declared necessary to wipe out all the Sioux in the Powder River country"—to their death. *The Bozeman Trail* goes into great detail about Fetterman's disobedience of Carrington's orders and

40. (*From left*) R. S. Ellison, E. A. Brininstool, Captain North, Major Ostrander, and Dr. Grace Hebard at the Fetterman Massacre Memorial, 1908. Hebard and Brininstool wrote the definitive history of the Bozeman Trail in two volumes in 1922 using sources directly shaped by Henry Carrington. Ostrander was a teenage private at Fort Phil Kearny who published his memoirs, *An Army Boy of the Sixties*, in 1924. Wyoming State Archives, Department of State Parks and Cultural Resources.

erroneously claims that Carrington "crossed the parade ground, and from a sentry platform, halted the troops and repeated to Fetterman his orders." This was the first publication to attribute the "eighty men" solely to Fetterman—the link to Brown was severed.[12]

In 1934 Stanley Vestal published *Warpath: The True Story of the Fighting Sioux*, a biography of the Sioux Chief White Bull who participated in the Battle of the Hundred-in-the-Hands against Fetterman. In Vestal's chapter on the battle, Fetterman is quoted as boastfully talking of "taking Red Cloud's scalp," and his by-now infamous statement, "with eighty men I can ride through the whole Sioux Nation" is once again positioned as "just the number" of men he led into ambush.[13] The same year Paul Wellman published *Death on the Prairie: The Thirty Years' Struggle for the Western Plains,* in which "the fire-eating Fetterman" was described as "eager," "reckless," and having "deliberately disobeyed orders." Again the "give me eighty men" statement was featured as evidence of Fetterman's arrogance.[14] In his 1946 biography of Jim Bridger, Vestal writes, "In his ignorance of Indian warfare, Fetterman was quite contemptuous of the Sioux. He declared that he was 'sure a single company of regulars could whip a thousand Indians.'" Vestal goes on to quote both Margaret and Frances Carrington exactly in his elaboration of Fetterman's boasts.[15]

During the next thirty years historians continued to portray Fetterman as arrogant. In the 1960s the members of the Potomac Corral of the Westerners published *Great Western Indian Fights* featuring Roy E. Appleman's frequently cited chapter on "The Fetterman Fight." Appleman's account documents Fetterman's "over-zealous disposition," by claiming he wanted to "lead a hundred mounted men against the whole Sioux Nation."[16] Dee Brown's 1962 *The Fetterman Massacre* is still considered to be the authoritative scholarly history of the event and his conclusions also follow the trail defined by the Carrington wives. Brown's book, unlike most of the other publications mentioned, provides detailed citations to support his analysis. Brown cited

Margaret Carrington's "single company of regulars" quote and Hebard and Brininstool's "eighty men" statement (which originated in Brady's work that was shaped directly by Carrington!) in his description of Fetterman's arrogance.[17] In 1971 Dorothy M. Johnson, a Montana native who became a popular author of western histories, published *The Bloody Bozeman: The Perilous Trail to Montana's Gold.* Johnson cited Fetterman's "eighty men" quote to portray Fetterman as a "fire-eater" who believed that he could surely "whip a bunch of savages." In fact, her chapter on the Fetterman Massacre is titled "The Fire-Eater Extinguished."[18] Robert Utley and Wilcomb Washburn published *Indian Wars*, a synthesis of three hundred years of Indian and Euro-American warfare commissioned by the American Heritage Library in 1977. Their version of the story of the Fetterman battle also incorporated the "eighty men" quote and characterized Fetterman as boastful and contemptuous of the fighting prowess of his adversaries. They claimed that Fetterman was easily lured by Crazy Horse over Lodge Trail Ridge and that "behind him, with rich irony, followed exactly eighty men."[19]

Current historical accounts of the incident continue to promulgate the Carringtons' claims. Stephen Ambrose's *Crazy Horse and Custer,* published in 1975 and republished in 1996, subtitled the chapter "Crazy Horse and the Fort Phil Kearny Battle" with Fetterman's quote, "With eighty men I can ride through the entire Sioux Nation." Ambrose specifically cites Cyrus Townsend Brady's *Indian Fights and Fighters* as his source for Fetterman's quote.[20] Yet, as described earlier, it was the Carrington wives' books and Henry Carrington himself who guided Brady in the development of the Fetterman story and Brady was the first to publish that it was eighty, not one hundred, men. Dee Brown's best-selling *The American West*, published in 1994, again cites the "eighty men" quote in depicting Fetterman's "reckless bravado" and his considerable "contempt for the 'untrained' Indian."[21]

Over the years, Fetterman's image evolved from Henry Carrington's eulogy of a refined gentleman whose character and duty was pure and without blemish and Margaret Carrington's noble gentleman reaching for laurels just out of his reach to that of a contemptuous and boastful buffoon. Best-selling western novels, such as Michael Straight's *Carrington* in 1960 and Larry McMurtry's *Boone's Lick* in 2000, portray Fetterman as a rude, arrogant, and mean-spirited bully.[22] In 2002 award-winning author Frederick J. Chiaventone published *Moon of Bitter Cold*, a well-written and historically researched novel in which Fetterman uses the "give me eighty men" quote in a disrespectful conversation with the universally esteemed, sagacious guide James Bridger who questions the new officer's overconfidence. Telling Bridger "now you have some real soldiers here" and barely concealing his contempt for Carrington, Fetterman is described as so jealous he was left "fairly quivering with rage."[23]

None of these characterizations fit in any way with primary sources describing his personality and performance. In addition to Fetterman's previously described exemplary record as a disciplined officer in the Civil War, soldiers and friends described him as caring, gentlemanly, refined, and intelligent. In an obituary written by a family friend who knew Fetterman since childhood, Fetterman was described as a man who formed many acquaintances who appreciated and endeared him:

> Colonel Fetterman well merited the title of a "Christian gentleman." He was as unobtrusive in his religion as in other things; but he was sincere, trustful, frank-hearted, and manly in every relation of his life. He did not stoop to imitate the fopperies of external fashionable gentility. While he was remarkably courteous to all who came in contact with him, and especially to the aged, it was easy to see that he had no sinister or selfish motive. He did not seek popularity; it simply followed him, in private life, as the result of a tenderly refined and loving heart. Those who knew him intimately could not avoid loving him deeply. He was a rare example of a truly noble and loving nature.[24]

Examining the story of Carrington, Fetterman, and their brief tenure at Fort Phil Kearny within the context of what is written about their personalities and the Victorian social values of the era creates an entirely different image of Fetterman from the one that evolved from the Carringtons' early efforts. Fetterman was equal to Carrington in manners, grace, dignity, and military bearing. However, the opposite perception has dominated the story and made it easy to portray the battle as the result of an arrogant fool blindly leading his men to their deaths.

In their haste to depict Fetterman as the culprit, historians have overlooked the real story behind the Fetterman Massacre. It is a story of political intrigue involving some of America's most beloved heroes and well-known men: Ulysses S. Grant, William T. Sherman, Edwin M. Stanton, and Andrew Johnson. The story of the debacle at Fort Phil Kearny is more about the clash of powerful personalities caught up in a rush of dramatic and historic post–Civil War events than it is the simple tale of one man's ignorance of the brilliance of Indian warfare tactics. Indeed, when searching for blame, it is unfair to point to the men in the field. As Commissioner Sanborn aptly stated in his final report on the incident, the difficulty "in a nutshell" was that Carrington's superiors did not provide the appropriate levels of support.[25] This was because they were too busy fighting their own political battles and posturing for control in the postwar quagmire of Washington politics. The ensuing cover-up at the highest levels of government operations positioned Carrington as a scapegoat and forced the Carringtons to push blame onto Fetterman. Thus, the Carrington wives changed the history of the Fetterman Massacre to ensure that Fetterman's performance remained shrouded in confusion.

Like Elizabeth Custer, the Carringtons were aware of the importance of history. They also knew that women's moral authority—derived from Victorian-era cultural values—empowered them to shape history. Their influence has continued for generations as later historians used the sources written by the Carrington wives almost without question. Like Custer's

Last Stand, the Fetterman Massacre became mythologized in popular culture. Books, novels, and articles have launched the story of Fetterman and this military debacle into the forefront of America's western heritage. The story that has been popularized is derived from history that was revised and controlled through the efforts of Margaret Carrington, Frances Grummond Carrington, and Frances Ten Eyck—women defending their men with the might of their pen.

⊱ NOTES ⊰

PREFACE

1. Utley, *Frontier Regulars*, 4.
2. Hebard and Brininstool, *The Bozeman Trail*, 2:90.
3. Leckie, *Elizabeth Bacon Custer and the Making of a Myth*; Dippie, *Custer's Last Stand*.

INTRODUCTION

1. Leckie, *Elizabeth Bacon Custer and the Making of a Myth*, xx.
2. Sibbald, "Camp Followers All: Army Women of the West," 56–67.
3. For sources on the myriad roles of women in the frontier army see Stallard, *Glittering Misery*; Nacy, *Members of the Regiment*; Stewart, "Army Laundresses: Ladies of the 'Soap Suds Row,'" 421–36; Miller, "Foragers, Army Women, and Prostitutes," in Jensen and Miller, eds., *New Mexico Women*, 141–68; Holmes, "And I Was Always with Him," 177–90.
4. Coffman, *The Old Army*, 25.
5. Coffman, *The Old Army*, 104.
6. *Vivandière* is a term from a mixture of French and Latin meaning "hospitality giver." For information about vivandières see Gail R. Jessee, "The Confederate Cantinieres," *Florida Frontier Gazette*, October 1998, www.floridafrontier.com, accessed 8 November 2006; Atkins, "Civil War Vivandieres and Daughters of the Regiment," www.vivandiere.net, accessed 8 November 2006; Battle, *Hearts of Fire*.
7. Carrington, *Absaraka, Home of the Crows*, 1, 41; Carrington, *My Army Life*, 61–62.
8. Coffman, *The Old Army*, 288.
9. Welter, "The Cult of True Womanhood: 1820–186," 151–74.
10. Fraser, *America and the Patterns of Chivalry*, 8.
11. Brooks, *Chivalric Days*, iii.
12. Mintz and Kellog, *Domestic Revolutions*, 56.

1. PRELUDE TO DISASTER

1. Harcey, Croone, Medicine Crow, *White-Man-Runs-Him*, 22. "Absaroka" has a varied synonymy, with "Absaraka," "Absarokee," "Apsáalooke," "Absaroga," and "Apsaroga" being a few of the more common versions. "Absaroka" is the most widely used spelling today.

2. Harcey, Croone, Medicine Crow, *White-Man-Runs-Him*, 19.

3. Carrington, *Absaraka*, 13. Margaret Carrington named her book "Absaraka, Home of the Crows" to emphasize her belief that Absaroka should be returned to the Crows after they had been dispossessed by the Lakota and the U.S. government.

4. White, "The Winning of the West," 342.

5. White, "The Winning of the West," 321; Hassrick, *The Sioux*, 7; Walker, DeMallie, *Lakota Society*, 14–17.

6. Harcey, Croone, Medicine Crow, *White-Man-Runs-Him*, 16–28; White, "The Winning of the West," 319–43.

7. Andrist, *The Long Death*, 18–20; Lavender, *Bent's Fort*, 319–23.

8. Hoxie, *Parading Through History*, 86–88; Linderman, *American*, 49.

9. For descriptions of the founding of the Bozeman Trail see Doyle, "Journeys to the Land of Gold," 54–67; Doyle, "The Bozeman Trail, 1863–1868," 5–11; Hebard and Brininstool, *The Bozeman Trail*, 1:201–35.

10. Olson, *Red Cloud and the Sioux Problem*, 23–24.

11. McGinnis, "Strike and Retreat," 30–41.

12. Athearn, *Sherman and the Settlement of the West*, 16.

13. Matloff, *American Military History*, 301.

14. Manzione, "I Am Looking to the North for My Life," 7–8.

15. Coffman, *The Old Army*, 218–19; Murray, *Military Posts in the Powder River Country*, 52; Utley, *Frontier Regulars*, 10–14.

16. Athearn, *Sherman and the Settlement of the West*, 6.

17. Athearn, *Sherman and the Settlement of the West*, 43.

18. Athearn, *Sherman and the Settlement of the West*, 39; Young, *The West of Philip St. George Cooke*, 326; Utley, *Frontier Regulars*, 12.

19. General Ulysses S. Grant, Department of the Army, Washington DC, to General William T. Sherman, Division of the Missouri, St. Louis, March 3, 1866, in Grant, *The Papers of Ulysses S. Grant*, 16:93.

20. Young, *The West of Philip St. George Cooke*, 19.

21. Foote, *The Civil War*, 1:472.

22. Quaife, Introduction to *Absaraka*, xxvi–xxvii.

23. McKeen, "Henry Beebee Carrington," 19–33.

24. McKeen, "Henry Beebee Carrington," 33–69.

25. McPherson, *The Battle Cry of Freedom*, 320–21.

26. McKeen, "Henry Beebee Carrington," 70–76.

27. McPherson, *The Battle Cry of Freedom*, 299–301.

28. Lord, *They Fought for the Union*, 1–8.

29. McKeen, "Henry Beebee Carrington," 77–80.

30. McKeen, "Henry Beebee Carrington," 80; Cabaniss, "The Eighteenth Regiment of the Infantry," 643. Cited from online transcription at the U.S. Army Center of Military History website, www.army.mil/cmh-pg/books/R&H/R&H-FM .htm, accessed April, 2001.

31. McDermott, "Price of Arrogance," 42–53; Carrington, *Absaraka*, 244.

32. McDermott, "The Life of William Judd Fetterman," 43.

33. Carrington, *Absaraka*, 244.

34. McDermott, "The Life of William Judd Fetterman," 44.

35. Lord, *They Fought for the Union*, 59, 110.

36. McKeen, "Henry Beebee Carrington," 61.

37. Carrington, *Absaraka*, 37.

38. General Order No. 33, Department of the Missouri, March 10, 1866. A copy of this order is published in U.S. Congress 50th, 1st sess Senate, *Indian Operations on the Plains* (Executive Document 33), Washington DC, 1888, 51–53. Referred to throughout Carrington's communications as "Senate Document 33," this document contains testimony and evidence gathered by Carrington. It contains more documents than "Senate Document 13," published twenty-one years earlier in 1867, and is annotated by Carrington throughout. Referred hereafter as *Indian Operations on the Plains (Senate Document 33)*.

39. General William T. Sherman, Division of the Missouri, St. Louis, to General Ulysses S. Grant, Department of the Army, Washington DC, March 10, 1866, in Grant, *The Papers of Ulysses S. Grant*, 16:97.

40. Ostrander, *An Army Boy of the Sixties*, 48–49.

41. Athearn, *Sherman and the Settlement of the West*, 99.

2. TO THE FRONTIER

1. Tenodor Ten Eyck Diary, May 11, 1866, Papers of Tenodor Ten Eyck, 1860–1890, MS008, Special Collections, University of Arizona Library, Tucson; Carrington, *Absaraka*, 41.

2. Olson, *Red Cloud and the Sioux Problem*, 29–32.

3. Carrington, *Absaraka*, 37.

4. Bisbee, "Items of Indian Service," 78.

5. Vestal, *Jim Bridger: Mountain Man*, 247.

6. Colonel Henry B. Carrington, Fort Kearny, Nebraska Territory, to Assistant Adjutant-General, Department of the Platte, Omaha, Nebraska, April 26, 1866, in U.S. Senate, *Indian Operations on the Plains (Senate Document 33)*, 3.

7. Carrington, *The Indian Question*, 3.

8. Colonel Henry B. Carrington, In camp near Fort Laramie, to H. G. Litchfield, Department of the Platte, Omaha, Nebraska, June 16, 1866, in U.S. Senate, *Indian Operations on the Plains (Senate Document 33)*, 6.

9. Rzeczkowski, "The Crow Indians and the Bozeman Trail," 30–47.

10. Colonel Henry B. Carrington, Fort Philip Kearny, Dakota Territory, to Major H. G. Litchfield, Assistant Adjutant-General, Department of the Platte, Omaha, Nebraska, November 5, 1866, in U.S. Senate, *Indian Operations on the Plains (Senate Document 33)*, 20–21; Carrillo, "Life in a War Zone," 50.

11. Dunn, *Massacres of the Mountains*, 485.

12. Dennison, "A History of Fort Phil Kearny," 1; Ostrander, *An Army Boy of the Sixties*, iii. If spelled "Kearny" the name denotes Irish descent; if spelled "Kearney" it is English. The second *e* in the name of Fort Kearney, Nebraska,

came about when an army engineer of English lineage, Lt. Col. James Kearney, drew up the plans for the new fort—to be named for Irish descendent Gen. Stephen Kearny—and the English spelling was forever attached to the post. It was used erroneously in so many official records that it became recognized as the standard spelling. Fort Phil Kearny was also frequently burdened with the additional *e*; the title of Frances Carrington's book even contains the misspelled "Fort Phil. Kearney."

13. Murray, *Military Posts in the Powder River Country*, 52; Utley, *Frontier Regulars*, 102.

14. Utley, *Frontier Regulars*, 70, 98.

15. Ostrander, *The Bozeman Trail Forts Under General Philip St. George Cooke*, 28.

16. Athearn, *Sherman and the Settlement of the West*, 68.

17. Ostrander, *The Bozeman Trail Forts Under General Philip St. George Cooke*, 31–32.

18. Colonel Henry B. Carrington, explanatory comments in U.S. Senate, *Indian Operations on the Plains (Senate Document 33)*, 16.

19. McDermott, "The Life of William Judd Fetterman," 44–45.

20. Ostrander, *An Army Boy of the Sixties*, 56–66.

21. Carrington, *My Army Life*, 27–29.

22. Seymour, *Incidents of a Trip Through the Great Platte Valley*, 7–9.

23. William J. Fetterman, Fort Phil Kearny via Fort Laramie, November 26, 1866, to Dr. Charles Terry, n.a., in McDermott, "Wyoming Scrapbook," 69–72.

24. Testimony of Lieutenant Frederick Phisterer and Captain Henry Haymond, May 10, 1867, Records of the Judge Advocate General's Office, GCMO 002236, National Archives and Records Administrations, as cited in Robert A. Murray, "Commentaries on the Col. Henry B. Carrington Image" in Murray, *The Army on the Powder River*, 4–5.

25. Colonel Henry B. Carrington, explanatory comments, in U.S. Senate, *Indian Operations on the Plains (Senate Document 33)*, 47.

26. William J. Fetterman, Fort Phil Kearny via Fort Laramie, November 26, 1866, to Dr. Charles Terry, n.a., in McDermott, "Wyoming Scrapbook," 68.

27. Colonel Henry B. Carrington, explanatory comments, in U.S. Senate, *Indian Operations on the Plains (Senate Document 33)*, 31; Colonel Henry B. Carrington, Fort Philip Kearny, to Major H. G. Litchfield, Assistant Adjutant-General, Department of the Platte, Omaha, Nebraska, November 25, 1866, in U.S. Senate, *Indian Operations on the Plains (Senate Document 33)*, 36.

3. LADIES OF THE REGIMENT

1. Hagan, "Pierre 'French Pete' Gazeau," in Fort Phil Kearny/Bozeman Trail Association, *Civilian, Military, Native American Portraits of Fort Phil Kearny*, 21–24; Murray and Curtiss, "Elisabeth A. Wheatley Breakenridge & George Breakenridge," in Fort Phil Kearny/Bozeman Trail Association, *Civilian, Military, Native American Portraits of Fort Phil Kearny*, 155–59; Murray, "New Facts about Civilians Killed in Fetterman Disaster," 5.

2. Roe, *Army Letters from an Officer's Wife*, 81.

3. Eales, *Army Wives on the American Frontier*, 137.

4. Stallard, *Glittering Misery*, 103.

5. Knight, *Life and Manners in the Frontier Army*, 42–43.

6. Stallard, *Glittering Misery*, 103.

7. Sullivant, *A Genealogy and Family Memorial*, 251.

8. Eales, *Army Wives*, 55.

9. Carrington, *Absaraka*, 173–74.

10. Carrington, *My Army Life*, 106.

11. Taylor, *Centennial History of Columbus*, 32.

12. McKeen, "Henry Beebee Carrington," 60–61; Columbus Compact Corporation, The Heritage Districts website, "Franklinton, Columbus' First Community," www.heritagedistricts.org/franklinton.htm, accessed March 3, 2004.

13. Taylor, *Centennial History of Columbus*, 52.

14. Stuckey, *First Botanists of Columbus*, "Lucas Sullivant and His Three Sons," 32–33.

15. Office of the Treasurer, Ohio State University website, www.treasurer.ohio-state.edu/TreaAdmin/PDFs/sullivant.pdf, accessed December 1, 2006.

16. Stuckey, *First Botanists of Columbus*, "Family Table of Joseph Sullivant."

17. Sullivant, *A Genealogy and Family Memorial*, 182.

18. Sullivant, *A Genealogy and Family Memorial*, 177.

19. McKeen, "Henry Beebee Carrington," 59; Sullivant, *A Genealogy and Family Memorial*, 176.

20. Stuckey, *First Botanists of Columbus*, 32; McKeen, "Henry Beebee Carrington," 61.

21. Kordik, "Frances C. Grummond Carrington," in Fort Phil Kearny/Bozeman Trail Association, *Civilian, Military, Native American Portraits*, 93–97; Carrington, *Atlas of Montgomery County*, 53; also "Carrington, Henry B.," *History of Montgomery County*, 246.

22. Carrington, *My Army Life*, 55; Carrington, *Atlas of Montgomery County*, 53; 1850 U.S. census, Williamson County, Tennessee, copy available at Wyoming Room, Fulmer Public Library, Sheridan WY; Tennessee State Library and Archives, *Tennessee Civil War Veterans' Questionnaires*, Manuscript Section AS. No. 420, W. W. Courtney.

23. Carrington, *My Army Life*, 55, 91, 105–6; *Tennessee Civil War Veterans' Questionnaires*, W. W. Courtney.

24. Cochnower, *Recollections Awakened*, 5; Franklin Old City Cemetery transcription, *Cemetery Records of Williamson Co TN*, Williamson County Historical Society, Franklin TN.

25. Kordik, "Frances C. Grummond Carrington," 93; Cochnower, *Recollections Awakened*, 1.

26. Cochnower, *Recollections Awakened*, 2.

27. Cochnower, *Recollections Awakened*, 4; Ohio State Historical Society Archives, *Correspondence to the Governor and Adjutant General of Ohio, September 30, 1861–November 13, 1861*, Series 147–16: 131; Dyer, "74th Regiment Infantry," 1531.

28. Tennessee State Library and Archives, *Tennessee Confederate Pension Applications: Soldiers and Widows*, Courtney, W. W., Pension #: S13899, Unit: 32nd Inf., Tennessee State Library and Archives website, www.state.tn.us/tsla/history/military/pen310.htm, accessed 20 December 2006; *Tennessee Civil War Veterans' Questionnaires*, W. W. Courtney; Cochnower, *Recollections Awakened*, 2.

29. Carrington, *My Army Life*, 38.

30. U.S. Department of War, *The War of the Rebellion: A Compilation of the Official Records of the Union and Confederate Armies*, 70 vols., 128 books, ser. 1, vol. 38, part 2, 495–507. Hereafter cited as *Official Records*.

31. Cochnower, *Recollections Awakened*, 4–6; Carrington, *Atlas of Montgomery County*, 53; Logsdon, "Fannie Courtney, 19, Franklin Resident," 18, 92–93, 101–2.

32. Carrington, *My Army Life*, 18–27; Marriage License, State of Tennessee, Williamson County, George W. Grummond and Fannie P. Courtney, in George W. Grummond Pension Records, Pension File 23 WC 111–43, National Archives and Records Administration, Washington DC.

33. Carrington, *My Army Life*, 94–95.

34. Carrington, *Absaraka*, 180–81.

35. Carrington, *My Army Life*, 94–95; Carrington, *Absaraka*, 83, 92.

36. Carrington, *Absaraka*, 137–38.

37. Carrington, *My Army Life*, 60, 64, 67, 88, 91–93.

4. OFFICERS AND GENTLEMEN

1. Hebard and Brininstool, *The Bozeman Trail*, 2:90–92; Colonel Henry B. Carrington, explanatory comments, in U.S. Senate, *Indian Operations on the Plains (Senate Document 33)*, 11–12.

2. Colonel Henry B. Carrington, Fort Philip Kearny, Dakota Territory, to Adjutant-General, U.S. Army, Washington DC, July 29, 1866; Colonel Henry B. Carrington, Fort Philip Kearny, Dakota Territory, to Major H. G. Litchfield, Acting Assistant Adjutant-General, Department of the Platte, Omaha, Nebraska, July 30, 1866, in U.S. Senate, *Indian Operations on the Plains (Senate Document 33)*, 12, 16.

3. McDermott, "Frederick Hallam Brown," in Fort Phil Kearny/Bozeman Trail Association, *Civilian, Military, Native American Portraits of Fort Phil Kearny*, 98–100; Colonel Henry B. Carrington, explanatory comments, in U.S. Senate, *Indian Operations on the Plains (Senate Document 33)*, 48; Carrington, *Absaraka*, 246–48; Carrington, "Response to Captain James Powell's Affidavit," in "Wyoming Opened–Carrington Scrapbook," Wyoming Room, Fulmer Public Library, Sheridan WY; also cited as Appendix B in Vaughn, *Indian Fights*, 211.

4. Tremaine, "Lt. William Henry Bisbee," in Fort Phil Kearny/Bozeman Trail Association, *Civilian, Military, Native American Portraits of Fort Phil Kearny*, 234–39.

5. Kimball, "Tenodor Ten Eyck," in Fort Phil Kearny/Bozeman Trail Association, *Civilian, Military, Native American Portraits of Fort Phil Kearny*, 114–19.

6. Kimball, "Susan Fitsgerald," in Fort Phil Kearny/Bozeman Trail Association, *Civilian, Military, Native American Portraits of Fort Phil Kearny*, 153–54.

7. Tenodor Ten Eyck Diary, Papers of Tenodor Ten Eyck, 1860–1890, MS008, Special Collections, University of Arizona Library, Tucson.

8. McDermott, "George Washington Grummond," in Fort Phil Kearny/Bozeman Trail Association, *Civilian, Military, Native American Portraits of Fort Phil Kearny*, 88–92.

9. Partridge, "Fetterman Debacle—Who Was to Blame?" 36–43; U.S. Department of War, *Official Records*, ser. 1, vol. 38, part 2, 497–500.

10. U.S. War Department, *Official Records*, ser. 1, vol. 98, part 1, 495–507.

11. U.S. Bureau of the Census, *Eighth Census of the United States, 1860*, National Archives and Records Administration, Washington DC, 1860, M653, 1,483 rolls, Census Place: Detroit Ward 8, Wayne, Michigan; Roll: M653_566; Page: o, Image: 598.

12. Dyer, "Michigan 14th Regiment Infantry," *Compendium of the War of the Rebellion*, vol. 3.

13. George W. Grummond Pension Records, Pension File 23 WC 111–43, National Archives and Records Administration, Washington DC.

14. Carrington, *My Army Life*, 18; Carrington, *Absaraka*, 249.

15. U.S. War Department, *Official Records*, ser. 1, vol. 38, part 1, 586–88.

16. William J. Fetterman, Fort Phil Kearny via Fort Laramie, November 26, 1866, to Dr. Charles Terry, n.a., in McDermott, "Wyoming Scrapbook," 68.

17. Hess, *The Union Soldier in Battle*, 118–20.

18. Hebard and Brininstool, *The Bozeman Trail*, 2:90.

19. Wilson, "Army Life in the Rockies," *National Tribune*, June 22, 1899, as cited in McDermott, "The Life of William Judd Fetterman," 45; Charles William Wilson, "Soldier's Memories," C. W. Wilson Papers, Ohio State Historical Society, Columbus OH.

20. Fetterman, "Wyoming Scrapbook," 68.

21. Testimony of Captain Henry Haymond, May 10, 1867, Records of the Judge Advocate General's Office, GCMO 002236, National Archives and Records Administrations, as cited in Murray, "Commentaries on the Carrington Image," 5.

22. Testimony of Lieutenant William F. Arnold, Minutes of the Meetings of the Special Commission, March 4, 1867, to June 12, 1867 (National Archives Microfilm Publication 740, "Records Relating to the Investigation of the Fort Philip Kearny Massacre, 1866–67"), Records of the Bureau of Indian Affairs, Record Group 75, National Archives and Records Administration, Washington DC.

23. Testimony of Captain William H. Bisbee, Minutes of the Meetings of the Special Commission, March 4, 1867, to June 12, 1867, "Records Relating to the Investigation of the Fort Philip Kearny Massacre, 1866–67."

24. Fetterman, "Wyoming Scrapbook," 68.

5. HARD LESSONS LEARNED

1. Carrington, *Absaraka*, 31.

2. Tenodor Ten Eyck Diary, November 18, 1866.

3. Lieutenant Alexander H. Wands, Fort Sanders, Dakota Territory, to Colonel

Henry B. Carrington, Wellingford, Connecticut, November 27, 1867, in "Wyoming Opened—Carrington Scrapbook," Wyoming Room, Fulmer Public Library, Sheridan WY; Tenodor Ten Eyck Diary, November 28, 1866.

4. Tenodor Ten Eyck Diary, December 13, 1866.

5. General Philip St. George Cooke, Headquarters Department of the Platte, Omaha, Nebraska, to Colonel H. B. Carrington, Fort Philip Kearney, Dakota Territory, September 27, 1866, in U.S. Congress 40th, 1st sess Senate, *Indian Hostilities.* (Executive Document 13) Washington DC, 1868, 31. Referred to throughout Carrington's communications as "Senate Document 13," this document contains testimony and evidence gathered by a congressionally mandated commission to investigate the massacre of Fetterman and his troops. Senate Document 13 was published on July 13, 1867, six months after the incident. Referred hereafter as *Indian Hostilities (Senate Document 13).*

6. Colonel Henry B. Carrington, explanatory comments; Colonel Henry B. Carrington, Fort Philip Kearny, Dakota Territory, to Major H.G. Litchfield, Assistant Adjutant-General, Department of the Platte, Omaha, Nebraska, September 25, 1866, in U.S. Senate, *Indian Operations on the Plains (Senate Document 33),* 33–34, 25–26.

7. Colonel Henry B. Carrington, Fort Philip Kearny, Dakota Territory, to Major H. G. Litchfield, Assistant Adjutant-General, Department of the Platte, Omaha, Nebraska, November 5, 1866, in U.S. Senate, *Indian Operations on the Plains (Senate Document 33),* 22.

8. Testimony of Lieutenant A. H. Wands, Military Court of Inquiry, May 1867, Records of Judge Advocate Generals Office, GCMO 002236, National Archives and Records Administration, as cited in Murray, "Commentaries on the Carrington Image," 5–6.

9. Murray, *Military Posts in the Powder River Country,* 81–82; Carrington, *My Army Life,* 111; General Order No. 38, November 11, 1866, in U.S. Senate, *Indian Operations on the Plains (Senate Document 33),* 33.

10. Brown, *The Fetterman Massacre,* 152–53.

11. Powell's report on Burke's case in third endorsement to Burke's petition for redress of grievance, March 8, 1867, Fort Philip Kearny, 1866–1868, Communication Register and Endorsement, Records of the U.S. Army Commands, Record Group 98, as cited in Murray, *Military Posts in the Powder River Country,* 81–82.

12. Carrington, *My Army Life,* 111; Colonel Henry B. Carrington, explanatory comments, in U.S. Senate, *Indian Operations on the Plains (Senate Document 33),* 48.

13. Carrington, "Response to Captain James Powell's Affidavit," in "Wyoming Opened-Carrington Scrapbook," Wyoming Room, Fulmer Public Library, Sheridan WY; also cited as Appendix B in Vaughn, *Indian Fights,* 206–23.

14. Carrington, "Response to Captain James Powell's Affidavit," in "Wyoming Opened-Carrington Scrapbook," Wyoming Room, Fulmer Public Library, Sheridan WY; also cited as Appendix B in Vaughn, *Indian Fights,* 206–23; Henry B. Carrington, Hyde Park, Massachusetts, to James Carrington, n.a., September

9, 1903, Carrington Family Papers, Manuscript Group No. 130, Manuscripts and Archives, Sterling Memorial Library, Yale University, New Haven.

15. Carrington, *My Army Life*, 106–7; Tenodor Ten Eyck Diary, September 6, 1866, Papers of Tenodor Ten Eyck, 1860–1890, MS008, Special Collections, University of Arizona Library, Tucson; Carrington, *Absaraka*, 141.

16. Young, *The West of Philip St. George Cooke*, 302–3.

17. Major H. G. Litchfield, Assistant Adjutant-General, Department of the Platte, Omaha, Nebraska, to Colonel Henry B. Carrington, Fort Philip Kearny, Dakota Territory, November 12, 1866, in U.S. Senate, *Indian Operations on the Plains (Senate Document 33)*, 34–35.

18. Carrington, *My Army Life*, 128–29.

19. Colonel Henry B. Carrington, Fort Philip Kearny, Dakota Territory, to Major H. G. Litchfield, Assistant Adjutant-General, Department of the Platte, Omaha, Nebraska, November 25, 1866, in U.S. Senate, *Indian Operations on the Plains (Senate Document 33)*, 36.

20. Hagan, "Prelude to a Massacre," 1–17. Hagan's monograph is an excellent reproduction of the fight, citing scores of unique military records and memoirs. It is the most in-depth scholarly analysis of the event.

21. Brown, *The Fetterman Massacre*, 164.

22. Hagan, "Prelude to a Massacre," 12.

23. Captain Wm. J. Fetterman, Fort Philip Kearny, Dakota Territory, to Post Adjutant Captain Wm. H. Bisbee, December 7, 1866, in U.S. Department of the Interior and U.S. Department of War, *Reports of the Secretaries of War and Interior*, 41–2.

24. Colonel Henry B. Carrington, Fort Philip Kearny, Dakota Territory, to Major H. G. Litchfield, Assistant Adjutant-General, Department of the Platte, Omaha, Nebraska, December 8, 1866, in U.S. Senate, *Indian Operations on the Plains (Senate Document 33)*, 36.

25. Colonel Henry B. Carrington, Fort Philip Kearny, Dakota Territory, to Major H. G. Litchfield, Assistant Adjutant-General, Department of the Platte, Omaha, Nebraska, November 5, 1866, in U.S. Senate, *Indian Operations on the Plains (Senate Document 33)*, 20–21.

26. Carrington, *Absaraka*, 195.

27. Brown, *The Fetterman Massacre*, 166.

6. THE BATTLE OF THE HUNDRED-IN-THE-HANDS

1. Carrington, *My Army Life*, 136.

2. Colonel Henry B. Carrington, Phil. Kearney. D. T., to A. A. General, Department of the Platte, Omaha, December 19, 1866, in U.S. Department of the Interior and U.S. Department of War, *Reports of the Secretaries of War and Interior*, 42–43.

3. General Philip St. George Cooke, Department of the Platte, Omaha, to A. A. General, Department of the Missouri, St. Louis, January 14, 1867, in U.S. Department of the Interior and U.S. Department of War, *Reports of the Secretaries of War and Interior*, 35–36.

4. Colonel Henry B. Carrington, explanatory comments, in U.S. Senate, *Indian Operations on the Plains (Senate Document 33)*, 39.

5. Evidence of Bvt. Major James Powell, July 24, 1867, Meetings of the Special Commission, March 4, 1867, to June 12, 1867, Record Group 75, Records of the Bureau of Indian Affairs, National Archives and Records Administration.

6. Colonel Henry B. Carrington, explanatory comments, in U.S. Senate, *Indian Operations on the Plains (Senate Document 33)*, 39.

7. Bisbee, "Items of Indian Service," 83.

8. Carrington, "Response to Captain James Powell's Affidavit," in "Wyoming Opened-Carrington Scrapbook," Wyoming Room, Fulmer Public Library, Sheridan WY; also cited as Appendix B in Vaughn, *Indian Fights*, 206–23; Carrington, *My Army Life*, 133.

9. Colonel Henry B. Carrington, explanatory comments, in U.S. Senate, *Indian Operations on the Plains (Senate Document 33)*, 40.

10. Testimony of Lieutenant A. H. Wands, Meetings of the Special Commission, March 4, 1867, to June 12, 1867, Record Group 75, Records of the Bureau of Indian Affairs, National Archives and Records Administration.

11. Evidence of Bvt. Major James Powell, July 24, 1867, Meetings of the Special Commission, March 4, 1867, to June 12, 1867, Record Group 75, Records of the Bureau of Indian Affairs, National Archives and Records Administration.

12. Colonel Henry B. Carrington, explanatory comments in U.S. Senate, *Indian Operations on the Plains (Senate Document 33)*, 44.

13. Carrington, *My Army Life*, 136.

14. Colonel Henry B. Carrington, explanatory comments, in U.S. Senate, *Indian Operations on the Plains (Senate Document 33)*, 39–40; Testimony of Capt. Ten Eyck, July 5, Minutes of the Meetings of the Special Commission, March 4, 1867, to June 12, 1867, in U.S. Department of the Interior, "Records Relating to the Investigation of the Fort Philip Kearny Massacre, 1866–67."

15. Vaughn, *Indian Fights*, 218; Murphy, "The Forgotten Battalion," M. A. Chapman Collection, B-M959-W, American Heritage Center, University of Wyoming, Laramie.

16. Colonel Henry B. Carrington, explanatory comments, in U.S. Senate, *Indian Operations on the Plains (Senate Document 33)*, 46; Murphy, "The Forgotten Battalion"; Testimony of Capt. Ten Eyck, July 5, Minutes of the Meetings of the Special Commission, March 4, 1867, to June 12, 1867, in U.S. Department of the Interior, "Records Relating to the Investigation of the Fort Philip Kearny Massacre, 1866–67."

17. McDermott, "The Life of William Judd Fetterman," 52.

18. Testimony of Lieutenant A. H. Wands, Meetings of the Special Commission, March 4, 1867, to June 12, 1867, Record Group 75, Records of the Bureau of Indian Affairs, National Archives and Records Administration.

19. Vaughn, *Indian Fights*, 14–90.

20. Belish, "American Horse (Wasechun-Tashunka)," 54–67; Cook, *Fifty Years on the Old Frontier*, 229; Agate Fossil Beds National Monument, 301 River Road,

Harrison NE; Evidence of Brvt. Maj. Samuel M. Horton, Asst. Surgeon U. S. A. on the Fort Phil. Kearney Massacre, Meetings of the Special Commission, March 4, 1867, to June 12, 1867, Record Group 75, Records of the Bureau of Indian Affairs, National Archives and Records Administration. American Horse's war club purportedly used to kill Fetterman was given to James Cook whose son subsequently gave it to the National Park Service where it is on display at the Visitor Center and Museum at the Agate Fossil Beds National Monument in Harrison, Nebraska.

21. Colonel Henry B. Carrington, Fort Philip Kearny, Dakota Territory, to Assistant Adjutant-General, Department of the Platte, Omaha, Nebraska, January 3, 1867, in U.S. Senate, *Indian Operations on the Plains (Senate Document 33)*, 41.

22. Carrington, *My Army Life*, 165–68; Stauffer, "Letter to Jack Leermakers, August 25, 1955," in *Letters of Mari Sandoz*, 276–77.

23. Cook, *Fifty Years on the Old Frontier*, 229; Sandoz, *Crazy Horse, Strange Man of the Oglalas*, 197; Tall Bull, *Northern Cheyenne History of the Battle of 100-In-The-Hand*, Fort Phil Kearny/Bozeman Trail Association website: www.philkearny.vcn.com/fpk-tallbull.htm, accessed August 1, 2007.

24. Carrington, *Absaraka*, 207

25. "Extract of Officer Assignments Under the Army Reorganization of 1866," *New York Times*, 9 December 1866, 3.

26. Colonel Henry B. Carrington, Fort Phil Kearney, D.T., to General U. S. Grant, December 21, 1866, in U.S. Senate, *Indian Hostilities (Senate Document 13)*, 26.

27. C. M. Hines, Fort Phil Kearny, D.T., to John Hines, n.a., January 1, 1867; Anonymous, Fort Phil Kearny, Dakota Territory, December 28, 1866, in U.S. Senate, *Indian Hostilities (Senate Document 13)*, 15, 34–35.

28. Carrington, *My Army Life*, 173.

29. Carrington, *Absaraka*, 218–25; Carrington, *My Army Life*, 176–77.

30. Carrington, *My Army Life*, 173–203; Carrington, *Absaraka*, 226–42.

7. BLAZING A PAPER TRAIL

1. Carrington, *Absaraka*, 211.

2. Carrington, *Absaraka*, 226; Carrington, *My Army Life*, 163; General Order No. 1, January 1, 1867, in U.S. Senate, *Indian Operations on the Plains (Senate Document 33)*, 42.

3. General Order No. 1, in U.S. Senate, *Indian Operations on the Plains (Senate Document 33)*, 42.

4. General William T. Sherman to General Ulysses S. Grant, January 17, 1867, telegram forwarding Colonel Henry B. Carrington, Fort Phil Kearney to Adjt. Gen. Department of the Platte, January 4, 1867, in Grant, *The Papers of Ulysses S. Grant*, 17:18–19.

5. U.S. Congress. 40th 2nd sess. Senate. *Message of the President* (Executive Document 1) Washington DC, 1867.

6. Carrington, *Absaraka*, 224.

7. Lewis V. Bogy, Commissioner of Indian Affairs, Department of the Interior,

n.a., to O. H. Browning, Secretary of the Interior, n.a., February 4, 1867, in U.S. Department of the Interior and U.S. Department of War, *Reports of the Secretaries of War and Interior*, 38.

8. Telegrams sent between General William T. Sherman, Division of the Missouri, St. Louis, and General Ulysses S. Grant, Department of the Army, Washington DC, December 28 and 29, 1866, in Grant, *The Papers of Ulysses S. Grant*, 16:422.

9. General Philip St. George Cooke, Department of the Platte, Omaha, Nebraska, to General J. A. Rawlins, Chief of Staff, General Commanding, Washington DC, December 27, 1866, in U.S. Senate, *Indian Hostilities (Senate Document 13)*, 29.

10. General William T. Sherman, Division of the Missouri, St. Louis, to General Ulysses S. Grant, Department of the Army, Washington DC, December 30, 1866, in Grant, *The Papers of Ulysses S. Grant*, 16:423.

11. Telegrams between General Philip St. George Cooke, Department of the Platte, Omaha, Nebraska, General William T. Sherman, Division of the Missouri, St. Louis, Missouri, and General Ulysses S. Grant, Department of the Army, Washington DC, January 7 and 8, 1867, in Grant, *The Papers of Ulysses S. Grant*, 17:18.

12. General William T. Sherman, Division of the Missouri, St. Louis, to General Grenville M. Dodge, Council Bluffs, Iowa, January 22, 1867, in Grant, *The Papers of Ulysses S. Grant*, 17:31.

13. General Philip St. George Cooke, Department of the Platte, Omaha, to A. A. General, Department of the Missouri, St. Louis, January 14, 1867, in U.S. Department of the Interior and U.S. Department of War, *Reports of the Secretaries of War and Interior*, 35–36.

14. General William T. Sherman, Division of the Missouri, St. Louis, January 9, 1867, endorsement to General Philip St. George Cooke, Department of the Platte, Omaha, to General William A. Nichols, Department of the Army, Washington DC, January 3, 1867, in Grant, *The Papers of Ulysses S. Grant*, 17:16–17.

15. Thorndike, *The Sherman Letters*, 275–316; Athearn, *Sherman and the Settlement of the West*, 190; Foner, *A Short History of Reconstruction*, 143; General William T. Sherman, Division of the Missouri, St. Louis, to General Ulysses S. Grant, Department of the Army, Washington DC, December 30, 1866, in Grant, *The Papers of Ulysses S. Grant*, 16:422–23; General Ulysses S. Grant, Department of the Army, Washington DC, to General William T. Sherman, Division of the Missouri, St. Louis, January 13, 1867, in Grant, *The Papers of Ulysses S. Grant*, 17:13–14.

16. General Ulysses S. Grant, Department of the Army, Washington, DC, to General William T. Sherman, Division of the Missouri, St. Louis, January 14, 1867, in Grant, *The Papers of Ulysses S. Grant*, 17:16.

17. General William T. Sherman, Division of the Missouri, St. Louis, to General Ulysses S. Grant, Department of the Army, Washington DC, January 17, 1867, in Grant, *The Papers of Ulysses S. Grant*, 17:15.

18. C. M. Hines, Fort Phil Kearney, D.T., to John Hines, n.a., January 1, 1867; Anonymous, Fort Phil Kearny, Dakota Territory, December 28, 1866, in U.S. Senate, *Indian Hostilities (Senate Document 13)*, 15, 34–35.

19. General Philip St. George Cooke to Adjutant General, January 19, 1867, General Ulysses S. Grant endorsement dated February 8, 1867, in Grant, *The Papers of Ulysses S. Grant,* 17:18.

20. General Philip St. George Cooke, Department of the Platte, to n.a., in U.S. Senate, *Letter from the Secretary of War* (Executive Document 97).

21. Carrington, "Wyoming Opened-Carrington Scrapbook," 8.

22. Colonel Henry B. Carrington, Fort Philip Kearny, Dakota Territory, to Assistant Adjutant-General, Department of the Platte, Omaha, January 3, 1867, in U.S. Senate, *Letter from the Secretary of War* (Executive Document 97).

23. Henry B. Carrington, "Wyoming Opened-Carrington Scrapbook," 33–42; also cited in Vaughn, *Indian Fights: New Facts on Seven Encounters,* 204–5.

24. U.S. Department of the Interior and U.S. Department of War, *Reports of the Secretaries of War and Interior,* 2.

25. U.S. Senate, *Letter from the Secretary of War* (Executive Document 97), 1, 2, 5. Dates are cited with each endorsement of the document as it was forwarded from Cooke to Sherman to Adjutant General to Grant to Stanton.

26. U.S. Department of the Interior and U.S. Department of War, *Reports of the Secretaries of War and Interior.*

27. General C. C. Augur, Department of the Platte, Omaha, to AAG, Division of the Missouri, St. Louis, February 19, 1867, as cited in Olson, *Red Cloud and the Sioux Problem,* 55.

28. Carrington, "Wyoming Opened-Carrington Scrapbook," 33–42; also cited in Vaughn, *Indian Fights,* 198.

29. General N. B. Buford, Special Commissioner, to E. M. Stanton, Secretary of War, Washington DC June 6, 1867, in U.S. Senate, *Indian Hostilities (Senate Document 13),* 57–60.

30. Colonel Ely S. Parker, n.a., to Adjutant General, Army Headquarters, Washington DC, March 14 and April 1, 1867, in Grant, *The Papers of Ulysses S. Grant,* 17:57–59.

31. General William T. Sherman, Division of the Missouri, St. Louis, to Major George Leet, Department of the Army, Washington DC, January 17, 1867, in Grant, *The Papers of Ulysses S. Grant,* 17:17–18.

32. Colonel Innis N. Palmer, Fort Laramie, to General Philip St. George Cooke, Department of the Platte, Omaha, December 26, 1866, cited in Murray, "Commentaries on the Carrington Image," 6.

33. John B. Sanborn, Washington DC, to Henry B. Carrington, Wallingford, Connecticut, July 16, 1867, Carrington Family Papers, Manuscript Group No. 130, Manuscripts and Archives, Sterling Memorial Library, Yale University, New Haven.

34. General William T. Sherman, Division of the Missouri, St. Louis, to General John Gibbon, President Court of Inquiry, n.a., n.d., in Grant, *The Papers of Ulysses S. Grant,* 17:325–26.

35. Ulysses S. Grant to Judge Advocate General Joseph Holt, endorsement, September 10, 1867, and responses dated September 26, 1867, in Grant, *The Papers of Ulysses S. Grant,* 17:325–26.

36. General William T. Sherman, Division of the Missouri, St. Louis, to General C. C. Augur, Department of the Platte, Omaha, February 23, 1867, Department of the Platte, Letters Received, Records of the Army Continental Command, Record Group 393, National Archives and Records Administration, Washington DC.

37. John B. Sanborn, Special Indian Commissioner, to O. H. Browning, Secretary of the Interior, Washington DC, July 8, 1867, in U.S. Senate, *Indian Hostilities (Senate Document 13)*, 60–74.

38. Henry B. Carrington, Hyde Park, Massachusetts, to C. G. Coutant, State Librarian, Cheyenne, Wyoming, June 6, 1902, Grace Raymond Hebard Collection, B-C235-hb, American Heritage Center, University of Wyoming, Laramie; also published in Hebard and Brininstool, *The Bozeman Trail*, 1:339–42.

8. WOMEN'S WORK

1. Eastman, *Dacotah*; Vielé, *Following the Drum*.

2. The Victorian ideals known as the "cult of true womanhood" is described in Welter, "The Cult of True Womanhood: 1820–186," 151–74. Some Victorian women took advantage of society's respect for their moral authority and achieved a public voice. Mintz and Kellog, *Domestic Revolutions*, 56; Davidson, "Preface: No More Separate Spheres!" 443–63. Although Davidson argues against the validity of the "binaric version of nineteenth-century American history" represented in the idea of the "separate spheres," she does not dispute the phenomenon of the Victorian woman writer.

3. Fahs, "The Feminized Civil War," 1461–94.

4. Kaplan, "Manifest Domesticity," 581–606. Identifying women's roles in American imperialism, Kaplan writes, "If domesticity plays a key role in imagining the nation as home, then women, positioned at the center of the home, play a major role in defining the contours of the nation and its shifting borders with the foreign." Margaret Carrington's book was the first of several post–Civil War frontier army wives' publications that helped shape the nation's positive perception of Manifest Destiny and their constantly shifting borders with the ever-shrinking Indian lands.

5. Leckie, *Elizabeth Bacon Custer and the Making of a Myth*, xx.

6. Carrington, *Absaraka*, 13–19.

7. Carrington, *Absaraka*, 171, 245, 202, 246.

8. Carrington, *Absaraka*, 1.

9. General William T. Sherman, Division of the Missouri, St. Louis, to Margaret Carrington, n.a., November 20, 1868, Carrington Family Papers, Yale University, New Haven.

10. Henry B. Carrington, Hyde Park, Massachusetts, to C. G. Coutant, State Librarian, Cheyenne, Wyoming, June 6, 1902, Grace Raymond Hebard Collection, B-C235-hb, American Heritage Center, University of Wyoming, Laramie; also published in Hebard and Brininstool, *The Bozeman Trail*, 1:339–42.

11. General William T. Sherman, Division of the Missouri, St. Louis, to Major George K. Leet, AAG, Army Headquarters, Washington DC, April 3, 1867, in Grant, *The Papers of Ulysses S. Grant*, 17:105.

12. Carrington, *Absaraka,* 225.

13. Captain R. L. Morris, Commander, Fort Casper, D.T., to AAG, Department of the Platte, Omaha, February 2, 1867, Department of the Platte, Letters Received, Records of the Army Continental Command, Record Group 393, National Archives and Records Administration, Washington DC.

14. George W. Grummond Pension Records, Pension File 23 WC 111–43, National Archives and Records Administration, Washington DC; Kordik, "Frances C. Grummond Carrington," in Fort Phil Kearny/Bozeman Trail Association, *Civilian, Military, Native American Portraits of Fort Phil Kearny,* 93–97.

15. Carrington, *My Army Life,* 217.

16. Murray, "Commentaries on the Carrington Image," 1–10.

17. General Philip St. George Cooke, Department of the Platte, to n.a., in U.S. Senate, *Letter from the Secretary of War* (Executive Document 97).

18. Carrington, "Explanation of Congressional Delay for Twenty Years," in "Wyoming Opened-Carrington Scrapbook," Wyoming Room, Fulmer Public Library, Sheridan WY.

19. Quaife, Introduction to *Absaraka, Home of the Crows* (Lakeside Press edition), xxxvii.

20. C. G. Coutant, *The History of Wyoming,* 574.

21. Henry B. Carrington, Hyde Park, Massachusetts,, to C. G. Coutant, State Librarian, Cheyenne, Wyoming, June 6, 1902, Grace Raymond Hebard Collection, B-C235-hb, American Heritage Center, University of Wyoming, Laramie; also published in Hebard and Brininstool, *The Bozeman Trail,* 1:339–42.

22. Carrington, "Explanation of Congressional Delay for Twenty Years," in "Wyoming Opened-Carrington Scrapbook," Wyoming Room, Fulmer Public Library, Sheridan WY.

23. Brady, *Indian Fights and Fighters,* 22–32.

24. Henry B. Carrington, Hyde Park, Massachusetts, to James Carrington, n.a., September 9, 1903, Carrington Family Papers, Manuscript Group No. 130, Manuscripts and Archives, Sterling Memorial Library, Yale University, New Haven.

25. Coutant, *The History of Wyoming,* 574.

26. U.S. Department of the Interior, National Park Service, "Handbook 107, Agate Fossil Beds National Monument, Nebraska," Washington DC.

27. Cook, *Fifty Years on the Old Frontier,* 229.

28. Cook Collection, Agate Fossil Beds National Monument, Harrison, Nebraska.

29. Eli S. Ricker Collection, MS008, Nebraska State Historical Society, Lincoln, Nebraska. (Hereafter cited as Ricker Collection.)

30. Frances Ten Eyck, Chicago, Illinois, to Mrs. Kate G. Cook, Crawford, Nebraska, February 22, 1906, copied by Eli S. Ricker, Ricker Collection, Box 18, Folder 209.

31. Frances Ten Eyck, Chicago, Illinois, to Eli S. Ricker, Chadron, Nebraska, February 22, 1906, Ricker Collection, Box 2, Series 1, Folder 30.

32. Henry B. Carrington, Hyde Park, Massachusetts to Frances Ten Eyck, Chicago, Illinois, February 15, 1906, hand-copied by Frances Ten Eyck and sent to Eli S. Ricker on May 16, 1906, Ricker Collection, Box 2, Series 1, Folder 30.

33. Carrington, *Absaraka*, 207.

34. Kimball, "Tenodor Ten Eyck," in Fort Phil Kearny/Bozeman Trail Association, *Civilian, Military, Native American Portraits of Fort Phil Kearny*, 118–19.

35. Excerpts of "Senate Documents 13 and 33" published in Carrington, *Absaraka*, 267; also published as an appendix in the updated editions, e.g., *Absaraka, or Wyoming Opened*, 6th ed., (Philadelphia: J.B. Lippincott Co., 1905), 369; also published in Carrington, *The Indian Question*, 26.

36. Colonel Henry B. Carrington, explanatory comments, in U.S. Senate, *Indian Operations on the Plains (Senate Document 33)*, 46; also cited in Carrington, *Absaraka*, 379; Carrington, *The Indian Question*, 26.

37. Frances Ten Eyck, Chicago, Illinois, to Eli S. Ricker, Chadron, Nebraska, June 1, 1906, Ricker Collection, Box 2, Series 1, Folder 30.

38. Obituary, "S. S. Peters Dead at Omaha, Veteran Neb. Newspaperman Who Served in Civil War," *State Journal*, August 9, 1910, 1.

39. S. S. Peters, Omaha, Nebraska to Frances Ten Eyck, Chicago, Illinois, May 16, 1906, hand-copied and mailed to Eli S. Ricker, Chadron, Nebraska, June 7, 1906, Ricker Collection, Box 2, Series 1, Folder 30.

40. Brady, *Indian Fights and Fighters*, 31.

41. Eli S. Ricker, Chadron, Nebraska to Henry B. Carrington, Hyde Park, Massachusetts, June 8, 1906, Ricker's handwritten extract kept for his own records, Ricker Collection, Box 2, Series 1, Folder 30.

42. Henry B. Carrington, Hyde Park, Massachusetts, to Eli S. Ricker, Chadron, Nebraska, June 30, 1906, Ricker Collection, Box 2, Series 1, Folder 30.

43. Frances Ten Eyck, Chicago, Illinois, to Eli S. Ricker, Chadron, Nebraska, June 27, 1908, Ricker Collection, Box 2, Series 1, Folder 31.

44. Henry B. Carrington, Hyde Park, Massachusetts, to Frances Ten Eyck, Chicago, Illinois, June 24, 1908, typed carbon copy sent by Frances Ten Eyck on June 27, 1908, to Eli S. Ricker, Ricker Collection, Box 2, Series 1, Folder 31.

45. Frances Ten Eyck, Chicago, Illinois, to C. G. Coutant, Sheridan, Wyoming, June 24, 1908, typed carbon copy sent by Frances Ten Eyck on Jun. 27, 1908, to Eli S. Ricker, Ricker Collection, Box 2, Series 1, Folder 31.

46. W. W. Robinson Jr., Chicago, Illinois, to General Charles Morton, n.a., June 27, 1908, typed carbon copies, sent from Frances Ten Eyck on June 27, 1908, to Eli S. Ricker, Ricker Collection, Box 2, Series 1, Folder 31.

47. S. S. Peters, Sheridan Wyoming, to Frances Ten Eyck, Chicago, Illinois, July 5, 1908, typed carbon copies of telegram, sent from Frances Ten Eyck on September 10, 1908, to Eli S. Ricker, Ricker Collection, Box 2, Series 1, Folder 31.

48. Frances Ten Eyck, Chicago, Illinois, to Eli S. Ricker, Chadron, Nebraska, September 10, 1908, Ricker Collection, Box 2, Series 1, Folder 31.

49. S. S. Peters, "Survivors of Famous Indian Fight Reunite at Scene of the Massacre," *Omaha Sunday Bee*, July 19, 1908.

50. Carrington, *My Army Life,* 253–54.

51. Carrington, *My Army Life,* 119, 136, 144.

52. Carrington, *The Indian Question,* 26.

53. Descriptions of Ten Eyck's actions and the unfortunate wording of Carrington's note can be found in Brown, *The Fetterman Massacre,* 63–65.

9. THE REST OF THE STORY

1. McDermott, "The Life of William Judd Fetterman," 46.

2. Colonel Henry B. Carrington, Fort Kearny, Nebraska Territory, to Assistant Adjutant-General, Department of the Platte, Omaha, Nebraska, January 3, 1867, in U.S. Senate, *Indian Operations on the Plains (Senate Document 33),* 40.

3. "Brevet Lieut. Col. William Judd Fetterman," *The Daily Cleveland (Ohio) Herald,* January 18, 1867, Issue 16, col. C.

4. Brown, *The Fetterman Massacre,* 163.

5. Carrington, *Absaraka,* 171.

6. McKeen, "Henry Beebee Carrington," 2.

7. Carrington, *My Army Life,* 148.

8. Carrington, *My Army Life,* 253.

9. Carrington, *My Army Life,* 119, 144.

10. Brady, *Indian Fights and Fighters,* 23.

11. Brady, *Indian Fights and Fighters,* 28.

12. Hebard and Brininstool, *The Bozeman Trail,* 1:303–7.

13. Vestal, *Warpath,* 59.

14. Wellman, *Death on the Prairie,* 38–39.

15. Vestal, *Jim Bridger, Mountain Man,* 270.

16. Appleman, "The Fetterman Fight," in The Publications Committee of the Potomac Corral of The Westerners, *Great Western Indian Fights,* 121–22.

17. Brown, *The Fetterman Massacre,* 150.

18. Johnson, *The Bloody Bozeman,* 231–33.

19. Utley and Washburn, *Indian Wars,* 213.

20. Ambrose, *Crazy Horse and Custer,* 225, 232.

21. Brown, *The American West,* 90.

22. Straight, *Carrington;* McMurtry, *Boone's Lick.*

23. Chiaventone, *Moon of Bitter Cold,* 263.

24. "Brevet Lieut. Col. William Judd Fetterman," *The Daily Cleveland (Ohio) Herald,* January 18, 1867, Issue 16, col. C.

25. John B. Sanborn, Special Indian Commissioner, to O. H. Browning, Secretary of the Interior, Washington DC, July 8, 1867, in U.S. Senate *Indian Hostilities (Senate Document 13),* 60–74.

⊱ BIBLIOGRAPHY ⊰

ARCHIVE COLLECTIONS

Carrington Family Papers. Manuscripts and Archives, Sterling Memorial Library, Yale University, New Haven CT.

"Wyoming Opened-Carrington Scrapbook." Wyoming Room, Fulmer Public Library, Sheridan WY.

M. A. Chapman Collection. American Heritage Center, University of Wyoming, Laramie WY.

Cook Collection. Agate Fossil Beds National Monument, 301 River Road, Harrison NE.

W. W. Courtney, Pension Record. Tennessee Confederate Pension Applications: Soldiers and Widows. Tennessee State Library and Archives. W. W. Courtney, Pension #: S13899, Unit: 32nd Inf.

George W. Grummond, Pension Records. Pension File 23 WC 111–43. National Archives and Records Administration, Washington DC.

Grace Raymond Hebard Collection. American Heritage Center, University of Wyoming, Laramie WY.

Eli S. Ricker Collection. Nebraska State Historical Society, Lincoln NE.

Correspondence to the Governor and Adjutant General of Ohio. Ohio State Historical Society Archives, Columbus OH.

Joseph Sullivant. A Genealogy and Family Memorial. Ohio State Historical Society Archives, Columbus OH.

Papers of Tenodor Ten Eyck, 1860–1890. Special Collections, University of Arizona Library, Tucson AZ.

Tennessee State Library and Archives. Tennessee Civil War Veterans' Questionnaires. Manuscript Section AS. No. 420: W. W. Courtney, Nashville TN.

Cemetery Records of Williamson Co, TN. Franklin Old City Cemetery transcription. Williamson County Historical Society, Franklin TN.

C. W. Wilson Papers. Ohio State Historical Society, Columbus OH.

PUBLISHED DOCUMENTS

Ambrose, Stephen E. *Crazy Horse and Custer: The Parallel Lives of Two American Warriors.* New York: Anchor Books, 1996.

Andrist, Ralph K. *The Long Death: The Last Days of the Plains Indians.* New York: Macmillan, 1964.

Appleman, Roy E. "The Fetterman Fight." In *Great Western Indian Fights,* ed. Members of the Potomac Corral of Westerners, 117–131. Washington DC: Potomac Corral of The Westerners, 1960; reprint, Lincoln: University of Nebraska Press, 1966.

Athearn, Robert G. *William Tecumseh Sherman and the Settlement of the West.* Norman: University of Oklahoma Press, 1956.

Battle, Kemp P. *Hearts of Fire: Great Women of American Lore and Legend.* New York: Harmony, 1997.

Belish, Elbert D. "American Horse (Wasechun-Tashunka): The Man Who Killed Fetterman." *Annals of Wyoming* (Spring 1991): 54–67.

Bisbee, William H. "Items of Indian Service." In *The Papers of the Order of Indian Wars,* comp. Order of Indian Wars. Fort Collins: Old Army Press, 1975.

———. *Through Four American Wars, The Impressions and Experiences of Brigadier General William Henry Bisbee.* Boston: Meador, 1931.

Brady, Cyrus Townsend. *Indian Fights and Fighters.* Lincoln: University of Nebraska Press, 1971; reprint, n.p.: McClure, Philips & Co., 1904.

Brooks, E. S. *Chivalric Days: and the Boys and Girls Who Helped to Make Them.* New York: Putnam, 1886.

Brown, Dee. *The Fetterman Massacre* formerly *Fort Phil Kearny: An American Saga.* New York: Putnam, 1962; reprint, Lincoln: University of Nebraska Press, 1971.

———. *The American West.* New York: Touchstone, 1994.

Cabaniss, Charles H., Jr. "The Eighteenth Regiment of the Infantry." In *The Army of the United States; Historical Sketches of Staff and Line with Portraits of Generals-In-Chief,* ed. Theophilus F. Rodenbough, 643–56. New York: Maynard, Merrill, 1896.

Carrillo, Jaime J. "Life in a War Zone: A Social History of Red Cloud's War 1866–67." Master's thesis, University of Texas at El Paso, 1996.

Carrington, Frances C. *My Army Life and the Fort Phil. Kearney Massacre with An Account of the Celebration of "Wyoming Opened."* Philadelphia: J. B. Lippincott, 1910.

Carrington, Henry B. *The Indian Question: Including a Report by the Secretary of the Interior on the Massacre of Troops Near Fort Kearny, December 1866.* Boston: DeWolfe & Fiske, 1884; reprint, New York: Sol Lewis, 1973.

———. "Carrington, Henry B." In *Atlas of Montgomery County*, 53. Chicago: Beers, 1878.

———. "Carrington, Henry B." In *History of Montgomery County, together with historic notes on the Wabash Valley; gleaned from early authors, old maps and manuscripts, private and official correspondence, and other authentic . . . sources.* Chicago: H.H. Hill and N. Iddings, 1881.

Carrington, Margaret I. *Absaraka, Home of the Crows.* Philadelphia: J. B. Lippincott, 1868.

———. *Absaraka, Home of the Crows.* With an introduction by Milo Milton Quaife (Lakeside Press edition). Chicago: R. R. Donnelley & Sons, 1950.

Chiaventone, Frederick J. *Moon of Bitter Cold.* New York: Tom Doherty, 2002.

Cochnower, Florence Octie Courtney. *Recollections Awakened by the Unveiling of the Thomas Statue! by the Army of the Cumberland.* Crawfordsville IN: n.p., 1879.

Coffman, Edward M. *The Old Army: A Portrait of the American Army in Peacetime, 1784–1898.* New York: Oxford University Press, 1986.

Columbus Compact Corporation, The Heritage Districts Website. "Franklinton, Columbus' First Community." Website: www.heritagedistricts.org/franklinton.htm, accessed March 3, 2004.

Cook, James H. *Fifty Years on the Old Frontier as Cowboy, Hunter, Guide, Scout, and Ranchman.* New Haven CT: Yale University Press, 1923.

Coutant, C. G. *The History of Wyoming.* Cheyenne WY: Chaplin, Spafford and Matthewson, 1899.

Davidson, Cathy N. "Preface: No More Separate Spheres!" *American Literature* vol. 70, no. 3 (September 1998): 443–63.

Dennison, John William. "A History of Fort Phil Kearny." Master's thesis, University of Omaha, 1957.

Doyle, Susan Badger. "Journeys to the Land of Gold: Emigrants on the Bozeman Trail, 1863–1866." *Montana: the Magazine of Western History* 41 (Autumn 1991): 54–67.

———. "The Bozeman Trail, 1863–1868," *Annals of Wyoming* 70 (Summer 1998): 5–11.

Dunn, J. P. *Massacres of the Mountains: A History of the Indian Wars of the Far West.* New York: Harper, 1886.

Dyer, Frederick H. *A Compendium of the War of the Rebellion.* 3 vols. Des Moines IA: Dyer Publishing Co., 1908; reprint, Dayton OH: Morningside, 1979.

Eales, Ann Brunner. *Army Wives on the American Frontier: Living by the Bugles.* Boulder CO: Johnson, 1996.

Eastman, Mary. *Dacotah; Life and Legends of the Sioux Around Fort Snelling.* New York: John Wiley, 1849.

Fahs, Alice. "The Feminized Civil War: Gender, Northern Popular Literature, and the Memory of the War, 1861–1900." *The Journal of American History* vol. 85, no. 4 (March 1999): 1461–94.

Foner, Eric. *A Short History of Reconstruction.* New York: Harper & Row, 1990.

Foote, Shelby. *The Civil War: A Narrative.* 3 vols. New York: Random House, 1958–1974.

Fort Phil Kearny/Bozeman Trail Association. *Civilian, Military, Native American Portraits of Fort Phil Kearny.* Banner WY: Fort Phil Kearny–Bozeman Trail Association, 1993.

Fraser, John. *America and the Patterns of Chivalry.* Cambridge: Cambridge University Press, 1982.

Grant, Ulysses S. *The Papers of Ulysses S. Grant,* ed. John Y. Simon. 24 vols. Carbondale: Southern Illinois University Press, 1967–.

Hagan, Father Barry. "Prelude to a Massacre—Fort Phil Kearny, December 6, 1866." *Journal of the Order of the Indian Wars* 1 (Fall 1980): 1–17.

Harcey, Dennis W., Brian R. Croone, and Joe Medicine Crow. *White-Man-Runs-Him; Crow Scout with Custer.* Evanston IL: Evanston, 1995.

Hebard, Grace Raymond, and E. A Brininstool. *The Bozeman Trail.* 2 vols. Cleveland: A. H. Clark, 1922.

Hess, Earl J. *The Union Soldier in Battle: Enduring the Ordeal of Combat.* Lawrence: University Press of Kansas, 1997.

Holmes, Alice D. "And I Was Always with Him: The Life of Jane Thorpy, Army Laundress." *Journal of Arizona History* 38 (1997): 177–90.

Hoxie, Frederick E. *Parading through History; The Making of the Crow Nation in America, 1805–1935.* Cambridge: Cambridge University Press, 1995.

Jensen, Joan M., and Darlis A. Miller, eds. *New Mexico Women: Intercultural Perspective.* Albuquerque: University of New Mexico Press, 1986.

Johnson, Dorothy M. *The Bloody Bozeman: The Perilous Trail to Montana's Gold.* New York: McGraw-Hill, 1971.

Kaplan, Amy. "Manifest Domesticity." *American Literature* vol. 70, no. 3, (September 1998): 581–606.

Knight, Oliver. *Life and Manners in the Frontier Army.* Norman: University of Oklahoma Press, 1978.

Lavender, David. *Bent's Fort.* New York: Doubleday, 1954.

Leckie, Shirley A. *Elizabeth Bacon Custer and the Making of a Myth.* Norman: University of Oklahoma Press, 1993.

Linderman, Frank B. *American: The Life Story of a Great Indian, Plenty-Coups, Chief of the Crows.* New York: John Day, 1930.

Logsdon, David R., ed. "Fannie Courtney, 19, Franklin Resident." *Eyewitnesses at the Battle of Franklin.* Nashville TN: Kettle Mills, 2000.

Lord, Francis A. *They Fought for the Union.* Harrisburg: Stackpole, 1960.

Manzione, Joseph. *"I Am Looking to the North for My Life": Sitting Bull, 1876–1881.* Salt Lake City: University of Utah Press, 1991.

Matloff, Maurice, ed. *American Military History.* Washington DC: U.S. Government Printing Office, Office of the Chief of Military History, U.S. Army, 1969.

McDermott, John D. "Price of Arrogance: The Short and Controversial Life of William Judd Fetterman." *Annals of Wyoming* (Spring 1991): 42–53.

——. "Wyoming Scrapbook: Documents Relating to the Fetterman Fight." *Annals of Wyoming* (Spring 1991): 69–72.

McGinnis, Anthony. "Strike and Retreat: Intertribal Warfare and the Powder River War, 1865–1868." *Montana: the Magazine of Western History* 30 (Autumn 1980): 30–41.

McKeen, Catherine. "Henry Beebee Carrington: A Soldier's Tale." Ph.D. dissertation, State University of New York at Stony Brook, 1998.

McMurtry, Larry. *Boone's Lick.* New York: Simon and Schuster, 2000.

McPherson, James M. *The Battle Cry of Freedom: The Civil War Era.* New York: Oxford University Press, 1988.

Mintz, Steven, and Susan Kellog. *Domestic Revolutions: A Social History of American Family Life.* New York: Free Press, 1988.

Miller, Darlis. "Foragers, Army Women, and Prostitutes." In *New Mexico Women: Intercultural Perspective,* ed. Joan M. Jensen and Darlis A. Miller, 141–68. Albuquerque: University of New Mexico Press, 1986.

Murray, Robert A. "Commentaries on the Carrington Image." In *The Army on the Powder River.* Bellevue NE: Old Army Press, 1969.

————. *Military Posts in the Powder River Country of Wyoming, 1865–1894*. Lincoln: University of Nebraska Press, 1968.

————. "New Facts about Civilians Killed in Fetterman Disaster," *Wyoming History News*, Wyoming State Historical Society, June 1993, 5.

Nacy, Michele J. *Members of the Regiment: Army Officers' Wives on the Western Frontier, 1865–1890*. Westport CT: Greenwood, 2000.

Ohio State University, Office of the Treasurer. "Treasurer 1870: Joseph Sullivant." Website: www.treasurer.ohio-state.edu/TreaAdmin/PDFs/sullivant.pdf, accessed December 1, 2006.

Olson, James C. *Red Cloud and the Sioux Problem*. Lincoln: University of Nebraska Press, 1965.

Ostrander, Alson B. *An Army Boy of the Sixties: A Story of the Plains*. Yonkers-on-Hudson NY: World Book, 1924.

————. *The Bozeman Trail Forts Under General Philip St. George Cooke in 1866*. Casper WY: Commercial Printing, 1932.

Partridge, Robert B. "Fetterman Debacle—Who Was to Blame?" *Journal of the Council on America's Military Past* 16.2 (1989): 36–43.

Quaife, Milo Milton. Introduction to *Absaraka, Home of the Crows* (Lakeside Press edition). Chicago: R.R. Donnelley & Sons, 1950.

Roe, Frances. *Army Letters from an Officer's Wife 1871–1888*. New York: Appleton, 1909.

Rzeczkowski, Frank. "The Crow Indians and the Bozeman Trail." *Montana: The Magazine of Western History* 49 (Winter 1999): 30–47.

Sandoz, Mari. *Crazy Horse, Strange Man of the Oglalas*. New York: Knopf, 1942; reprint, Lincoln: University of Nebraska Press, 1992.

Seymour, Silas. *Incidents of a Trip Through the Great Platte Valley, to the Rocky Mountains and Larame Plains, in the Fall of 1866, with a Synoptical Statement of the Various Pacific Railroads, and an Account of the Great Union Pacific Railroad Excursion to the One Hundredth Meridian of Longitude*. New York: D. Van Nostrand, 1867.

Sibbald, John. "Camp Followers All: Army Women of the West." *American West* (Spring 1966): 56–67.

Stallard, Patricia. *Glittering Misery: Dependents of the Indian-Fighting Army*. Fort Collins CO: Old Army Press, 1978.

Stauffer, Helen Winter, ed. *Letters of Mari Sandoz*. Lincoln: University of Nebraska Press, 1992.

Stewart, Miller J. "Army Laundresses: Ladies of the 'Soap Suds Row.'" *Nebraska History* 61 (1980): 421–36.

Straight, Michael. *Carrington*. New York: Knopf, 1960.

Stuckey, Ronald L. *First Botanists of Columbus: A Sullivant Family Scrapbook.* Columbus OH: R. L. Stuckey, 1987.

Tall Bull, Bill (Feather Wolf). *Northern Cheyenne History of the Battle of 100-In-The-Hand (the Fetterman Battle): We Are The Ancestors Of Those Yet To Be Born.* Sheridan WY: Fort Phil Kearny–Bozeman Trail Association, 1989.

Taylor, William Alexander. *Centennial History of Columbus and Franklin County, Ohio.* 2 vols. Chicago: S. J. Clarke, 1909.

Thorndike, Rachel Sherman. *The Sherman Letters; Correspondence Between General Sherman and Senator Sherman from 1837 to 1891.* New York: n.p., 1894; reprint, New York: Da Capo, 1969.

U.S. Bureau of the Census. *Seventh Census of the United States, 1850.* National Archives and Records Administration, Washington DC. Records of Williamson County TN.

U.S. Bureau of the Census. *Eighth Census of the United States, 1860.* National Archives and Records Administration, Washington DC, 1860, M653, 1,483 rolls, Census Place: Detroit Ward 8, Wayne, Michigan; Roll M653_566, p. 0, image 598.

U.S. Congress. Senate. *Message of the President.* 40th Congress, 2nd session, 1867. Senate Document 1. Washington DC.

U.S. Congress. Senate. *Indian Hostilities.* 40th Congress, 1st session, 1868. Senate Document 13. Washington DC.

U.S. Congress. Senate. *Letter from the Secretary of War Transmitting in response to Resolution of February 11, 1887, report of Colonel Carrington on the Massacre near Fort Philip Kearny.* 49th Congress, 2nd session, 1887. Senate Document 97. Washington DC.

U.S. Congress. Senate. *Letter from the Acting Secretary Of The Interior, Transmitting In Response To Resolution Of February 11, 1887, Papers Relative To Indian Operations On The Plains.* 50th Congress, 1st Session, 1888. Senate Document 33. Washington DC.

U.S. Congress. Senate. *Message of the President.* 40th Congress, 2nd session, 1867. Executive Document 1. Washington DC.

U.S. Congress. Senate. *Letter from The Secretary of War Transmitting in Response to Resolution of Februrary 11, 1887, Report of Colonel Carrington on the Massacre New Fort Philip Kearny.* 49th Congress, 2nd Session. 1887. Executive Document 97. Washington DC, 1887.

U.S. Department of the Interior, National Park Service. "Handbook 107,

Agate Fossil Beds National Monument, Nebraska." Washington DC: Interior Department, National Park Service, Division of Publications.

U.S. Department of the Interior. *Records Relating to the Investigation of the Fort Philip Kearny Massacre, 1866–67.* National Archives Microfilm Publication 740. Records of the Bureau of Indian Affairs. Record Group 75. National Archives and Records Administration, Washington DC.

U.S. Department of the Interior and U.S. Department of War. *Reports of the Secretaries of War and Interior in Answer to Resolutions of the Senate and House of Representatives in Relation to the Massacre at Fort Phil. Kearney, on December 21, 1866 with the views of Commissioner Lewis V. Bogy, in Relation to the Future Policy to be Pursued by the Government for the Settlement of the Indian Question, also Reports of Gen. John Pope and Col. Eli S. Parker, on Same Subject.* Washington DC: Government Printing Office, 1867.

U.S. Department of War. *The War of the Rebellion: A Compilation of the Official Records of the Union and Confederate Armies.* 70 vols., 128 books. 1880–1901.

U.S. Department of War. Department of the Platte. Letters Received. Records of the Army Continental Command. Record Group 393. National Archives and Records Administration, Washington DC.

Utley, Robert M. *Frontier Regulars: The United States Army and the Indian, 1866–1891.* New York: Macmillan, 1973; reprint, Lincoln: University of Nebraska Press, 1984.

Utley Robert M., and Wilcomb E. Washburn. *Indian Wars.* New York: Houghton Mifflin, 1977.

Vaughn, J. W. *Indian Fights: New Facts on Seven Encounters.* Norman: University of Oklahoma Press, 1966.

Vestal, Stanley. *Jim Bridger: Mountain Man.* New York: W. Morrow & Company, 1946; reprint, Lincoln: University of Nebraska Press, 1970.

——. *Warpath: The True Story of the Fighting Sioux Told in a Biography of Chief White Bull.* Boston: Houghton Mifflin, 1934; reprint, Lincoln: University of Nebraska Press, 1984.

Vielé, Teresa Griffin. *Following the Drum.* New York: Rudd & Carleton, 1858.

Welter, Barbara. "The Cult of True Womanhood: 1820–1860," *American Quarterly* vol. 18, no. 2.1 (Summer 1996): 151–74.

Wellman, Paul I., Jr. *Death on the Prairie: The Thirty Years' Struggle for the Western Plains*. New York: Macmillan, 1934; reprint, Lincoln: University of Nebraska Press, 1987.

White, Richard. "The Winning of the West: The Expansion of the Western Sioux in the Eighteenth and Nineteenth Centuries." *The Journal of American History* 65 (September 1978): 319–43.

Young, Otis E. *The West of Philip St. George Cooke, 1809–1895*. Glendale CA: Arthur H. Clark, 1955.

⊱ INDEX ⊰

Carrington (Straight), 197
Carrington, Frances Courtney Grummond. *See* Grummond, Frances Courtney
Carrington, Henry (son of Henry B. Carrington), 48
Carrington, Henry B., 7, 14, *183*, *185*; antislavery views of, 15–16; appointed colonel of the 18th Infantry Regiment, 17; appointed commander of the Mountain district, 13, 15, 23–24; at Camp Thomas, 19–20, 21–22; children of, 21, 46–47; communications to General Cooke, 29, 79, 87, 123–24, 128–29; concern over conflict with the Indians, 29–30; counterattacks commanded by, 87–91; defenders of, 190–92; defense of his actions before the Fetterman massacre, 99–100, 102, 147, 188–89, 190; design of Fort Phil Kearny by, *32*, 33–34, 79; disapproval of Fetterman's plans, 102; education and personal life, 15; expedition toward the Bozeman Trail, 27–28; at Fort Kearney, 22, 23–24; at Fort McPherson, 127, 151, 152; information and evidence provided by, 134, 141–46, 164–67; leadership skills of, 70–74; leaves Fort Phil Kearny, 127; lobbying for position in the western frontier, 21–22; Margaret Carrington's book on, 159–61, 186–87, 188, 191; marriage to Frances Grummond, 163; marriage to Margaret Sullivant, 45, 48; military ability of, 38–39; officers accompanying, 38–39; officers reassigned away from, 38–39, 58–59, 92; as Ohio state adjutant general, 16–17; ordered to take offensive action, 85–86; political activism, 15–16; reassigned to Fort

Casper, 122, 124; recovery of bodies from the Fetterman massacre by, 122; recruits Fetterman, 19; relationship with William Fetterman, 71–74, 98; report on the Fetterman massacre, 128, 129–30, 141, 143; reports submitted by, 95–96; requests for more soldiers, 34; and the Sanborn Commission, 147, 150–52; shoots himself in the thigh, 127; shortages reported by, 34–35; support for Ten Eyck, 175–78, 182–84; takes leave of absence, 152; William Dennison and, 158
Carrington, James (son of Henry B.), 48
Carrington, Joseph Sullivant (son of Henry B.), 47
Carrington, Margaret, 15, 19, 21, 22, *43*, 76; book on the Fetterman massacre, 158, 186–87, 199; children of, 21, 46, 46–47; death of, 46–47; education of, 48; on Fetterman's analysis of the Indians, 93, 191, 197; on the Fort Laramie Treaty, 26; on Fred Brown, 189; on George Grummond, 68; on Indian warfare, 56; marriage to Henry Carrington, 45, 48; on the recovery of bodies from the Fetterman massacre, 122; relationships with other officers' wives, 42–44, 55–57; on report of Lewis V. Bogy, 131; on social life at Fort Phil Kearny, 85; socioeconomic background of, 44–48
Carrington, Margaret Irvin (daughter of Henry Carrington), 47
Carrington, Mary McDowell, 47
Carrington, Morton (son of Henry B.), 47
Carrington, William, 163
Chase, Salmon, 15–16, 17
Cheyenne Indians, 3; Sand Creek Massacre of, 5–6

Gatchell, Jim, 118
Gazeau, Pierre, 41
Gibbon, John, 151
Glover, Ridgeway, 31
gold rush: 1849 California, 3; 1862 Idaho, 4–5, 6
Granger, Robert, 66–67
Grant, Ulysses S., 9, 10, 22–23, 135, 137, 148, 165, 198; Carrington's suspicions of, 191; death of, 167; informed about the Fetterman massacre, 123–24; James W. Powell and, 165–66; portrayed by the media, 155; reactions to the Fetterman massacre, 132–39; report on Fetterman massacre received by, 130; request by Sherman to, 34; and the Sanborn Commission, 150–51, 153–54; suppression of information by, 143, 145
Great Western Indian Fights (Potomac Corral of the Westerners), 195
Grummond, Delia, 67, 68, 163
Grummond, Frances Courtney, 48, 51, 119, 183, 199; defense of Henry Carrington by, 191–92; at Fort Phil Kearney, 54–57; George W. Grummond and, 52–55, 67, 102, 126; leaves Fort Phil Kearny, 125; marriage to George Grummond, 68; marriage to Henry Carrington, 163; memoir published by, 186; socioeconomic background of, 49–50
Grummond, George W., 52–55, 53, 66–69, 78, 84; assigned to Fort Phil Kearney, 68–69; assigned to replace Ten Eyck, 94; burial sites of, 126; children of, 68; death of, 107, 122; and the Fetterman massacre, 98, 99–100, 108, 110, 111–12; and the first counterattack against Lakotas, 88–91; marriage to Delia Grummond, 67, 68, 163; marriage to Frances Courtney, 68
Grummond, William Wands, 163

Hancock, Winfield Scott, 12, 23
Harney, William S., 149
Harper's Weekly, 109, 135, 144, 155
Haymond, Henry, 38–39, 58–59, 71
Hazen, William, 59, 79
Hebard, Grace Raymond, 193, 194, 196
Hines, C. M., 61, 102, 103, 124, 139; leaves Fort Phil Kearny, 127
History of Wyoming (Coutant), 167, 169, 170, 171, 184, 193
Homer, Winslow, 109
Horton, Samuel, 61, 84, 85, 113, 118

Idaho Territory, 4–5, 6
impeachment of Andrew Johnson, 135, 137
Indian Fights (Vaughn), 108
Indian Fights and Fighters (Brady), 168, 193, 196
The Indian Question (Henry B. Carrington), 164, 167, 187, 188
Indian Wars (Utley and Washburn), 196
investigation into the Fetterman massacre, 208n5; Carrington's report and, 128, 129–30, 141, 143; Congressional report on, 145–46; politics and, 131–39, 208n5; Sanborn Commission and, 147, 150–53; suppression of information during, 143, 145, 164–67; tension between the Departments of War and the Interior during, 130–31, 138, 143–46

Jackson, Andrew, 65
Johnson, Andrew, 6–7, 9, 130, 147, 154, 198; battle with Congress over Reconstruction, 136; impeachment of, 135, 137; proclamation of peace on the Plains by, 154; Ulysses S. Grant and, 136; William Sherman and, 138

Johnson, Dorothy M., 196
Jonesboro, battle of, 21, 39

Kearny, Stephen Watts, 33, 204n12
King, Charles, 42
Kinney, J. F., 147, 150, 168
Kinney, J. T., 85
Knight, Oliver, 42

Lakota Indians: ambush at Crazy
    Woman's Creek, 59; attacks of
    military regiments by, 30, 76, 80;
    celebrations after the Fetterman
    massacre, 120, 122; conflicts with
    the Crows, 5; counterattacks by
    Carrington's soldiers' on, 87–91;
    and the Fetterman massacre,
    105–13; negotiations with the U.S.,
    4, 149; in the Seven Council Fires, 3
leadership skills of Henry B. Car-
    rington, 70–74
Leckie, Shirley, 160
Letter from the Acting Secretary of the
    Interior, 166
Letter from the Secretary of War, 164
Letter of the Secretary of the Interior, 156
Life and Manners in the Frontier Army
    (Knight), 42
Lincoln, Abraham, 16, 17, 65
Lippincott, J. B., 159
literature and women, 159–61
Little Wound, 115
livestock and horses at Fort Phil
    Kearny, 61, 79
Lodge Trail Ridge, 96–97, 99, 102,
    103–5, 108, 110, 156. See also
    Fetterman massacre

Madison, James, 45
Man Afraid of His Horses, 5, 115
Manzione, Joseph, 8
Matloff, Maurice, 7
Matson, Lieutenant, 103
Maynadier, Henry E., 26

McClellan, George, 13, 16–17
McDermott, John D., 111, 188
McDowell, Irvin, 45
McKeen, Catherine, 191
McMurtry, Larry, 197
Metzger, Adolph, 119
Mexican War, 13
military: Army Reorganization Act
    and, 35–36; buildup at the start
    of the Civil War, 16–17, 19; Eigh-
    teenth Regiment, 17–21, 35, 38,
    70; geographical commands, 9–12;
    leaders after the Civil War, 9–13;
    restructuring after the Civil War,
    7–10, 39–40; U.S. Indian policy
    enforced by, 8. See also specific forts;
    United States
Mizner, Henry, 67
Moon of Bitter Cold (Chiaventone), 197
Mormons, 13
Morton, Charles, 182
Morton, Oliver, 21
Mountain District, Montana, 4–5, 6;
    dissolution, 78; General Order No.
    33, 22–23. See also Bozeman Trail
Murray, Robert A., 81–82
My Army Life and the Fort Phil. Kearney
    Massacre (F. Grummond), 57, 106,
    185, 186, 187, 188, 191, 192

Nakota Indians, 3
Nast, Thomas, 109
North, Captain, 194

Oceti Sakowin, 3
Office of Indian Affairs, 26, 29
officers assigned to Fort Phil Kearny,
    38–39, 58–61
Ostrander, Alson, 34, 194

Palmer, I. N., 124, 151
Parker, Ely S., 147, 150–51
Paulus, Jacob, 77
Pearson's Magazine, 168

234   Index

Peters, S. S., 176, 178, 179, 182, 184, 186
Phillips, John, 120, 121, 122–23
Phisterer, Frederick, 38–39, 58–59
politics: after the Civil War, 6–7, 39–40, 65; after the Fetterman massacre, 132–39, 198; and the Indian Question, 164; Johnson's impeachment and, 135, 137
Pope, John, 22–23, 23
Powder River Basin, 4, 26, 29
Powell, James W., 39, 78, 80, 83; assigned commander of the cavalry, 95; Bully 38 and, 81–82; refusals to take field commands, 98–99; remains at Fort Phil Kearny after the Fetterman massacre, 127; testimony against Carrington by, 85, 95–97, 140, 164–67, 190–91

Red Cloud, 114, 115, 116; army trained by, 36; and the Fetterman massacre, 105–10, 113, 120; fighters attacked by Carrington's soldiers, 87–91; James Cook and, 170; as leader of the Sioux, 5; mistrust of the U.S., 6; negotiations with the U.S., 26, 27, 29–30, 149
Reports of the Secretaries of War and Interior, 145
Ricker, Eli S., 113, 172–74, 176–79, 184, 186
Robinson, W. W., 182
Roe, Frances, 42

Sample, Archibald, 104, 105
Sanborn, John B., 147, 153, 165
Sanborn Commission, 147, 150–53, 190
Sand Creek Massacre, 5–6
Sandoz, Mari, 120
Seven Council Fires, 3
Seymour, Silas, 37
Sheridan, Philip, 148

Sherman, William Tecumseh, 148, 149, 198; *Absaraka* (M. Carrington) dedicated to, 161; at Fort Laramie, 34; at Fort Phil Kearny, 25; informed about the Fetterman massacre, 123–24; march on Atlanta, 52, 68; Margaret Carrington and, 161–62; reactions to the Fetterman massacre, 132–39; report on Fetterman massacre received by, 130; responsibilities after the Civil War, 9–10, 12, 22–23; retirement of, 167; suppression of information by, 143, 145; underestimation of the Indians by, 35
Sioux Indians: conflicts with the U.S., 5–6; leadership of, 5; and negotiations with the U.S., 4; tribes of, 3
Skinner, Prescott, 59
Smith, John E., 122
social atmosphere at Fort Phil Kearny, 84–85
Spotted Tail, 5
Stallard, Patricia Y., 42
Stanton, Edwin, 9, 132, 135–37, 145, 154, 165–66, 198
Starling, Sarah, 45
Stead, Jack, 75
Straight, Michael, 197
Stuart, J. E. B., 11, 13
Sullivant, Joseph, 44–45
Sullivant, Lucas, 44
Sullivant, Margaret. *See* Carrington, Margaret
Sullivant, Margaret Irvin McDowell (mother of Margaret Carrington), 44–45
Sullivant, Michael, 45
Sullivant, William, 45
Sully, Alfred, 147, 150

Taylor, E. B., 26
Templeton, George, 59

In the Women in the West series

When Montana and I Were Young:
A Frontier Childhood
By Margaret Bell
Edited by Mary Clearman Blew

Martha Maxwell,
Rocky Mountain Naturalist
By Maxine Benson

The Enigma Woman: The Death
Sentence of Nellie May Madison
By Kathleen A. Cairns

Front-Page Women Journalists, 1920–1950
By Kathleen A. Cairns

The Cowboy Girl:
The Life of Caroline Lockhart
By John Clayton

The Art of the Woman:
The Life and Work of Elisabet Ney
By Emily Fourmy Cutrer

Emily: The Diary of a
Hard-Worked Woman
By Emily French
Edited by Janet Lecompte

The Important Things of Life: Women,
Work, and Family in Sweetwater County,
Wyoming, 1880–1929
By Dee Garceau

The Adventures of The Woman
Homesteader: The Life and Letters of
Elinore Pruitt Stewart
By Susanne K. George

Flowers in the Snow: The Life of Isobel
Wylie Hutchison, 1889–1982
By Gwyneth Hoyle

Domesticating the West: The Re-Creation
of the Nineteenth-Century American
Middle Class
By Brenda K. Jackson

Engendered Encounters: Feminism and
Pueblo Cultures, 1879–1934
By Margaret D. Jacobs

Riding Pretty: Rodeo Royalty in the
American West
By Renée Laegreid

The Colonel's Lady on the Western
Frontier: The Correspondence of
Alice Kirk Grierson
Edited by Shirley A. Leckie

Their Own Frontier: Women Intellectuals
Re-Visioning the American West
Edited by Shirley A. Leckie and
Nancy J. Parezo

A Stranger in Her Native Land:
Alice Fletcher and the American Indians
By Joan Mark

So Much to Be Done: Women Settlers
on the Mining and Ranching Frontier,
Second Edition
Edited by Ruth B. Moynihan,
Susan Armitage, and
Christiane Fischer Dichamp

Women and Nature:
Saving the "Wild" West
By Glenda Riley

The Life of Elaine Goodale Eastman
By Theodore D. Sargent

Give Me Eighty Men: Women and the
Myth of the Fetterman Fight
By Shannon D. Smith

Moving Out: A Nebraska Woman's Life
By Polly Spence
Edited by Karl Spence Richardson

Eight Women, Two Model Ts,
and the American West
By Joanne Wilke